Lecture Notes in Artificial Intelligence   9785

Subseries of Lecture Notes in Computer Science

More information about this series at http://www.springer.com/series/1244

Ahlame Douzal-Chouakria · José A. Vilar
Pierre-François Marteau (Eds.)

Advanced Analysis and Learning on Temporal Data

First ECML PKDD Workshop, AALTD 2015
Porto, Portugal, September 11, 2015
Revised Selected Papers

 Springer

Editors
Ahlame Douzal-Chouakria
Laboratoire d'Informatique de Grenoble
Université Grenoble Alpes (UGA)
Grenoble
France

Pierre-François Marteau
IRISA
Université de Bretagne-Sud
Vannes
France

José A. Vilar
Universidade da Coruna
Coruna
Spain

ISSN 0302-9743   ISSN 1611-3349   (electronic)
Lecture Notes in Artificial Intelligence
ISBN 978-3-319-44411-6   ISBN 978-3-319-44412-3   (eBook)
DOI 10.1007/978-3-319-44412-3

Library of Congress Control Number: 2016947506

LNCS Sublibrary: SL7 – Artificial Intelligence

Printed on acid-free paper

This Springer imprint is published by Springer Nature
The registered company is Springer International Publishing AG Switzerland

Preface

This book brings together advances and new perspectives in machine learning, statistics, and data analysis on temporal data. Temporal data arise in several domains such as bio-informatics, medicine, finance, and engineering, among many others. They are naturally present in applications covering language, motion, and vision analysis, and particularly in emerging applications such as energy-efficient building, smart cities, dynamic social media, or Internet of Things. Contrary to static data, temporal data are of a complex nature, they are generally noisy, of high dimensionality, they may be nonstationary (i.e., first-order statistics vary with time) and irregular (involving several time granularities), they may have several invariant domain-dependent factors such as time delay, translation, scale, or tendency effects. These temporal peculiarities make limited the majority of standard statistical models and machine learning approaches, that mainly assume *i.i.d.* data, homoscedasticity, normality of residuals, etc. To tackle such challenging temporal data, one appeals for new advanced approaches at the bridge of statistics, time series analysis, signal processing, and machine learning. Defining new approaches that transcend boundaries between several domains to extract valuable information from temporal data will undeniably be a hot topic in the near future, that has, however, been the subject of active research this past decade.

The aim of this book is to present recent challenging issues and advances in temporal data analysis addressed in machine learning, data mining, pattern analysis and statistics. Analysis and learning from temporal data cover a wide scope of tasks including learning metrics, learning representations, unsupervised feature extraction, clustering, and classification. This book is organized as follows. The first part focuses on learning new representations and embeddings for time series classification, clustering, or dimensionality reduction. The second chapter presents several approaches to classification and clustering with challenging applications in medicine or earth observation data. These works show different ways to consider temporal dependency in clustering or classification processes. The last part of the book is dedicated to metric learning and time series comparison, it addresses the problem of speeding up the dynamic time warping or dealing with multimodal and multiscale metric learning for time series classification and clustering. The papers presented were reviewed by at least two independent reviewers, leading to the selection of 11 papers among 22 initial submissions. An index of authors is provided at the end of this book.

The editors are grateful to the authors of the papers selected in this volume for their contributions and for their willingness to respond so positively to the time constraints in preparing the final version of their papers. We are especially grateful to the reviewers, listed herein, for their careful reviews that helped us greatly in selecting the papers included in this volume. We also thank all the staff at Springer for their support and dedication in publishing this volume in the series–Lecture Notes in Artificial Intelligence.

July 2015

Ahlame Douzal-Chouakria
José A. Vilar
Pierre-François Marteau
Ann E. Maharaj
Andrés M. Alonso
Edoardo Otranto
Irina Nicolae

Organization

Program Committee

Ahlame Douzal-Chouakria	Université Grenoble Alpes, France
José Antonio Vilar Fernández	University of A Coruña, Spain
Pierre-François Marteau	IRISA, Université de Bretagne-Sud, France
Ann Maharaj	Monash University, Australia
Andrés M. Alonso	Universidad Carlos III de Madrid, Spain
Edoardo Otranto	University of Messina, Italy

Reviewing Committee

Massih-Reza Amini	Université Grenoble Alpes, France
Manuele Bicego	University of Verona, Italy
Gianluca Bontempi	MLG, ULB University, Belgium
Antoine Cornuéjols	LRI, AgroParisTech, France
Pierpaolo D'Urso	La Sapienza University, Italy
Patrick Gallinari	LIP6, Université Pierre et Marie Curie, France
Eric Gaussier	Université Grenoble Alpes, France
Christian Hennig	London's Global University, UK
Frank Höeppner	Ostfalia University of Applied Sciences, Germany
Paul Honeine	ICD, Université de Troyes, France
Vincent Lemaire	Orange Lab, France
Manuel García Magariños	University of A Coruña, Spain
Mohamed Nadif	LIPADE, Université Paris Descartes, France
François Petitjean	Monash University, Australia
Fabrice Rossi	SAMM, Université Paris 1, France
Allan Tucker	Brunel University, UK

Contents

X   Contents

Time Series Representation and Compression

Symbolic Representation of Time Series: A Hierarchical Coclustering Formalization

Alexis Bondu[1,2,3(✉)], Marc Boullé[1,2,3], and Antoine Cornuéjols[1,2,3]

[1] EDF R&D, 1 avenue du Général de Gaulle, 92140 Clamart, France
alexis.bondu@edf.fr
[2] Orange Labs, 2 avenue Pierre Marzin, 22300 Lannion, France
marc.boulle@orange.com
[3] AgroParisTech, 16 rue Claude Bernard, 75005 Paris, France
antoine.cornuejols@agroparistech.fr

Abstract. The choice of an appropriate representation remains crucial for mining time series, particularly to reach a good trade-off between the dimensionality reduction and the stored information. Symbolic representations constitute a simple way of reducing the dimensionality by turning time series into sequences of symbols. SAXO is a data-driven symbolic representation of time series which encodes typical distributions of data points. This approach was first introduced as a heuristic algorithm based on a regularized coclustering approach. The main contribution of this article is to formalize SAXO as a hierarchical coclustering approach. The search for the best symbolic representation given the data is turned into a model selection problem. Comparative experiments demonstrate the benefit of the new formalization, which results in representations that drastically improve the compression of data while keeping useful information for classification tasks.

Keywords: Time series · Symbolic representation · Coclustering

1 Introduction

The choice of the representation of time series remains crucial since it impacts the quality of supervised and unsupervised analysis [1]. Time series are particularly difficult to deal with due to their inherently high dimensionality when they are represented in the time-domain [2,3]. Virtually all data mining and machine learning algorithms scale poorly with the dimensionality. During the last two decades, numerous high level representations of time series have been proposed to overcome this difficulty. The most commonly used approaches are: the Discrete Fourier Transform [4], the Discrete Wavelet Transform [5,6], the Discrete Cosine Transform [7], the Piecewise Aggregate Approximation (PAA) [8]. Each representation of time series encodes some information derived from the raw data[1]. According to [1], mining time series heavily relies on the choice of

---

[1] *"Raw data"* designates a time series represented in the time-domain by a vector of real values.

© Springer International Publishing Switzerland 2016
A. Douzal-Chouakria et al. (Eds.): AALTD 2015, LNAI 9785, pp. 3–16, 2016.
DOI: 10.1007/978-3-319-44412-3_1

a representation and a similarity measure. Our objective is to find a **compact** and **informative** representation which is driven by the data. The symbolic representations constitute a simple way of reducing the dimensionality of the data by turning time series into sequences of symbols [9]. In such representations, each symbol corresponds to a time interval and encodes information which summarize the related sub-series. Without making hypothesis on the data, such a representation does not allow one to quantify the loss of information. This article focuses on a less prevalent symbolic representation which is called SAXO[2]. This approach optimally discretizes the time dimension and encodes typical distributions[3] of data points with the symbols [10]. SAXO offers interesting properties. Since this representation is based on a **regularized** Bayesian coclustering[4] approach called MODL[5] [11], a good trade-off is naturally reached between the dimensionality reduction and the information loss. SAXO is a parameter-free and data-driven representation of time series. In practice, this symbolic representation proves to be highly **informative** for training classifiers. In [10], SAXO was evaluated on public datasets and favorably compared with the SAX representation.

Originally, SAXO was defined as a heuristic algorithm. The two main contributions of this article are: (i) the **formalization** of SAXO as a hierarchical coclustering approach; (ii) the evaluation of its **compactness** in terms of coding length and its **informativeness** for classification tasks. The most probable SAXO representation given the data is defined by minimizing the new evaluation criterion. Our objective is to yield better SAXO representations, which improve the compression of time series while preserving the advantage of coding typical distributions. This article is organized as follows. Section 2 briefly introduces the symbolic representations of time series and presents the original SAXO heuristic algorithm. Section 3 formalizes the SAXO approach resulting in a new evaluation criterion which is the main contribution of this article. Experiments are conducted in Sect. 4 on real datasets in order to compare the SAXO evaluation criterion with that of the MODL coclustering approach. Lastly, perspectives and future works are discussed in Sect. 5.

2   Related Work

Numerous compact representations of time series deal with the curse of dimensionality by discretizing the time and by summarizing the sub-series within each time interval. For instance, the Piecewise Aggregate Approximation (PAA) encodes the mean values of data points within each time interval. The Piecewise Linear Approximation (PLA) [12] is an other example of compact representation which encodes the gradient and the y-intercept of a linear approximation

---

[2] SAXO *Symbolic Aggregate approXimation Optimized by data.*

[3] The SAXO approach produces clusters of time series within each time interval which correspond to the symbols.

[4] The coclustering problem consist in reordering rows and columns of a matrix in order to satisfy a homogeneity criterion.

[5] *Minimum Optimized Description Length.*

of sub-series. In both cases, the representation consist of numerical values which describe each time interval. In contrast, the symbolic representations characterize the time intervals by categorical variables [9]. For instance, the Shape Definition Language (SDL) [13] encodes the shape of sub-series by symbols.

The SAX Approach. The Symbolic Aggregate approXimation approach is one of the main symbolic representations of time series. It provides a distance measure that lower bounds the Euclidian distance defined in the time-domain. This approach consists of two steps: (i) time discretization using PAA; (ii) discretization of the outcome mean values into symbols. First, the PAA transform reduces the dimensionality of the original time series $S = \{x_1, ..., x_{m_*}\}$ by considering a vector $\bar{S} = \{\bar{x}_1, ..., \bar{x}_w\}$ of w mean values ($w < m_*$) calculated on regular time intervals. Then, the SAX approach discretizes the mean values $\{\bar{x}_i\}$ obtained from the PAA transform into a set of α equiprobable symbols. The interval of values corresponding to each symbol can be analytically calculated under the assumption that the time series have a Gaussian distribution [9]. An alternative method consists in empirically calculating the quantiles of values in the dataset.

Figure 1 plots an example of SAX transform based on a set of three symbols *(i.e. $\{a, b, c\}$)*. The left part of this figure illustrates that the distribution of values is supposed to be known, and is divided into equiprobable intervals corresponding to each symbol. Then, these intervals are exploited to discretize the mean values into symbols within each time interval. The concatenation of symbols **baabccbc** constitutes the SAX representation of the original time series. The SAX representation has become an essential tool for time series data mining. This approach has been exploited to implement various tasks on large time series datasets, including similarity clustering [14], anomaly detection [15,16], discovery of motifs [17], visualization [18], stream processing [9]. Originally, the SAX approach was designed for indexing very large sets of time series [19], and remains a reference in this field.

The symbolic representations appear to be really helpful for processing large datasets of time series owing to dimensionality reduction. However, these approaches suffer several limitations.

- Most of these representations are lossy compression approaches unable to quantify the loss of information without strong hypothesis on the data.
- The discretization of the time dimension into regular intervals is not data driven.
- The symbols have the same meaning over time irrespectively of their rank *(i.e. the ranks of the symbols may be used to improve the compression)*.

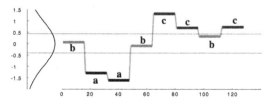

Fig. 1. Example of SAX representation.

– Most of these representations involve user parameters which affect the stored information *(ex: for the SAX representation, the number of time intervals and the size of the alphabet must be specified).*

The SAXO approach overcomes these limitations by optimizing the time discretization, and by encoding typical distributions of data points within each time interval [10]. SAXO was first defined as a heuristic which exploits the MODL coclustering approach.

Figure 2 provides an overview of this approach by illustrating the main steps of the learning algorithm. The joint distribution of the identifiers of the time series C, the values X, and the timestamp T is estimated by a trivariate coclustering model. The time discretization resulting from the first step is retained, and the joint distribution of X and C is estimated within each time interval by using a bivariate coclustering model. The resulting clusters of time series are characterized by piecewise constant distributions of values and correspond to the symbols. A specific representation allows one to re-encode the time series as a sequence of symbols. Then, the typical distribution that best represents the data points of the time series is selected within each time interval. Figure 3(a) plots an example of recoded time series. The original time series *(represented by the blue curve)* is recoded by the **"abba"** SAXO word. The time is discretized into four intervals *(the vertical red lines)* corresponding to each symbol. Within time intervals, the values are discretized *(the horizontal green lines)*: the number of intervals of values and their locations are not necessary the same. The symbols correspond to typical distributions of values: conditional probabilities of X are associated with each cell of the grid *(represented by the gray levels)*; Fig. 3b gives an example of the alphabet associated with the second time interval. The four available symbols correspond to typical distributions which are both represented by gray levels and by histograms. By considering Figs. 3a and b, **b** appears to be the closest typical distribution of the second sub-series.

As in any heuristic approach, the original algorithm finds a suboptimal solution for selecting the most suitable SAXO representation given the data. Solving this problem in an exact way appears to be intractable, since it is comparable to the coclustering problem which is NP-hard. The main contribution of this paper is to **formalize** the SAXO approach within the MODL framework. We claim this formalization is a first step to improving the quality of the SAXO representations learned from data. In this article, we define a new evaluation

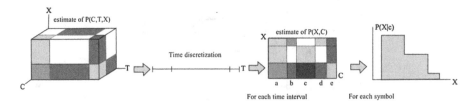

Fig. 2. Main steps of the SAXO learning algorithm.

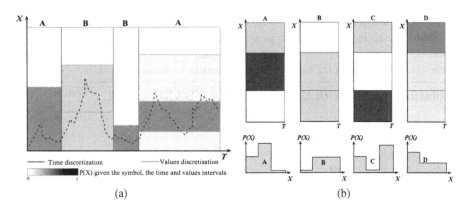

Fig. 3. Example of a SAXO representation (a) and the alphabet of the second time interval (b). (Color figure online)

criterion denoted by C_{saxo} *(see Sect. 3)*. The most probable SAXO representation given the data is defined by minimizing C_{saxo}. We expect to reach better representations by optimizing C_{saxo}, instead of exploiting the original heuristic algorithm.

3 Formalization of the SAXO Approach

This section presents **the main contribution** of this article: the SAXO approach is formalized as a hierarchical coclustering approach. As illustrated in Fig. 4, the originality of the SAXO approach is that the groups of identifiers *(variable C)* and the intervals of values *(variable X)* are allowed to change over time. By contrast, the MODL coclustering approach forces the discretization of C and X to be the same within time intervals. Our objective is to reach better models by removing this constraint.

A SAXO model is hierarchically instantiated by following two successive steps. First, the discretization of time is determined. The bivariate discretization $C \times X$ is then defined within each time interval. Additional notations are required to describe the sequence of bivariate data grids.

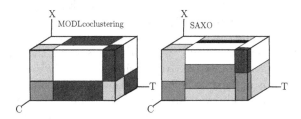

Fig. 4. Examples of a MODL coclustering model *(left part)* and a SAXO model *(right part)*.

> **Notations for time series:** *In this article, the input dataset $\mathcal{D}$ is considered to be a collection of N time series denoted S_i (with $i \in [1,N]$). Each time series consists of m_i data points, which are couples of values X and timestamps T. The total number of data points is denoted by $m = \sum_{i=1}^{N} m_i$.*

> **Notations for the *t-th* time interval of a SAXO model:**
>
> - k_T : *number of time intervals;*
> - k_C^t : *number of clusters of time series;*
> - k_X^t : *number of intervals of value;*
> - $k_C(i,t)$: *index of the cluster that contains the sub-series of S_i;*
> - $\{n_{i_C}^t\}$: *number of time series in each cluster i_C^t;*
> - m_t : *number of data point;*
> - m_i^t : *number of data points of each time series S_i;*
> - $m_{i_C}^t$: *number of data points in each cluster i_C^t;*
> - $\{m_{j_X}^t\}$: *number of data points in the intervals j_X;*
> - $\{m_{i_C j_X}^t\}$: *number of data points belonging to each cell (i_C, j_X).*

Eventually, a SAXO model M' is first defined by a number of time intervals and the location of their bounds. The bivariate data grids $C \times X$ within each time interval are defined by: (i) the partition of the time series into clusters; (ii) the number of intervals of values; (iii) the distribution of the data points on the cells of the data grid; (iv) for each cluster, the distribution of the data points on the time series belonging to the same cluster. Section 3.1 presents the prior distribution of the SAXO models. The likelihood of a SAXO model given the data is described in Sect. 3.2. A new evaluation criterion which defines the most probable model given the data is proposed in Sect. 3.3.

3.1   Prior Distribution of the SAXO Models

The proposed prior distribution $P(M')$ exploits the hierarchy of the parameters of the SAXO models and is uniform at each level. The prior distribution of the number of time intervals k_T is given by Eq. 1. The parameter k_T belongs to $[1,m]$, with m representing the total number of data points. All possible values of k_T are considered as equiprobable. By using combinatorics, the number of possible locations of the bounds can be enumerated given a fixed value of k_T. Once again, all possible locations are considered as equiprobable. Equation 2 represents the prior distribution of the parameter $\{m^t\}$ given k_T. Within each time interval t, the number of intervals of values k_X^t is uniformly distributed *(see Eq. 3)*. The value of k_X^t belongs to $[1, m^t]$, with m^t representing the number of data points within the t-th time interval. All possible values of k_X^t are equiprobable. The same approach is applied to define the prior distribution of the number of clusters within each time interval *(see Eq. 4)*. The value of k_C^t belongs to $[1, N]$, with N denoting the total number of time series. Once again, all possible values of k_C^t are equiprobable. The possible ways of partitioning the N time series into k_C^t clusters can be enumerated, given a fixed number of clusters in the

t-th time interval. The term $B(N, k_C^t)$ in Eq. 5 represents the number of possible partitions of N elements into k_C^t possibly empty clusters[6]. Within each time interval, all distributions of the m^t data points on the cells of the bivariate data grid $C \times X$ are considered as equiprobable. Equation 6 enumerates the possible ways of distributing $\{m^t\}$ data points on $k_X^t.k_C^t$ cells. Given a time interval t and a cluster i_C^t, all distributions of the data points on the time series belonging to the same cluster are equiprobable. Equation 7 enumerates the possible ways of distributing m_i^t data points on $n_{i_C}^t$ time series.

$$P(k_T) = \frac{1}{m} \tag{1}$$

$$P(\{m^t\}|k_T) = \frac{1}{\binom{m+k_T-1}{k_T-1}} \tag{2}$$

$$P(\{k_X^t\}|k_T, \{m^t\}) = \prod_{t=1}^{k_T} \frac{1}{m^t} \tag{3}$$

$$P(\{k_C^t\}|k_T) = \prod_{t=1}^{k_T} \frac{1}{N} \tag{4}$$

$$P\left(k_C(i,t)|k_T, \{k_C^t\}\right) = \prod_{t=1}^{k_T} \frac{1}{B(N, k_C^t)} \tag{5}$$

$$P\left(\{m_{j_C,j_X}^t\}|k_T, \{m^t\}, \{k_X^t\}, \{k_C^t\}\right) = \prod_{t=1}^{k_T} \frac{1}{\binom{m^t+k_C^t.k_X^t-1}{k_C^t.k_X^t-1}} \tag{6}$$

$$P\left(\{m_i^t\}|k_T, \{k_C^t\}, k_C(i,t), \{m_{j_C,j_X}^t\}\right) = \prod_{t=1}^{k_T}\prod_{i=1}^{k_C^t}\frac{1}{\binom{m_{i_C}^t+n_{i_C}^t-1}{n_{i_C}^t-1}} \tag{7}$$

In the end, the prior distribution of the SAXO models M' is given by Eq. 8.

$$P(M') = \frac{1}{m} \times \frac{1}{\binom{m+k_T-1}{k_T-1}}$$

$$\times \prod_{t=1}^{k_T}\left[\frac{1}{m^t} \times \frac{1}{N} \times \frac{1}{B(N,k_C^t)} \times \frac{1}{\binom{m^t+k_C^t.k_X^t-1}{k_C^t.k_X^t-1}} \times \prod_{i=1}^{k_C^t}\frac{1}{\binom{m_{i_C}^t+n_{i_C}^t-1}{n_{i_C}^t-1}}\right] \tag{8}$$

---

[6] The second kind of Stirling numbers $S\{^v_k\}$ enumerates the possible partitions of v elements into k clusters and $B(N, k_C^t) = \sum_{i=1}^{k_C^t} S\{^N_i\}$.

3.2 Likelihood of Data Given a SAXO Model

A SAXO model matches with several possible datasets. Intuitively, the likelihood $P(D|M')$ enumerates all the datasets which are compatible with the parameters of the model M'. The first term of the likelihood represents the distribution of the ranks of the values of T. In other words, Eq. 9 codes all the possible permutations of the data points within each time interval. The second term enumerates all the possible distributions of the m data points on the k_T time intervals, which are compatible with the parameter $\{m^t\}$ (see Eq. 10). In the same way, Eq. 11 enumerates the distributions of the m^t data points on the $k_X^t.k_C^t$ cells of the bivariate data grids $C \times X$ within each time interval. The considered distributions are compatible with the parameter $\{m_{i_C,j_X}^t\}$. For each time interval and for each cluster, Eq. 12 enumerates all the possible distributions of the data points on the time series belonging to the same cluster. Equation 13 enumerates all the possible permutations of the data points in the intervals of X, within each time interval. This information must also be coded over all the time intervals, which is equivalent to enumerating all the possible fusions of k_T stored lists in order to constitute a global stored list (see Eq. 14). In the end, the likelihood of the data given a SAXO models M' is characterized by Eq. 15.

$$\frac{1}{\prod_{t=1}^{k_T} m^t!} \tag{9}$$

$$\frac{1}{\frac{m!}{\prod_{t=1}^{k_T} m^t!}} \tag{10}$$

$$\prod_{t=1}^{k_T} \frac{1}{\frac{m^t!}{\prod_{i_C=1}^{k_C^t} \prod_{j_X=1}^{k_X^t} m_{i_C,j_X}^t!}} \tag{11}$$

$$\prod_{t=1}^{k_T} \frac{1}{\frac{\prod_{i_C=1}^{k_C^t} m_{i_C}^t!}{\prod_{i=1}^{N} m_i^t!}} \tag{12}$$

$$\prod_{t=1}^{k_T} \frac{1}{\prod_{j_X=1}^{k_X^t} m_{j_X}^t!} \tag{13}$$

$$\frac{1}{\frac{m!}{\prod_{t=1}^{k_T} m^t!}} \tag{14}$$

$$P(D|M') = \frac{1}{m!^2} \times \prod_{t=1}^{k_T} \left[\frac{\prod_{i_C=1}^{k_C^t} \prod_{j_X=1}^{k_X^t} m_{i_C,j_X}^t! \times \prod_{i=1}^{N} m_i^t!}{\prod_{j_X=1}^{k_X^t} m_{j_X}^t! \times \prod_{i_C=1}^{k_C^t} m_{i_C}^t!} \right] \tag{15}$$

3.3   Evaluation Criterion

The SAXO evaluation criterion is the negative logarithm of $P(M') \times P(D|M')$ (see Eq. 16). The first three lines correspond to the prior term $-log(P(M'))$ and the last two lines represent the likelihood term $-log(P(M'|D))$. The most probable model given the data is found by minimizing $C_{saxo}(M')$ over the set of all possible SAXO models denoted by $\mathbb{M}'$.

$$
\begin{aligned}
C_{saxo}(M') = {} & log(m) + log\binom{m + k_T - 1}{k_T - 1} + \sum_{t=1}^{k_T} log(m^t) \\
& + k_T.log(N) + \sum_{t=1}^{k_T} log\left(B(N, k_C^t)\right) + \sum_{t=1}^{k_T} log\binom{m^t + k_C^t.k_X^t - 1}{k_C^t.k_X^t - 1} \\
& + \sum_{t=1}^{k_T}\sum_{i_C=1}^{k_C^t} log\binom{m_{i_C}^t + n_{i_C}^t - 1}{n_{i_C}^t - 1} \\
& + 2.log(m!) - \sum_{t=1}^{k_T}\sum_{i_C=1}^{k_C^t}\sum_{j_X=1}^{k_X^t} log(m_{i_C,j_X}^t!) \\
& + \sum_{t=1}^{k_T}\left[\sum_{i_C=1}^{k_C^t} log(m_{i_C}^t!) - \sum_{i=1}^{N} log(m_i^t!) + \sum_{j_X=1}^{k_X^t} log(m_{j_X}^t!)\right]
\end{aligned}
\tag{16}
$$

Key ideas to retain: Rather than having a heuristic decomposition of the SAXO approach in a two-step algorithm, we propose a single evaluation criterion based on the MODL framework. Once optimized, this criterion should yield better representations of time series. We compare the ability of both criterion to compress data. We aim at evaluating the interest of optimizing C_{saxo} rather than the original trivariate coclustering criterion [20] (denoted by C_{modl}).

---

4   Comparative Experiments on Real Datasets

According to the information theory and since both criteria are a negative logarithm of a probability, C_{saxo} and C_{modl} represent the coding length of the models. In Sect. 4.1, both approaches are compared in terms of coding length. Then, Sect. 4.2 evaluates the informativeness of several symbolic representations for classification tasks.

4.1   Coding Length Evaluation

The 20 processed datasets come from the *UCR Time Series Classification and Clustering repository* [21]. Some datasets are relatively small, we have selected the ones which include at least 800 learning examples. Originally, these datasets are divided into training and test sets which have been merged in our experiments. The objective of this section is to compare C_{saxo} and C_{modl} for each dataset. On the one hand, the criterion C_{modl} is optimized by using the greedy heuristic and a neighborhood exploration mentioned described in [11]. The coding length of the most probable MODL model *(denoted by MAP_{modl})* is then calculated by using C_{modl}. On the other hand, the criterion C_{saxo} is optimized by exploiting the original heuristic algorithm illustrated in Fig. 2 [10]. The coding length of best SAXO model *(denoted by MAP_{saxo})* is given by the criterion C_{saxo}. Notice that both algorithms have a $\mathcal{O}(m\sqrt{m}\log m)$ time complexity. The order of magnitude of the coding length depends on the size of the data set and can not be easily compared over all datasets. We choose to exploit the compression gain [22] which consists in comparing the coding length of a model M with the coding length of the simplest model M_{sim}. This key performance indicator varies in the interval $[0, 1]$. The compression gain is similarly defined for the MODL and the SAXO approaches such that:

$$\mathcal{G}ain_{modl}(M) = 1 - C_{modl}(M)/C_{modl}(M_{sim})$$

$$\mathcal{G}ain_{saxo}(M') = 1 - C_{saxo}(M')/C_{saxo}(M_{sim})$$

Our experiments evaluate the variation of the compression gain between the SAXO and the MODL approaches. This indicator is denoted by Δ_G and represents the relative improvement of the compression gain provided by SAXO. The value of Δ_G can be negative, which means that SAXO provides a worse compression gain than the MODL approach.

$$\Delta_G = \frac{\mathcal{G}ain_{saxo}(MAP_{saxo}) - \mathcal{G}ain_{modl}(MAP_{modl})}{\mathcal{G}ain_{modl}(MAP_{modl})}$$

Table 1 presents the results of our experiments and includes a particular case with a missing value for the dataset "TwoPatterns". In this case, the first step of the heuristic algorithm which optimizes C_{saxo} *(see Fig. 2)* leads to the simplest trivariate coclustering model that includes a single cell. This is a side effect

Table 1. Coding length evaluation.

Dataset	Δ_G	Dataset	Δ_G
Starlight curves	63.86%	CBF	−1.43%
uWaveGestureX	191.41%	AllFace	383.24%
uWaveGestureY	157.79%	Symbols	23.16%
uWaveGestureZ	185.13%	50 Words	400.68%
ECG Five Days	−1.80%	Wafer	37.03%
MoteStrain	627.84%	Yoga	63.40%
CincEGCtorso	32.93%	FacesUCR	−18.39%
MedicalImages	191.32%	Cricket Z	290.22%
WordSynonym	264.93%	Cricket X	285.87%
TwoPatterns	missing	Cricket Y	296.40%

due to the fact that the MODL approach is regularized. A possible explanation is that the temporal representation of time series is not informative for this dataset. Other representations such as the Fourier or the wavelet transforms could be tried. In most cases, Δ_G has a positive value which means SAXO provides a better compression than the MODL approach. This trend emerges clearly, the average compression improvement reaches 183 %. We exploit the *Wilcoxon signed-ranks test* to reliably comparing both approaches over all datasets [23]. If the output value *(denoted by z)* is smaller than -1.96, the gap in performance is considered as significant. Our experiments give $z = -3.37$ which is highly significant. In the end, the compression of data provided by SAXO appears to be intrinsically better than the MODL approach. The prior term of C_{saxo} induces an additional cost in terms of coding length. This additional cost is far outweighed by a better encoding of the likelihood.

4.2 Supervised Learning Evaluation

This section aims to evaluate several symbolic representations conditionally to a supervised learning task. The same 19 datasets as in Sect. 4.1 are exploited. Each dataset is randomly split into a training set *(70 %)* and a test set *(30 %)*. The input datasets are sequentially recoded into multiple symbolic versions *(the class value is ignored at this step)*. The SAXO representation is first computed and is used to fix the parameters of SAX. Namely, the SAX approach is applied while keeping the same number of time intervals *(w = k_T)*, the parameter α is fixed as the average size of the alphabet within the time intervals of SAXO. The third representation *(denoted by MODL)* encodes the data by using a constant alphabet. This approach exploits the same time discretization as SAXO with a symbol per interval. But the time series are recoded by using a MODL coclustering model which estimates $P(C, T, X)$. In each time interval, a sub-series is associated with the symbol which corresponds to the closest joint distribution $P(T, X|C)$. In contrast, the symbols of SAXO correspond to univariate distributions $P(X|T, C)$. Our objective is to compare the MODL representation with SAXO which defines specific alphabets within each time interval. A naive Bayes classifier is trained on each version of the recoded datasets. In all cases, the symbols are exploited as categorical input variables. The classifiers are evaluated by using the multi-class AUC *(Area Under ROC Curves)* [24].

Table 2 shows the AUC reached by the naive Bayes classifier considering the various representations of the time series. A color code gives the rank of each approach. SAXO reaches the best AUC in 84 % of cases. The *Wilcoxon signed-ranks test* gives $z = -2.86$ when SAXO is compared with the MODL representation. This significant gap in performance demonstrates the interest of defining specific alphabets within each time interval. The formalisation of SAXO as a hierarchical coclustering approach proves to be more informative than the original MODL coclustering approach. SAXO and MODL are favorably compared with SAX *(respectively $z = -3.63$ and $z = -3,29$)*. This comparison must be moderated because these representations do not satisfy the same practical needs: (i) SAXO is the most informative representation but involves a relatively

Table 2. Evaluation on supervised learning tasks.

Dataset	SAXO	MODL	SAX
MoteStrain	0.8216	0.8274	0.7343
Yoga	0.8953	0.8957	0.7703
FacesUCR	0.9469	0.9655	0.7770
AllFace	0.9768	0.9474	0.9659
uWaveGestureY	0.8025	0.7095	0.7426
uWaveGestureX	0.9307	0.9187	0.8966
uWaveGestureZ	0.8470	0.8220	0.7189
Starlight curves	0.9521	0.9503	0.9350
ECG Five Days	0.8697	0.8616	0.7350
CincEGCtorso	0.9128	0.9017	0.7023
MedicalImages	0.8439	0.8280	0.7055
WordSynonym	0.8507	0.8420	0.6863
CBF	0.8657	0.8324	0.6694
Symbols	0.9940	0.9739	0.9504
50 Words	0.9437	0.9270	0.8937
Wafer	0.9924	0.9919	0.9350
Cricket Z	0.8818	0.8501	0.8237
Cricket X	0.9838	0.9785	0.8011
Cricket Y	0.8883	0.8468	0.7758

important training time complexity; (ii) SAXO is challenging to use in a sliding window scenario, where no absolute time points exist. In order to improve the interpretability of our approach, C_{saxo} could be optimized while limiting the number of symbols within each time interval. Such an optimization algorithm necessarily degrades the quality of the compression. In the end, the main challenge of the symbolic representations of time series is to reach a good tradeoff between the compression and the interpretability.

5 Conclusion and Perspectives

SAXO is a data-driven symbolic representation of time series which extends SAX in three ways: (i) the discretization of time is optimized by a Bayesian approach rather than considering regular intervals; (ii) the symbols within each time interval represents typical distributions of data points rather than average values; (iii) the number of symbols may differ per time interval. The parameter settings is automatically optimized given the data. SAXO was first introduced as an heuristic algorithm. This article formalizes this approach within the MODL framework as a hierarchical coclustering approach *(see Sect. 3)*. A Bayesian approach is applied leading to an analytical evaluation criterion. This criterion must be minimized in order to define the most probable representation given the data. This new criterion is evaluated on real datasets in Sect. 4. Our experiments compare the SAXO representation with the original MODL coclustering approach.

The SAXO representation appears to be significantly better in terms of data compression and in terms of informativeness when it is exploited for classification tasks. In future work, we plan to use the SAXO criterion in order to define a similarity measure. Numerous learning algorithms, such as K-means and K-NN, could use such an improved similarity measure defined over time series. We plan to explore potential gains in areas such as: (i) the detection of atypical time series; (ii) the query of a database by similarity; (iii) the clustering of time series.

References

1. Liao, T.: Clustering of time series data: a survey. Pattern Recogn. **38**, 1857–1874 (2005)
2. Bosq, D.: Linear Processes in Function Spaces: Theory and Applications. LNS. Springer, New York (2000)
3. Ramsay, J., Silverman, B.: Functional Data Analysis. Springer Series in Statistics. Springer, New York (2005)
4. Frigo, M., Johnson, S.: The design and implementation of FFTW3. Proc. IEEE **93**(2), 216–231 (2005). Special issue on "Program Generation, Optimization, and Platform Adaptation"
5. Polikar, R.: The story of wavelets. In: Mastorakis, N. (ed.) Physics and Modern Topics in Mechanical and Electrical Engineering. World Scientific and Engineering Society Press, New York (1999)
6. Chan, K., Fu, W.: Efficient time series matching by wavelets. In: Proceedings of the 15th International Conference on Data Engineering, ICDE 1999. IEEE Computer Society (1999)
7. Ahmed, N., Natarajan, T., Rao, K.R.: Discrete cosine transfom. IEEE Trans. Comput. **23**(1), 90–93 (1974)
8. Guo, C., Li, H., Pan, D.: An improved piecewise aggregate approximation based on statistical features for time series mining. In: Bi, Y., Williams, M.-A. (eds.) KSEM 2010. LNCS, vol. 6291, pp. 234–244. Springer, Heidelberg (2010)
9. Lin, J., Keogh, E., Lonardi, S., Chiu, B.: A symbolic representation of time series, with implications for streaming algorithms. In: 8th ACM SIGMOD Workshop on Research Issues in Data Mining and Knowledge Discovery, San Diego (2003)
10. Bondu, A., Boullé, M., Grossin, B.: SAXO: an optimized data-drivensymbolic representation of time series. In: IJCNN, International Joint Conference on Neural Networks. IEEE (2013)
11. Boullé, M.: Data grid models for preparation and modeling in supervised learning. In: Guyon, I., Cawley, G., Dror, G., Saffari, A. (eds.) Hands on Pattern Recognition. Microtome, Brookline (2010)
12. Shatkay, H., Zdonik, S.B.: Approximate queries and representations for large data sequences. In: 12th International Conference on Data Engineering (ICDE), pp. 536–545 (1996)
13. Agrawal, R., Psaila, G., Wimmers, E.L., Zait, M.: Querying shapes of histories. In: 21th International Conference on Very Large Data Bases (VLDB 1995), pp. 502–514 (1995)
14. Ratanamahatana, C., Keogh, E., Bagnall, T., Lonardi, S.: A novel bit level time series representation with implications for similarity search and clustering. In: PAKDD (2005)

15. Cortes, C., Fisher, K., Pregibon, D., Rogers, A., Smith, F.: Hancock: a language for extracting signatures from data streams. In: 6th ACMSIGKDD International Conference on Knowledge Discovery and Data Mining, Boston, pp. 9–17 (2000)

16. Keogh, E., Lin, J., Fu, A.: HOT SAX: efficiently finding the most unusualtime series subsequence. In: 5th IEEE International Conference on Data Mining, Houston, Texas, pp. 226–233 (2005)

17. Chiu, B., Keogh, E., Lonardi, S.: Probabilistic discovery of time series motifs. In: 9th ACM SIGKDD International Conference on Knowledge Discovery and Data Mining, Washington, pp. 493–498 (2003)

18. Keogh, E., Wei, L., Xi, X., Lonardi, S., Shieh, J., Sirowy, S.: IntelligentIcons: integrating lite-weight data mining and visualization into GUI operating systems. In: International Conference on Data Mining (2006)

19. Camerra, A., Palpanas, T., Shieh, J., Keogh, E.: iSAX 2.0: indexing andmining one billion time series. In: International Conference on DataMining (2010)

20. Boullé, M.: Functional data clustering via piecewise constant nonparametric density estimation. Pattern Recogn. 45(12), 4389–4401 (2012)

21. Keogh, E., Zhu, Q., Hu, B., Hao, Y., Xi, X., Wei, L., Ratanamahatana, C.A.: The UCR Time Series Classification/Clustering Homepage (2011). http://www.cs.ucr.edu/~eamonn/time_series_data/

22. Boullé, M.: Optimum simultaneous discretization with data grid models in supervised classification: a Bayesian model selection approach. Adv. Data Anal. Classif. 3(1), 39–61 (2009)

23. Demšar, J.: Statistical comparisons of classifiers over multiple data sets. J. Mach. Learn. Res. 7, 1–30 (2006)

24. Fawcett, T.: Roc graphs: notes and practical considerations for data mining researchers. Technical Report HPL-2003-4, HP Labs (2003). http://citeseer.ist.psu.edu/fawcett03roc.html

Dense Bag-of-Temporal-SIFT-Words for Time Series Classification

Adeline Bailly[1,3](✉), Simon Malinowski[2](✉), Romain Tavenard[1],
Laetitia Chapel[3], and Thomas Guyet[4]

[1] Université de Rennes 2, IRISA, LETG-Rennes COSTEL, Rennes, France
adeline.bailly@univ-rennes2.fr
[2] Université de Rennes 1, IRISA, Rennes, France
simon.malinowski@irisa.fr
[3] Université de Bretagne-Sud, IRISA, Vannes, France
[4] Agrocampus Ouest, IRISA, Rennes, France

Abstract. The SIFT framework has shown to be effective in the image classification context. In [4], we designed a Bag-of-Words approach based on an adaptation of this framework to time series classification. It relies on two steps: SIFT-based features are first extracted and quantized into words; histograms of occurrences of each word are then fed into a classifier. In this paper, we investigate techniques to improve the performance of Bag-of-Temporal-SIFT-Words: dense extraction of keypoints and different normalizations of Bag-of-Words histograms. Extensive experiments show that our method significantly outperforms nearly all tested standalone baseline classifiers on publicly available UCR datasets.

Keywords: Time series classification · Bag-of-Words · SIFT · Dense features · BoTSW · D-BoTSW

1 Introduction

Classification of time series has received an important amount of interest over the past years due to many real-life applications, such as medicine [29], environmental modeling [11], speech recognition [16]. A wide range of algorithms have been proposed to solve this problem. One simple classifier is the k-nearest-neighbor (kNN), which is usually combined with Euclidean Distance (ED) or Dynamic Time Warping (DTW) similarity measure. The combination of the kNN classifier with DTW is one of the most popular methods since it achieves high classification accuracy [24]. However, this method has a high computation cost which makes its use difficult for large-scale real-life applications.

Above-mentioned techniques compute similarity between time series based on point-to-point comparisons. Classification techniques based on higher level structures (*e.g.* feature vectors) are most of the time faster, while being at least as accurate as DTW-based classifiers. Hence, various works have investigated the extraction of local and global features in time series. Among these works, the Bag-of-Words (BoW) approach (also called Bag-of-Features) consists in representing documents using a histogram of word occurrences. It is a very common

© Springer International Publishing Switzerland 2016
A. Douzal-Chouakria et al. (Eds.): AALTD 2015, LNAI 9785, pp. 17–30, 2016.
DOI: 10.1007/978-3-319-44412-3_2

technique in text mining, information retrieval and content-based image retrieval because of its simplicity and performance. For these reasons, it has been adapted to time series data in some recent works [5,6,18,26,29]. Different kinds of features based on simple statistics, computed at a local scale, are used to create the words.

In the context of image retrieval and classification, scale-invariant descriptors have proved their accuracy. Particularly, the Scale-Invariant Feature Transform (SIFT) framework has led to widely used descriptors [21]. These descriptors are scale and rotation invariant while being robust to noise. In [4], we build upon this framework to design a BoW approach for time series classification where words correspond to quantized versions of local features. Features are built using the SIFT framework for both detection and description of the keypoints. This approach can be seen as an adaptation of [27], which uses SIFT features associated with visual words, to time series. In this paper, we improve on our previous work by applying enhancement techniques for BoW approaches, such as dense extraction and BoW normalization. To validate this approach, we conduct extensive experiments on a wide range of publicly available datasets.

This paper is organized as follows. Section 2 summarizes related work, Sect. 3 describes the proposed Bag-of-Temporal-SIFT-Words (BoTSW) method and its improved version (D-BoTSW) and Sect. 4 reports experimental results. Finally, Sect. 5 concludes and discusses future work.

2   Related Work

Our approach for time series classification builds on two well-known methods in computer vision: local features are extracted from time series using a SIFT-based approach and a global representation of time series is produced using Bag-of-Words. This section first introduces state-of-the-art distance-based methods in Time Series Classification (TSC), then presents previous works that make use of Bag-of-Words approaches for TSC and finally introduces some ensemble classifiers adapted to TSC.

2.1   Distance-Based Time Series Classification

Data mining community has, for long, investigated the field of time series classification. Early works focus on the use of dedicated similarity measures to assess similarity between time series. In [24], Ratanamahatana and Keogh compare Dynamic Time Warping to Euclidean Distance when used with a simple kNN classifier. While the former benefits from its robustness to temporal distortions to achieve high accuracy, ED is known to have much lower computational cost. Cuturi [9] shows that, although DTW is well-suited to retrieval tasks since it focuses on the best possible alignment between time series, it fails at precisely quantifying dissimilarity between non-matching sequences (which is backed by the fact that DTW-derived kernel is not positive definite). Hence, he introduces the Global Alignment Kernel that takes into account all possible alignments in order to produce a reliable similarity measure to be used at the core of standard kernel methods such as Support Vector Machines (SVM). Instead of building classification decision on similarities between time series, Ye and Keogh [31] use a decision tree in which the partitioning of time series is performed with respect to the presence (or absence) of discriminant sub-sequences (named shapelets) in the series. Though accurate, the method is very computational demanding as building the decision tree requires one to check for all candidate shapelets. Douzal and Amblard [10] define a dedicated similarity measure for time series which is then used in a classification tree.

2.2   Bag-of-Words for Time Series Classification

Inspired by text mining, information retrieval and computer vision communities, recent works have investigated the use of Bag-of-Words (BoW) for time series classification [5,6,18,25,26,29]. These works are based on two main operations: converting time series into BoW and building a classifier upon this BoW representation. Usually, standard techniques such as random forests, SVM or kNN are used for the classification step. Yet, many different ways of converting time series into BoW have been introduced. Among them, Baydogan $et\ al.$ [6] propose a framework to classify time series denoted TSBF where local features such as mean, variance and extrema are computed on sliding windows. These features are then quantized into words using a codebook learned by a class probability estimate distribution. In [29], discrete wavelet coefficients are extracted on sliding windows and then quantized into words using k-means. Quantized Fourier coefficients are used as words in the BOSS representation introduced in [25]. In [18,26], words are constructed using the Symbolic Aggregate approXimation (SAX) representation [17] of time series. SAX symbols are extracted from time series and histograms of n-grams of these symbols are computed to form a Bag-of-Patterns (BoP). In [26], Senin and Malinchik combine SAX with Vector Space Model to form the SAX-VSM method. In [5], Baydogan and Runger design a symbolic representation of multivariate time series (MTS), called SMTS, where MTS are transformed into a feature matrix, whose rows are feature vectors containing a time index, the values and the gradient of time series at this time index (on all dimensions). Random samples of this matrix are given to decision trees whose leaves are seen as words. A histogram of words is output when the different trees are learned.

Local feature extraction has been investigated for long in the computer vision community. One of the most powerful local feature for image is SIFT [21]. It consists in detecting keypoints as extremum values of the Difference-of-Gaussians (DoG) function and describing their neighborhoods using histograms of gradients. Xie and Beigi [30] use similar keypoint detection for time series. Keypoints are then described by scale-invariant features that characterize the shapes surrounding the extremum. In [8], extraction and description of time series keypoints in a SIFT-like framework is used to reduce the complexity of DTW: features are used to match anchor points from two different time series and prune the search space when searching for the optimal path for DTW.

2.3   Ensemble Classifiers for Time Series

Recently, ensemble classifiers have been designed for time series classification. They typically rely on standalone classifiers (such as the ones described above) and fuse information from their outputs to build a more reliable classification decision. Lines and Bagnall [19] propose an ensemble classifier based on a family of elastic distance measures, named Proportional Elastic Ensemble (PROP). Bagnall *et al.* [3] propose a meta ensemble classifier that is a collection of 35 classifiers for time series (COTE).

In this paper, we build upon BoW of SIFT-based descriptors. We propose an adaptation of SIFT to mono-dimensional signals that preserves their robustness to noise and their scale invariance. We then use BoW to gather information from many local features into a single global one.

3   Bag-of-Temporal-SIFT-Words (BoTSW)

The proposed method is based on three main steps: (i) extraction of keypoints in time series, (ii) description of these keypoints through gradient magnitude at a specific scale and (iii) representation of time series by a BoW, where words correspond to quantized version of the description of keypoints. These steps are depicted in Fig. 1 and detailed below.

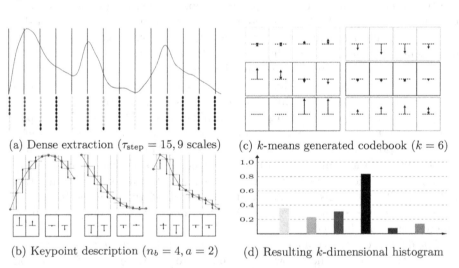

(a) Dense extraction ($\tau_{\text{step}} = 15, 9$ scales)   (c) k-means generated codebook ($k = 6$)

(b) Keypoint description ($n_b = 4, a = 2$)   (d) Resulting k-dimensional histogram

Fig. 1. Approach overview: (a) A time series and its dense-extracted keypoints. (b) Keypoint description is based on the time series filtered at the scale at which the keypoint is extracted. Descriptors are quantized into words. (c) Codewords obtained *via* k-means, the color is associated with the dots under each keypoint in (a). (d) Histograms of word occurrences are given to a classifier (linear SVM) that learns boundaries between classes. Best viewed in color. (Color figure online)

3.1   Keypoint Extraction in Time Series

The first step of our method consists in extracting keypoints in time series. Two approaches are described here: the first one is based on scale-space extrema detection (as in [4]) and the second one proposes a dense extraction scheme.

Scale-Space Extrema Detection. Following the SIFT framework, keypoints in time series can be detected as local extrema in terms of both scale and (temporal) location. These scale-space extrema are identified using a DoG function, and form a list of scale-invariant keypoints. Let $L(t, \sigma)$ be the convolution ($*$) of a time series $S(t)$ with a Gaussian function $G(t, \sigma)$ of width σ:

$$L(t, \sigma) = S(t) * G(t, \sigma) \tag{1}$$

where $G(t, \sigma)$ is defined as

$$G(t, \sigma) = \frac{1}{\sqrt{2\pi}\,\sigma}\, e^{-t^2/2\sigma^2}. \tag{2}$$

Lowe [20] proposes the Difference-of-Gaussians (DoG) function to detect scale-space extrema in images. Adapted to time series, a DoG function is obtained by subtracting two time series filtered at consecutive scales:

$$D(t, \sigma) = L(t, k_{\mathrm{sc}}\sigma) - L(t, \sigma), \tag{3}$$

where k_{sc} is a parameter of the method that controls the scale ratio between two consecutive scales.

Keypoints are then detected at time index t in scale j if they correspond to extrema of $D(t, k_{\mathrm{sc}}^j \sigma_0)$ in both time and scale, where σ_0 is the width of the Gaussian corresponding to the reference scale. At a given scale, each point has two neighbors: one at the previous and one at the following time instant. Points also have neighbors one scale up and one scale down at the previous, same and next time instants, leading to a total of eight neighbors. If a point is higher (or lower) than all of its neighbors, it is considered as an extremum in the scale-space domain and hence a keypoint.

Dense Extraction. Previous works have shown that accurate classification could be achieved by using densely extracted local features [14,28]. In this section, we present the adaptation of this setup to our BoTSW scheme. Keypoints selected with dense extraction no longer correspond to extrema but are rather systematically extracted at all scales every τ_{step} time steps on Gaussian-filtered time series $L(\cdot, k_{\mathrm{sc}}^j \sigma_0)$.

Unlike scale-space extrema detection, regular sampling guarantees a minimal amount of keypoints per time series. This is especially crucial for smooth time series from which very few keypoints are detected when using scale-space extrema detection. In all cases, description of these keypoints (*cf.* Sect. 3.2) covers the description of scale-space extrema if τ_{step} is small enough, which leads to a more robust representation. A dense extraction scheme is represented in Fig. 1. In the following, when dense extraction is performed, we will refer to our method as D-BoTSW (for dense BoTSW).

3.2 Description of the Extracted Keypoints

Next step in our process is the description of keypoints. A keypoint at time index t and scale j is described by gradient magnitudes of $L(\cdot, k_{sc}{}^j \sigma_0)$ around t. To do so, n_b blocks of size a are selected around the keypoint. Gradients are computed at each point of each block and weighted using a Gaussian window of standard deviation $\frac{a \times n_b}{2}$ so that points that are farther in time from the detected keypoint have lower influence. Then, each block is described by two values: the sum of positive gradients and the sum of negative gradients. Resulting feature vector is hence of dimension $2 \times n_b$.

3.3 Bag-of-Temporal-SIFT-Words for Time Series Classification

Training features are used to learn a codebook of k words using k-means clustering. Words represent different local behaviors in time series. Then, for a given time series, each feature vector is assigned the closest word in the codebook. The number of occurrences of each word in a time series is computed. (D-)BoTSW representation of a time series is the normalized histogram of word occurrences.

Bag-of-Words Normalization. Dense sampling on multiple Gaussian-filtered time series provides considerable information to process. It also tends to generate words with little informative power, as stop words do in text mining applications. In order to reduce the impact of those words, we compare two normalization schemes for BoW: Signed Square Root normalization (SSR) and Inverse Document Frequency normalization (IDF). These normalizations are commonly used in image retrieval and classification based on histograms [12,13,23,27].

Jégou et al. [13] and Perronin et al. [23] show that reducing the influence of frequent codewords before ℓ_2 normalization could be profitable. They apply a power $\alpha \in [0,1]$ on their global representation. SSR normalization corresponds to the case where $\alpha = 0.5$, which leads to near-optimal results [13,23]. IDF normalization also tends to lower the influence of frequent codewords. To do so, document frequency of words is computed as the number of training time series in which the word occurs. BoW are then updated by diving each component by its associated document frequency. SSR and IDF are both applied before ℓ_2 normalization. Note that normalizing histograms using SSR followed by ℓ_2 can be seen as an explicit feature map for the Hellinger kernel between ℓ_1-normalized histograms [1]. We show in the experimental part of this paper that using BoW normalization improves the accuracy of our method.

Normalized histograms finally feed a classifier that learns how to discriminate classes from this BoW representation.

Time Complexity. The process of computing (D-)BoTSW representation for a time series has linear time complexity in the number of features extracted. When using dense extraction, this number depends on the length of the time series. For a time series of length T, features will be computed at $\lfloor T/\tau_{\text{step}} \rfloor$ different time instants. At each time instant, features will be computed at all scales and the number of scales is $\left\lfloor \frac{\log(T/8\sigma_0)}{\log k_{\text{sc}}} \right\rfloor$. Finally, time complexity of computing D-BoTSW for a time series of length T is in $O(T \log T)$.

4 Experiments and Results

In this section, we investigate the impact of both dense extraction of keypoints and normalizations of the Bag-of-Words on classification performance. We then compare our results to the ones obtained by 9 relevant baselines.

Experiments are conducted on the 86 currently available datasets from the UCR repository [15], the largest online database for time series classification. It includes a wide variety of problems, such as sensor reading (*ECG*), image outline (*ArrowHead*), human motion (*GunPoint*), as well as simulated problems (*TwoPatterns*). All datasets are split into a training and a test set, whose size varies between less than 20 and more than 8000 time series. For a given dataset, all time series have the same length, ranging from 24 to more than 2500 time instants. Following results should be interpreted in the light of the potential bias that is implied by using such a setup, especially when few training data are available [2].

For the sake of reproducibility, C++ source code used for (D-)BoTSW in these experiments and all raw numbers are made available for download[1]. To provide illustrative timings for our methods, we ran it on a personal computer, for a given set of parameters, using dataset *Cricket_X* [15] that is made of 390 training time series and 390 test ones. Each time series in the dataset is of length 300. Extraction and description of dense keypoints take around 2 s for all time series in the dataset. Then, 75 s are necessary to learn a k-means and fit a linear SVM classifier using training data only. Finally, classification of all D-BoTSW corresponding to test time series takes less than 1 s.

4.1 Experimental Setup

Parameters a, n_b, k and C_{SVM} of (D-)BoTSW are learned, whereas we set $\sigma_0 = 1.6$ and $k_{\text{sc}} = 2^{1/3}$, as these values have shown to produce stable results [21]. Parameters a, n_b, k and C_{SVM} vary inside the following sets: $\{4, 8\}$, $\{4, 8, 12, 16, 20\}$, $\{2^i, \forall i \in \{5..10\}\}$ and $\{1, 10, 100\}$ respectively. A linear SVM is used to classify time series represented as (D-)BoTSW. For our approach, the best sets (in terms of accuracy) of $(a, n_b, k, C_{\text{SVM}})$ parameters are selected by performing cross-validation on the training set. Due to the heterogeneity of the datasets, leave-one-out cross-validation is performed on datasets where the

---

[1] http://github.com/a-bailly/dbotsw.

training set contains less than 300 time series, and 10-fold cross-validation is used otherwise. These best sets of parameters are then used to build the classifier on the training set and evaluate it on the test set. For datasets with little training data, it is likely that several sets of parameters yield best performance during the cross-validation process. For example, when using *DiatomSizeReduction* dataset, BoTSW has 150 out of 180 parameter sets yielding best performance, while there are 42 such sets for D-BoTSW with SSR normalization. In both cases, the number of *best* parameter sets is too high to allow a fair parameter selection. When this happens, we keep all parameter sets with best performance at training and perform a majority voting between their outputs at test time.

Parameters a and n_b both influence the descriptions of the keypoints; their optimal values vary between sets so that the description of keypoints can fit the shape of the data. If the data contains sharp peaks, the size of the neighborhood on which features are computed (equal to $a \times n_b$) should be small. On the contrary, if it contains smooth peaks, descriptions should take more points into account. The number k of codewords needs to be large enough to precisely represent the different features. However, it needs to be small enough in order to avoid overfitting. We consequently allow a large range of values for k.

In the following, BoTSW denotes the approach where keypoints are selected as scale-space extrema and BoW histograms are ℓ_2-normalized. For all experiments with dense extraction, we set $\tau_{\text{step}} = 1$, and we extract keypoints at all scales. Using such a value for τ_{step} enables one to have a sufficient number of keypoints even for small time series, and guarantees that keypoint neighborhoods overlap so that all subparts of the time series are described.

4.2   Dense Extraction *vs.* Scale-Space Extrema Detection

Figure 2 shows a pairwise comparison of error rates between BoTSW and its dense counterpart D-BoTSW for all datasets in the UCR repository. A point on

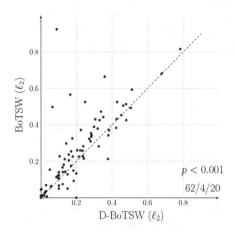

Fig. 2. Error rates of BoTSW compared to D-BoTSW.

the diagonal means that methods obtain equal error rates. A point above the diagonal illustrates a dataset for which D-BoTSW outperforms BoTSW. One-sided Wilcoxon signed rank test's p-value and Win/Tie/Lose scores are given in the bottom-right corner of the figure. D-BoTSW reaches better performance than BoTSW on 62 datasets, equivalent performance on 4 datasets and worse on 20 datasets. If the p-value is less than the 5 % significance level, the method on the x-axis is considered significantly better than the one on the y-axis, *e.g.* Fig. 2 shows that D-BOTSW (ℓ_2) is significantly better than BoTSW (ℓ_2). D-BoTSW improves classification on a large majority of datasets. In the following, we show how to further improve these results thanks to BoW normalization.

4.3   Impact of the BoW Normalization

As can be seen in Fig. 3, both SSR and IDF normalizations improve classification performance (though the improvement of using IDF is not statistically significant). Lowering the influence of largely-represented codewords hence leads to more accurate classification with D-BoTSW. IDF normalization only leads to a small improvement in classification accuracy, whereas SSR normalization significantly improves classification accuracy. This is backed by Fig. 4, which shows that SSR normalization tends to spread energy across BoW dimensions, leading to a more balanced representation than other two normalization schemes.

4.4   Comparison with State-of-the-Art Methods

In the following, we will refer to dense SSR-normalized BoTSW as D-BoTSW, since this setup is the one providing the best classification performance. We now compare D-BoTSW to the most popular state-of-the-art methods for time series classification (a detailed comparison of time series classification algorithms can be found in [2]). The UCR repository provides error rates for the

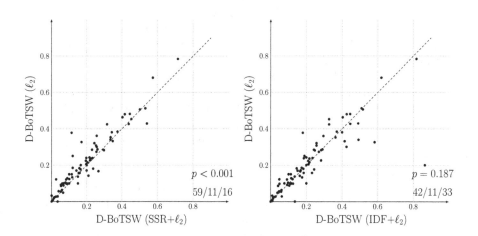

Fig. 3. Error rates of D-BoTSW with and without normalization.

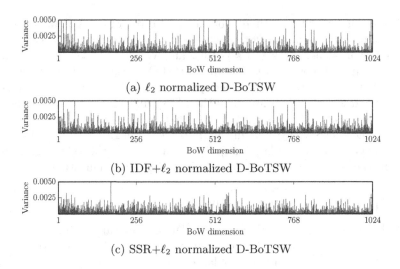

(a) ℓ_2 normalized D-BoTSW

(b) IDF+ℓ_2 normalized D-BoTSW

(c) SSR+ℓ_2 normalized D-BoTSW

Fig. 4. Per-dimension energy of D-BoTSW vectors extracted from dataset *ShapesAll*. The same codebook is used for all normalization schemes so that dimensions are comparable across all three sub-figures.

86 datasets with Euclidean distance 1NN (EDNN) and Dynamic Time Warping 1NN (DTWNN) [24]. We use published error rates for TSBF (45 datasets) [6], SAX-VSM (51 datasets) [26], SMTS (45 datasets) [5], BoP (20 datasets) [18], BOSS (83 datasets) [25], PROP (46 datasets) [19] and COTE (45 datasets) [3].

As BoP only provides classification performance for 20 datasets, we decided not to plot pairwise comparison of error rates between D-BoTSW and BoP. Note however that the Win/Tie/Lose score is 15/2/3 in favor of D-BoTSW and this difference is statistically significant ($p < 0.001$).

Figure 5 shows that D-BoTSW performs better than 1NN combined with ED (EDNN) or DTW (DTWNN), TSBF, SAX-VSM and SMTS. This difference is statistically significant. We can also notice from Fig. 5 that BOSS and D-BoTSW have comparable Win/Tie/Lose performance. Note that, if D-BoTSW is not significantly better than BOSS ($p = 0.791$), the reverse is also true ($p = 0.209$). It is striking to realize that D-BoTSW not only improves classification accuracy, but might improve it considerably. Error rate on *Shapelet Sim* dataset drops from 0.461 (EDNN) and 0.35 (DTWNN) to 0 (D-BoTSW), for example. Pairwise comparisons of methods show that D-BoTSW is significantly better than almost all state-of-the-art standalone classifiers, excepted BOSS that exhibits equivalent performance compared to D-BoTSW.

In Fig. 6, we compare our standalone classifier D-BoTSW to ensemble classifiers. Wilcoxon tests show that D-BoTSW is not statistically better than neither PROP nor COTE. Testing the reverse hypothesis that D-BoTSW is outperformed by these methods gives significance for COTE ($p = 0.046$) but not for PROP ($p = 0.725$). In all cases, ensemble classifiers can benefit from the design of new standalone classifiers as D-BoTSW.

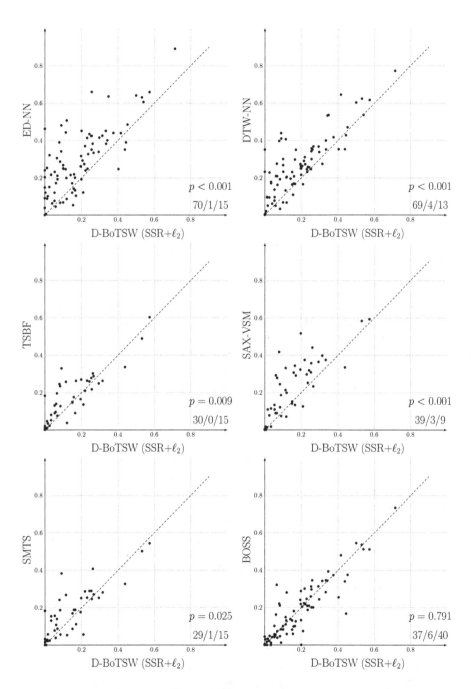

Fig. 5. Error rates for D-BoTSW with SSR normalization versus standalone baseline classifiers (ED-NN, DTW-NN, TSBF, SAX-VSM, SMTS and BOSS).

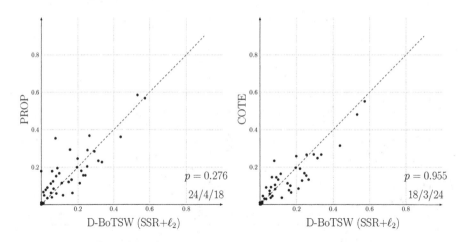

Fig. 6. Error rates for D-BoTSW with SSR normalization versus baseline ensemble classifiers (PROP and COTE).

We noticed that D-BoTSW performs especially well in the presence of large amounts of training data. On the contrary, when faced with smaller training sets, it is more likely (though still a minority) that non-parametric methods such as DTWNN or EDNN are competitive against D-BoTSW.

These experiments, conducted on a wide variety of time series datasets, show that D-BoTSW significantly outperforms most considered standalone classifiers.

5   Conclusion

In this paper, we presented the D-BoTSW technique, which transforms time series into histograms of quantized local features. The association of SIFT keypoints and Bag-of-Words has been widely used and is considered as a standard technique in image domain; however it has never been investigated for time series classification. We carried out extensive experiments and showed that dense keypoint extraction and SSR normalization of Bag-of-Words lead to the best performance for our method. We compared the results with standard techniques for time series classification and show that D-BoTSW significantly outperforms most standalone state-of-the-art time series classification algorithms.

We believe that classification performance could be further improved by taking more time information into account. Indeed, only local temporal information is embedded in our model and the global structure of time series is ignored. Moreover, more detailed global representations for feature sets than BoW have been proposed in the computer vision community [13,22], and such global features could be used in our framework. Future work also includes the evaluation of our method on multidimensional signals: a straightforward extension would be to consider one dimension at a time and describe it, as done for HSV-SIFT [7].

Acknowledgments. This work has been partly funded by ANR project ASTERIX (ANR-13-JS02-0005-01), Région Bretagne and CNES-TOSCA project VEGIDAR. Authors also thank anonymous reviewers for their fruitful comments as well as data donators.

References

1. Arandjelović, R., Zisserman, A.: Three things everyone should know to improve object retrieval. In: Proceedings of the IEEE Conference on Computer Vision and Pattern Recognition, pp. 2911–2918 (2012)
2. Bagnall, A., Bostrom, A., Large, J., Lines, J.: The great time series classification bake off: an experimental evaluation of recently proposed algorithms. Extended Version. CoRR, abs/1602.01711 (2016)
3. Bagnall, A., Lines, J., Hills, J., Bostrom, A.: Time-series classification with COTE: the collective of transformation-based ensembles. IEEE Trans. Knowl. Data Eng. **27**(9), 2522–2535 (2015)
4. Bailly, A., Malinowski, S., Tavenard, R., Guyet, T., Chapel, L.: Bag-of-Temporal-SIFT-Words for time series classification. In: Proceedings of the ECML-PKDD Workshop on Advanced Analytics and Learning on Temporal Data (2015)
5. Baydogan, M.G., Runger, G.: Learning a symbolic representation for multivariate time series classification. Data Min. Knowl. Discov. **29**(2), 400–422 (2015)
6. Baydogan, M.G., Runger, G., Tuv, E.: A Bag-of-Features framework to classify time series. IEEE Trans. Pattern Anal. Mach. Intell. **35**(11), 2796–2802 (2013)
7. Bosch, A., Zisserman, A., Muoz, X.: Scene classification using a hybrid generative/discriminative approach. IEEE Trans. Pattern Anal. Mach. Intell. **30**(4), 712–727 (2008)
8. Candan, K.S., Rossini, R., Sapino, M.L.: sDTW: computing DTW distances using locally relevant constraints based on salient feature alignments. In: Proceedings of the International Conference on Very Large DataBases, vol. 5, pp. 1519–1530 (2012)
9. Cuturi, M.: Fast global alignment kernels. In: Proceedings of the International Conference on Machine Learning, pp. 929–936 (2011)
10. Douzal-Chouakria, A., Amblard, C.: Classification trees for time series. Elsevier Pattern Recogn. **45**(3), 1076–1091 (2012)
11. Dusseux, P., Corpetti, T., Hubert-Moy, L.: Temporal kernels for the identification of grassland management using time series of high spatial resolution satellite images. In: Proceedings of the IEEE International Geoscience and Remote Sensing Symposium, pp. 3258–3260 (2013)
12. Jégou, H., Chum, O.: Negative evidences and co-occurrences in image retrieval: the benefit of PCA and whitening. In: Proceedings of the European Conference on Computer Vision, pp. 774–787 (2012)
13. Jégou, H., Douze, M., Schmid, C., Pérez, P.: Aggregating local descriptors into a compact image representation. In: Proceedings of the IEEE Conference on Computer Vision and Pattern Recognition, pp. 3304–3311 (2010)
14. Jurie, F., Triggs, B.: Creating efficient codebooks for visual recognition. In: Proceedings of the International Conference on Computer Vision, pp. 604–610 (2005)
15. Keogh, E., Zhu, Q., Hu, B., Hao, Y., Xi, X., Wei, L., Ratanamahatana, C.A.: The UCR Time Series Classification/Clustering Homepage (2011). www.cs.ucr.edu/~eamonn/time_series_data/

16. Le Cun, Y., Bengio, Y.: Convolutional networks for images, speech, and time series. In: Arbib, M.A. (ed.) The Handbook of Brain Theory and Neural Networks, pp. 255–258. MIT Press, Cambrdige (1995)

17. Lin, J., Keogh, E., Lonardi, S., Chiu, B.: A symbolic representation of time series, with implications for streaming algorithms. In: Proceedings of the ACM SIGMOD Workshop on Research Issues in Data Mining and Knowledge Discovery, pp. 2–11 (2003)

18. Lin, J., Khade, R., Li, Y.: Rotation-invariant similarity in time series using Bag-of-Patterns representation. Int. J. Inf. Syst. **39**, 287–315 (2012)

19. Lines, J., Bagnall, A.: Time series classification with ensembles of elastic distance measures. Data Min. Knowl. Dis. **29**(3), 565–592 (2014)

20. Lowe, D.G.: Object recognition from local scale-invariant features. In: Proceedings of the International Conference on Computer Vision, pp. 1150–1157 (1999)

21. Lowe, D.G.: Distinctive image features from scale-invariant keypoints. Int. J. Comput. Vis. **60**(2), 91–110 (2004)

22. Perronnin, F., Dance, C.: Fisher kernels on visual vocabularies for image categorization. In: Proceedings of the IEEE Conference on Computer Vision and Pattern Recognition, pp. 1–8 (2007)

23. Perronnin, F., Liu, Y., Sanchez, J., Poirier, H.: Large-scale image retrieval with compressed Fisher vectors. In: Proceedings of the IEEE Conference on Computer Vision and Pattern Recognition, pp. 3384–3391 (2010)

24. Ratanamahatana, C.A., Keogh, E.: Everything you know about dynamic time warping is wrong. In: Proceedings of the Workshop on Mining Temporal and Sequential Data, pp. 22–25 (2004)

25. Schäfer, P.: The BOSS is concerned with time series classification in the presence of noise. Data Min. Knowl. Dis. **29**(6), 1505–1530 (2014)

26. Senin, P., Malinchik, S.: SAX-VSM: interpretable time series classification using SAX and vector space model. In: Proceedings of the IEEE International Conference on Data Mining, pp. 1175–1180 (2013)

27. Sivic, J., Zisserman, A.: Video google: a text retrieval approach to object matching in videos. In: Proceedings of the International Conference on Computer Vision, pp. 1470–1477 (2003)

28. Wang, H., Ullah, M.M., Klaser, A., Laptev, I., Schmid, C.: Evaluation of local spatio-temporal features for action recognition. In: Proceedings of the British Machine Vision Conference, pp. 124.1–124.11 (2009)

29. Wang, J., Liu, P., She, M.F.H., Nahavandi, S., Kouzani, A.: Bag-of-Words representation for biomedical time series classification. Biomed. Sig. Process. Control **8**(6), 634–644 (2013)

30. Xie, J., Beigi, M.: A scale-invariant local descriptor for event recognition in 1D sensor signals. In: Proceedings of the IEEE International Conference on Multimedia and Expo, pp. 1226–1229 (2009)

31. Ye, L., Keogh, E.: Time series shapelets: a new primitive for data mining. In: Proceedings of the ACM SIGKDD International Conference on Knowledge Discovery and Data Mining, pp. 947–956 (2009)

Dimension Reduction in Dissimilarity Spaces for Time Series Classification

Brijnesh Jain$^{(\boxtimes)}$ and Stephan Spiegel

Electrical Engineering and Computer Science, Technische Universität Berlin,
Fak. IV, TEL 14, Ernst-Reuter Platz 7, 10587 Berlin, Germany
jain@dai-labor.de

Abstract. Time series classification in the dissimilarity space combines the advantages of elastic dissimilarity functions such as the dynamic time warping distance and the rich mathematical structure of Euclidean spaces. We applied dimension reduction using PCA followed by support vector learning on dissimilarity representations to 42 UCR datasets. The results suggest that time series classification in dissimilarity space has potential to complement the state-of-the-art, because the SVM classifiers perform better on the 42 datasets with higher confidence than the nearest-neighbor classifier based on the dynamic time warping distance.

Keywords: Time series classification · Dynamic time warping distance · Dissimilarity space · PCA · SVM

1 Introduction

Time series classification finds many applications in diverse domains such as speech recognition, medical signal analysis, and recognition of gestures [10,12,22]. Surprisingly, the simple nearest-neighbor method together with the dynamic time warping (DTW) distance still belongs to the state-of-the-art and is reported to be *exceptionally difficult to beat* [1,25,35]. This finding is in stark contrast to classification in Euclidean spaces, where nearest neighbor methods often serve as baseline. One reason for this situation is that nearest neighbor methods in Euclidean spaces compete against a plethora of powerful statistical learning methods. The majority of these statistical learning methods apply the concept of derivative, which is not available for warping-invariant functions on time series. Prominent examples of such statistical methods include logistic regression, neural networks, and SVM.

The dissimilarity space approach proposed by [8,9,28] offers to combine the advantages of the DTW distance with the rich mathematical structure of Euclidean spaces. The basic idea is to first select a set of k reference time series, called prototypes. Then the dissimilarity representation of a time series consists of k features, each of which represents its DTW distance from one of the k prototypes. Since dissimilarity representations are vectors from $\mathbb{R}^k$, we can resort to the whole arsenal of mathematical tools for statistical data analysis.

© Springer International Publishing Switzerland 2016
A. Douzal-Chouakria et al. (Eds.): AALTD 2015, LNAI 9785, pp. 31–46, 2016.
DOI: 10.1007/978-3-319-44412-3_3

The dissimilarity space approach has been systematically applied to the graph domain using graph matching [26,32]. Though first work has been presented [15,19,21], a similar systematic study of the dissimilarity space approach for time series endowed with the DTW distance is still missing.

In [15,21] the full pairwise DTW distance matrix is used for support vector learning. This contribution extends prior work [19] on exploring the effects of dimensionality reduction applied to the pairwise distance matrix. The proposed approach applies principal component analysis (PCA) for dimension reduction of the dissimilarity representations followed by training a linear and non-linear support vector machine (SVM). Experimental results on 42 datasets show that SVM classifiers performed better on average than the nearest-neighbor classifier using DTW distance. In addition, we show that the dissimilarity approach induces prototype dependent kernels on time series in a natural way. The results in conjunction with the findings in [21] suggest that combining the advantages of both, the DTW distance and statistical pattern recognition methods on dissimilarity representations, can result in powerful classifiers that complement the state-of-the-art.

The rest of this paper is structured as follows: Sect. 2 discusses related work. Section 3 describes the dissimilarity space approach. Experiments are presented and discussed in Sect. 4. Finally, Sect. 5 concludes with a summary of main results and future directions of research.

2   Related Work

Following [36], three main directions of time series classification are (1) model-based classification, (2) dissimilarity-based classification, and (3) feature-based classification. Model-based classification refers to statistical models such as Hidden Markov Models. Dissimilarity-based methods predominantly apply k-nearest-neighbor classifiers or support vector machines if the underlying similarity function is a positive definite kernel. Finally, feature-based methods embed time series into Euclidean spaces by means of extracting features from time series. Then the repertoire of standard classification methods can be applied to the feature representations. Recently, a novel approach that extends gradient-based learning to time series spaces has been proposed [20].

Works related to this contribution combine approach (2) and (3) in the sense that the features of a time series are its dissimilarities to other time series. One prominent approach combining (2) and (3) are kernel methods [2,6]. Kernel methods are limited to positive semi-definite kernels and therefore can not be directly applied to general dissimilarity data. This limitation of kernel methods led to the dissimilarity representation introduced by Duin and co-workers [8,28]. Pairwise dissimilarities extend kernels to dyadic kernels [13,14,17], indefinite kernels [11,16,18,23,27], and kernels on dissimilarity representations [28]. Kernelizing indefinite pairwise dissimilarity matrices by Eigenspectrum corrections is reviewed in [5].

Dissimilarity representations have been applied, for example, in the domain of graphs using variants of the graph edit distance [3,26,31,32], to strings using the edit distance [33], and to time series using variants of the dynamic time warping (DTW) distance [15,19,21]. The approaches [15,21] apply support vector classification on the full pairwise DTW distance matrix. In [21] the dissimilarity representations are additionally combined with the symbolic aggregate approximation method proposed by [24]. This contribution, extends the idea of our prior work [19] on investigating how dimensionality reduction of dissimilarity representations using principal component analysis affects the generalization performance of a support vector classifier. Using principal component analysis for dimensionality reduction prior support vector learning can result in better performance as shown in [4,34].

3   Dissimilarity Representations of Time Series

3.1   The Basic Idea

Figure 1 illustrates the basic idea of dissimilarity representations. Suppose that $\mathcal{T}$ is a space of time series endowed with a distance function d. The time series space is depicted by the gray shaded area. Since the distance space $(\mathcal{T}, d)$ is not a normed vector space and in general not even a metric space, the majority of learning algorithms are not directly applicable for time series classification. Consequently, the simple nearest-neighbor classifier belongs to the state-of-the art.

One way to overcome the lack of powerful learning methods in time series spaces is by means of dissimilarity representations living in some Euclidean space. For this, we need to specify an ordered set of reference time series, called

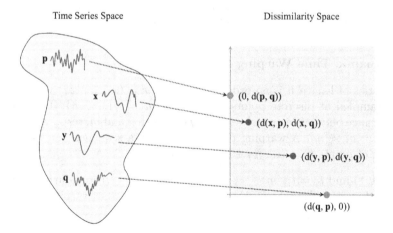

Fig. 1. Embedding of time series into the dissimilarity space. Prototypes p and q in the time series spaces are shown by blue curves and their respective embeddings in the dissimilarity space by blue balls. Arbitrary time series and their embeddings are shown in red. (Color figure online)

prototypes, that define the coordinates of the dissimilarity space. In Fig. 1 we consider two prototypes p and q shown by the blue curves. Since we have two different prototypes, the dissimilarity space is a subset of the two-dimensional Euclidean space, as we will see shortly.

The red shaded curves represent example time series x and y we want to embed into the dissimilarity space. The position of the time series in Fig. 1 reflect their pairwise distances. We see that, for example, time series x is closer to prototype p than to prototype q.

We embed time series x into the dissimilarity space by computing its distances from both prototypes. In doing so, we obtain a two-dimensional feature vector

$$\phi(x) = \big(d(x, p), d(x, q)\big).$$

The vector $\phi(x) \in \mathbb{R}^2$ is the dissimilarity representation of x with respect to the prototypes p and q. The dissimilarity representations of the prototypes themselves and the example time series are shown as blue and red shaded balls in Fig. 1. As indicated by the plot, the embedding is not isometric, that is the pairwise Euclidean distances of the dissimilarity representations distort the topological structure of the time series space. However, since dissimilarity representations reside in some Euclidean space, we can access the plethora of powerful data analysis tools not available in time series spaces. Then two cases can occur: (1) the dissimilarity representation is a better representation for the underlying classification problem, (2) the distortion arising by the dissimilarity representation is not a better representation for classification. In the latter case, sophisticated learning algorithms may partially compensate for distortions of the topological structure arising by non-isometric embeddings.

In the remainder of this section, we introduce the dynamic time warping distance, formalize the basic idea of dissimilarity representations, and describe how to solve classification problems in the dissimilarity space.

3.2   Dynamic Time Warping Distance

A time series of length n is an ordered sequence $x = (x_1, \ldots, x_n)$ with features $x_i \in \mathbb{R}$ sampled at discrete points of time $i \in [n] = \{1, \ldots, n\}$. To define the DTW distance between time series x and y of length n and m, resp., we construct a grid $\mathcal{G} = [n] \times [m]$. A warping path in grid $\mathcal{G}$ is a sequence $\phi = (t_1, \ldots, t_p)$ consisting of points $t_k = (i_k, j_k) \in \mathcal{G}$ such that

1. $t_1 = (1, 1)$ and $t_p = (n, m)$ (boundary conditions)
2. $t_{k+1} - t_k \in \{(1, 0), (0, 1), (1, 1)\}$ (warping conditions)

for all $1 \leq k < p$. The length p of a warping path ϕ is a number from the interval $[\max(n, m), n + m]$. The cost (error) of warping $x = (x_1, \ldots, x_n)$ and $y = (y_1, \ldots, y_m)$ along ϕ is defined by

$$d_\phi(x, y) = \sum_{(i,j) \in \phi} (x_i - y_j)^2,$$

where $(x_i - y_j)^2$ is the local transformation cost of assigning features x_i to y_j. Then the distance function

$$d(\boldsymbol{x}, \boldsymbol{y}) = \min_{\phi} d_\phi(\boldsymbol{x}, \boldsymbol{y}),$$

is the dynamic time warping (DTW) distance between $\boldsymbol{x}$ and $\boldsymbol{y}$, where the minimum is taken over all warping paths in $\mathcal{G}$.

3.3 Dissimilarity Representations

Let $(\mathcal{T}, d)$ be a time series space $\mathcal{T}$ endowed with the DTW distance d. Suppose that we are given a subset

$$\mathcal{P} = \{\boldsymbol{p}_1, \ldots, \boldsymbol{p}_k\} \subseteq \mathcal{T}$$

of k reference time series $\boldsymbol{p}_i \in \mathcal{T}$, called prototypes henceforth. The set $\mathcal{P}$ of prototypes gives rise to a function of the form

$$\phi : \mathcal{T} \to \mathbb{R}^k, \quad \boldsymbol{x} \mapsto (d(\boldsymbol{x}, \boldsymbol{p}_1), \ldots, d(\boldsymbol{x}, \boldsymbol{p}_k)),$$

where $\mathbb{R}^k$ is the *dissimilarity space* of $(\mathcal{T}, d)$ with respect to $\mathcal{P}$. The k-dimensional vector $\phi(\boldsymbol{x})$ is the *dissimilarity representation* of $\boldsymbol{x}$. The i-th feature of $\phi(\boldsymbol{x})$ represents the dissimilarity $d(\boldsymbol{x}, \boldsymbol{p}_i)$ between $\boldsymbol{x}$ and the i-th prototype $\boldsymbol{p}_i$.

3.4 Learning Classifiers in Dissimilarity Space

Suppose that

$$\mathcal{X} = \{(\boldsymbol{x}_1, y_1), \ldots, (\boldsymbol{x}_n, y_n)\} \subseteq \mathcal{T} \times \mathcal{Y}.$$

is a training set consisting of n time series $\boldsymbol{x}_i$ with corresponding class labels $y_i \in \mathcal{Y}$. Learning in the dissimilarity space proceeds in three steps:

1. *Prototype selection*:
   Select a set $\mathcal{P} = \{\boldsymbol{p}_1, \ldots, \boldsymbol{p}_k\}$ of k prototypes using the training set $\mathcal{X}$.
2. *Dissimilarity representation*:
   Represent each time series $\boldsymbol{x}$ by the vector $\phi(\boldsymbol{x}) = (d(\boldsymbol{x}, \boldsymbol{p}_1), \ldots, d(\boldsymbol{x}, \boldsymbol{p}_k))$.
3. *Learning*:
   Train a classifier $h : \mathbb{R}^k \to \mathcal{Y}$ using the dissimilarity representations of the training examples.

After a classifier h has been learned, we can predict the class label of an unseen test time series $\boldsymbol{x} \in \mathcal{T}$ by computing $h(\phi(\boldsymbol{x}))$. That is, we first embed the time series $\boldsymbol{x}$ into the dissimilarity space and obtain its dissimilarity representation $\phi(\boldsymbol{x})$. Then we apply the trained classifier h to the dissimilarity representation $\phi(\boldsymbol{x})$ of time series $\boldsymbol{x}$.

The performance of a classifier learned in dissimilarity spaces crucially depends on a proper dissimilarity representation of the time series. We distinguish between two common approaches:

1. *Prototype selection*: construct a set of prototypes $\mathcal{P}$ from the training set $\mathcal{X}$.
2. *Dimension reduction*: perform dimension reduction in the dissimilarity space.

There are numerous strategies for prototype selection. Naive examples include all elements of the training set $\mathcal{X}$ and sampling a random subset of $\mathcal{X}$. For more sophisticated selection methods, we refer to [29]. It is important to note that the prototypes need not to be elements of the training set. For example, one can use class means of time series as prototypes. For algorithms that compute a mean of a sample of time series, we refer to [30].

Dissimilarity embeddings typically use all training examples as prototypes. Dimension reduction is performed on the dissimilarity representations using methods such as, for example, principal component analysis (PCA).

3.5   Prototype Dependent Kernels

Once we consider the dissimilarity representations of time series, we have a large amount of learning algorithms at out disposal. We can choose among standard classifiers such as, for example, Bayes classifiers, decision trees, neural networks and deep learning, ensemble methods, and support vector machines (SVM). Here, we focus on SVM classifiers [2,6] and show how we can construct positive-definite kernels on time series that depend on a given set of prototypes.

Support Vector Machines. To describe SVM classifiers, we consider two-class classification problems in the k-dimensional Euclidean space $\mathbb{R}^k$. We assume that

$$\mathcal{X} = \{(\boldsymbol{z}_1, y_1), \ldots, (\boldsymbol{z}_n, y_n)\} \subseteq \mathbb{R}^k \times \mathcal{Y}.$$

is a training set consisting of n feature vectors $\boldsymbol{z}_i \in \mathbb{R}^k$ with corresponding class labels $y_i \in \mathcal{Y} = \{\pm 1\}$. Training a support vector machines amounts in solving the optimization problem

$$\min_{\boldsymbol{w}, b, \boldsymbol{\lambda}} \quad \frac{1}{2} \|\boldsymbol{w}\|^2 + C \sum_{i=1}^{n} \lambda_i$$
$$\text{subject to} \quad y_i \left(\boldsymbol{w}^T \psi\left(\boldsymbol{z}_i\right) + b\right) \geq 1 - \lambda_i$$
$$\lambda_i \geq 0$$

Here, $\boldsymbol{w}$ is the weight vector and b is the bias. The feature map $\psi : \mathbb{R}^k \to \mathcal{H}$ sends the training elements $\boldsymbol{z}_i$ into a (possibly higher or even infinite dimensional) feature space $\mathcal{H}$. The constant C is the regularization parameter that trades margin maximization against error minimization. The feature map ψ induces a positive-definite kernel function

$$k(\boldsymbol{z}, \boldsymbol{z}') = \psi(\boldsymbol{z})^T \psi(\boldsymbol{z}').$$

Two examples of kernel functions that can be evaluated in $\mathbb{R}^k$ are as follows:

1. Linear function: $k(\boldsymbol{z}, \boldsymbol{z}') = \boldsymbol{z}^T \boldsymbol{z}'$
2. Radial basis function: $k(\boldsymbol{z}, \boldsymbol{z}') = \exp\left(-\gamma \|\boldsymbol{z} - \boldsymbol{z}'\|^2\right)$

Here, γ is a kernel parameter that need to be selected carefully.

Prototype Dependent Kernels. Suppose that $\mathcal{P} = \{p_1, \ldots, p_k\}$ is a set of k prototypes. The set $\mathcal{P}$ gives rise to a dissimilarity function $\phi : \mathcal{T} \to \mathbb{R}^k$. Let $k(z, z') = \psi(z)^T \psi(z')$ be a positive-definite kernel function on $\mathbb{R}^k$ induced by the feature map $\psi : \mathbb{R}^k \to \mathcal{H}$. Then

$$k_{\mathcal{P}} : \mathcal{T} \times \mathcal{T} \to \mathcal{H}, \quad (x, x') \mapsto k\big(\phi(x), \phi(y)\big)$$

is a positive-definite kernel function on the time series space $\mathcal{T}$, because

$$k_{\mathcal{P}}(x, y) = k\left(\phi(x), \phi(y)\right) = \psi\big(\phi(x)\big)^T \psi\big(\phi(y)\big).$$

We call $k_{\mathcal{P}}$ the time series kernel induced by the kernel k and the protoype set $\mathcal{P}$.

4   Experiments

The goal of this experiment is to validate dissimilarity representations for time series classification.

4.1   Data

We used 42 datasets from the UCR time series datasets [22] shown in Table 1.

4.2   Classifiers

We considered the following classifiers:

1	NN-DTW	NN classifier with DTW distance in time series space
2	NN-EUC	NN classifier with Euclidean distance in dissimilarity space
3	SVM-LIN	SVM with linear kernel
4	SVM-RBF	SVM with radial-basis-function
5	PCA+LIN	PCA for dimension reduction followed by SVM-LIN
6	PCA+RBF	PCA for dimension reduction followed by SVM-RBF

4.3   Experimental Protocol

Each dataset shown in Table 1 comes with a pre-defined training and test set. To embed the time series of a dataset into a dissimilarity space, we used the whole training set as prototype set. Then we embedded each training and test example by computing their DTW distances to the training examples (prototypes).

We trained the linear and non-linear support vector machine using the embedded training examples. We selected the parameters γ and C of SVM-RBF over a two-dimensional grid with points $(\gamma_i, C_j) = (2^i, 2^j)$, where i, j are 30 equidistant values from $[-15, 15]$. For each parameter configuration (γ_i, C_j)

we performed 10-fold cross-validation and selected the parameters (γ_*, C_*) with the lowest average classification error. Then we trained the non-linear SVM on the whole embedded training set using the selected parameters (γ_*, C_*). Finally, we applied the learned model to the embedded test examples for estimating the generalization performance. We adopted the same procedure for selecting the regularization parameter C of SVM-LIN and for training.

When performing PCA for dimension reduction prior training of the SVM classifier, we applied the following procedure: We considered the q first dimensions with highest variance, where $q \in \{a, 2a, \ldots, 19a\}$ with a being the closest integer of $k/20$ and k is the dimension of the dissimilarity space. For each q, we performed hyperparameter selection for the SVM as described above. We selected the parameter configuration (q_*, γ_*, C_*) for SVM-RBF and (q_*, C_*) for SVM-LIN, resp., that gave the lowest classification error. Then we applied PCA on the whole embedded training set, retained the first q_* dimensions and trained the SVM on the embedded training set after dimension reduction. Finally we reduced the dimension of the embedded test examples and applied the learned model.

4.4   Results

Table 1 shows the error rates of all six classifiers on all 42 classification problems. These results form the basic data used in the subsequent discussion.

Pairwise Comparisons. Figure 2 shows the results of pairwise comparisons between the six classifiers using the error rates from Table 1 as performance measure. Table 2 ranks the six classifiers with respect to the average percentage of pairwise wins, average percentage of pairwise losses, and number of pairwise wins. We made the following observations:

1. The nearest-neighbor classifier NN-EUC in the dissimilarity space is not competitive. In particular, the nearest-neighbor classifier NN-DTW in the time series space performed better than NN-EUC in 78.6 % of all cases. Dissimilarity spaces endowed with the Euclidean distance form a distorted representation of the time series space endowed with the DTW distance in such a way that neighborhood relations are not properly preserved. In most cases, these distortions impact classification results negatively, often by a large margin (see Table 1). In the few cases where the distortions improve classification results, the improvements are only small and could also be occurred by chance due to the random sampling of the training and test set.
2. All four SVM classifiers performed better than the nearest-neighbor classifier NN-DTW with respect to the rankings in Table 2. Moreover, reducing the dimension using PCA gives better representations for SVM classification when directly compared to NN-DTW. These results suggest that sophisticated learning algorithms, which exploit the rich mathematical structure of inner product spaces can compensate poor dissimilarity representations.
3. Finally, PCA+RBF performed best among all classifiers under consideration. In particular, PCA+RBF is better than NN-DTW in 2/3 of all cases.

Table 1. Error rates in percentages. The first two columns refer to the NN-classifiers NN-DTW in time series space and NN-EUC in the dissimilarity space. The next two columns refer to the SVM classifiers SVM-LIN and SVM-RBF. The last two columns refer to PCA+LIN and PCA+RBF.

Data	NN		SVM		PCA	
	DTW	EUC	LIN	RBF	LIN	RBF
50words	31.0	42.9	33.6	33.4	30.8	31.0
Adiac	39.6	40.2	32.7	34.0	40.2	37.6
Beef	50.0	56.7	60.0	60.0	43.3	40.0
CBF	0.3	0.2	1.7	1.4	0.2	0.2
ChlorineConcentration	35.2	48.3	29.6	28.9	35.3	30.2
CinC ECG torso	34.9	44.0	35.7	41.4	43.0	39.8
Coffee	17.9	39.3	10.7	32.1	10.7	17.9
Cricket X	22.3	38.5	22.8	24.1	26.2	23.6
Cricket Y	20.8	37.9	18.7	20.0	20.5	19.7
Cricket Z	20.8	34.9	20.5	20.8	20.3	18.2
DiatomSizeReduction	3.3	4.2	4.2	10.8	6.2	13.7
ECG	23.0	20.0	16.0	16.0	14.0	18.0
ECGFiveDays	23.2	22.4	23.8	24.9	26.2	14.1
Face (all)	19.2	28.9	23.8	23.8	23.3	10.9
Face (four)	17.1	19.3	13.6	13.6	12.5	17.0
FacesUCR	9.5	17.1	12.8	13.4	9.7	9.0
Fish	16.7	32.6	17.1	17.7	17.1	14.3
Gun-point	9.3	20.0	10.7	6.7	8.0	8.7
Haptics	62.3	58.4	50.3	54.9	52.3	54.9
InlineSkate	61.6	61.8	67.5	65.5	67.3	68.4
ItalyPowerDemand	5.0	8.4	6.6	6.5	5.5	6.3
Lighting 2	13.1	18.0	27.9	14.8	29.5	16.4
Lighting 7	27.4	37.0	23.3	23.3	24.7	20.5
Mallat	6.6	4.6	5.8	5.6	6.5	5.5
Medical images	26.3	27.9	25.5	24.9	27.8	21.7
MoteStrain	16.5	24.8	15.4	17.2	13.5	14.1
Olive oil	13.3	13.3	13.3	10.0	13.3	13.3
OSU leaf	40.9	45.0	36.4	36.0	36.8	38.0
SonyAIBORobotSurface	27.5	16.3	22.1	22.3	25.3	25.3
SonyAIBORobotSurface II	16.9	19.4	23.3	17.4	13.7	19.3
Swedish leaf	21.0	27.2	14.4	14.4	14.9	18.7
Symbols	5.0	5.3	4.2	8.7	4.5	5.3
Synthetic control	0.7	1.7	1.3	1.3	1.3	2.0
Trace	0.0	1.0	0.0	1.0	0.0	0.0
TwoLeadECG	9.6	0.0	4.5	7.7	3.2	7.1
TwoPatterns	0.0	18.7	0.0	0.0	0.0	0.0
uWaveGestureLibrary X	27.3	28.9	21.4	20.8	22.4	20.6
uWaveGestureLibrary Y	36.6	40.5	28.6	28.6	29.1	28.5
uWaveGestureLibrary Z	34.2	34.6	26.2	27.0	28.4	26.9
Wafer	2.0	1.5	1.3	1.1	1.5	1.5
WordsSynonyms	35.1	43.9	38.4	39.0	36.2	34.3
Yoga	16.4	20.0	19.4	14.0	22.7	14.8

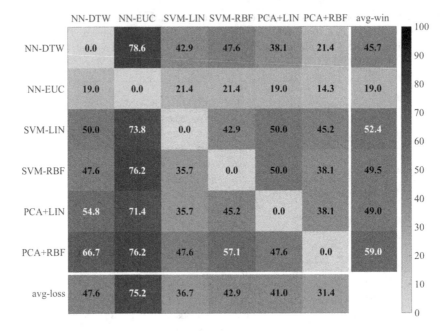

Fig. 2. Results on pairwise comparisons of the six classifiers. Consider row i and column j, where $1 \leq i, j \leq 6$. The value p_{ij} of the heat-map shows the percentage that the classifier in row i has lower error rate than the classifier in column j. For example, row 3 refers to SVM-LIN and column 1 to NN-DTW. The value $p_{13} = 50.0$ means that SVM-LIN performed better than NN-DTW in 50 % of all classification problems. The percentage of identical error rate for two classifiers i and j is given by $100 - p_{ij} - p_{ji}$. The seventh column (row) of the heat-map shows the average percentage of wins (losses) of every classifier.

Table 2. Ranking of the classifiers with respect to average percentage of pairwise wins (avg-win), average percentage of pairwise losses (avg-loss), and number of pairwise wins (wins). Classifier i won against classifier j if $p_{ij} > p_{ji}$, that is classifier i was more often better than classifier j.

#	Classifier	avg-win	#	Classifier	avg-loss	#	Classifier	Wins
1	PCA+RBF	59.0	1	PCA+RBF	31.4	1	PCA+RBF	5
2	SVM-LIN	52.4	2	SVM-LIN	36.7	2	SVM-LIN	4
3	SVM-RBF	49.5	3	PCA+LIN	41.0	3	SVM-RBF	2
4	PCA+LIN	49.0	4	SVM-RBF	42.9	4	PCA+LIN	2
5	NN-DTW	45.7	5	NN-DTW	47.6	5	NN-DTW	1
6	NN-EUC	19.0	6	NN-EUC	75.2	6	NN-EUC	0

Performance Profiles. Rankings based on pairwise competitions discard information about differences in solution quality. We use performance profiles introduced by [7] to compare the difference in the classification accuracies of different classifiers. Performance profiles are useful for studying the robustness of a classifier and to which extent a classifier is superior. We refer to Appendix A for a detailed description of performance profiles.

Figure 3 shows the performance profiles of NN-DTW, NN-EUC, and the best SVM classifier PCA+RBF using classification accuracy as performance metric. It is sufficient to keep the following facts in mind to have a good interpretation of performance profiles:

- Each curve represents a classifier and the higher the curve, the better its performance.
- $P_c(0)$ is the fraction of problems on which classifier c performed best.
- $P_c(\tau)$ is the fraction of problems on which the performance of classifier c deviates at most by factor $\tau \in [0, 1]$ from the best performance.
- τ_{max} with $P_c(\tau_{max}) = 1$ is the maximum factor by which classifier c deviates from the best performance.

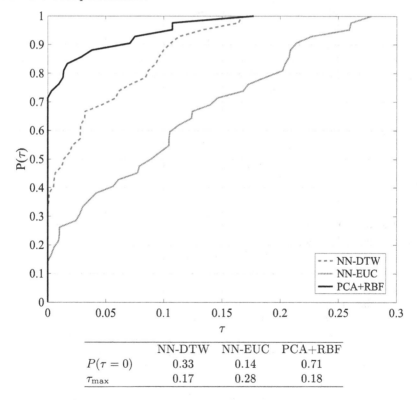

	NN-DTW	NN-EUC	PCA+RBF
$P(\tau = 0)$	0.33	0.14	0.71
τ_{max}	0.17	0.28	0.18

Fig. 3. Performance profile of NN-DTW, NN-EUC, and PCA+RBF using classification accuracy as performance metric. The table shows the fraction of wins and the maximum deviation τ_{max} of each classifier.

We made the following observations:

1. The SVM classifier PCA+RBF had the most wins. The fraction of problems on which PCA+RBF won is 0.71, whereas the fraction of problems on which the nearest-neighbor classifiers NN-DTW and NN-EUC were best is 0.33 and 0.14, respectively. It is important to note that more than one classifier can obtain the best solution for a given problem. From the previous discussion, we know that PCA+RBF is better than NN-DTW in 66.7 % of all cases.
2. The classification accuracies of PCA+RBF and NN-DTW deviated from the best solution not more than by a factor τ of 0.18 and 0.17, respectively. In contrast, NN-EUC has a maximum deviation of $\tau_{max} = 0.28$. The estimated probability that a solution of PCA+RBF deviates more than 15 % from a solution of NN-DTW is 0.02. Similarly, the estimated probability that a solution of NN-DTW deviates more than 15 % from a solution of PCA+RBF is 0.05. These results indicate that PCA+RBF and NN-DTW are comparable with respect to robustness.
3. The solutions of PCA+RBF deviated at most 5 % from the best solutions with high confidence 90 %. In contrast, the solutions of NN-DTW and NN-EUC deviated at most 5 % from the best solutions with confidence 70 % and 40 %, respectively.
4. The performance profile of PCA+RBF is consistently better than the performance profile of NN-DTW except for one problem that lead to a worse maximum factor. Both classifier have performance profiles that are consistently better than the performance profile of NN-EUC.

Comparison of SVM Classifiers. Figure 4 shows the performance profiles of the four SVM classifiers SVM-LIN, SVM-RBF, PCA+LIN, and PCA+RBF using classification accuracy as performance metric. We made the following observations:

1. PCA+RBF had the most wins with fraction 0.36 and is most robust with smallest maximum deviation $\tau_{max} = 0.1$. In addition, PCA+RBF has almost always the best performance profile.
2. Dimension reduction using PCA results in more robust SVM classifiers in the sense that the maximum deviation from the best solution is more strongly bounded. In the worst case, classification accuracy of SVM classifiers without PCA deviated from the best solution by factor $\tau_{max} = 0.33$, whereas τ_{max} is 0.17 for PCA+LIN and 0.1 for PCA+RBF.
3. In 80 % of all cases, the four SVM classifiers perform comparable in the sense that none of the classifiers deviates more than 5 % from the best classifier. For the remaining 20 %, the choice of kernel and dimension reduction has a substantial effect on the generalization performance.
4. PCA has a consistent positive effect on the performance profile of non-linear SVMs with rbf-kernel, but not on linear SVMs.

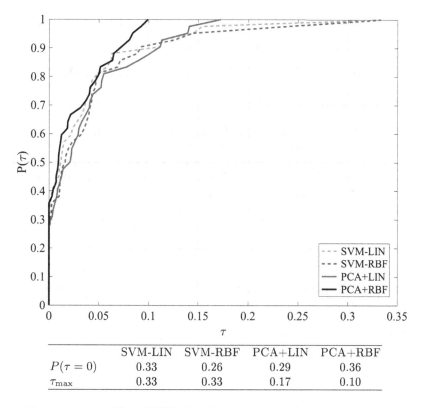

	SVM-LIN	SVM-RBF	PCA+LIN	PCA+RBF
$P(\tau = 0)$	0.33	0.26	0.29	0.36
$\tau_{\max}$	0.33	0.33	0.17	0.10

Fig. 4. Performance profile of SVM classifiers using classification accuracy as performance metric. The table shows the faction of wins and the maximum factor $\tau_{\max}$ of each classifier.

5   Conclusion

This paper is a first step to explore dissimilarity space learning for time series classification. Results combining PCA with SVM on dissimilarity representations are promising and complement nearest neighbor methods using DTW in time series spaces. Key findings are: PCA+RBF performs better than NN-DTW with high confidence. Pairwise comparisons against NN-DTW suggest that all four SVM classifiers perform better or equally well as NN-DTW. These findings are notable for two reasons: (i) the results obtained by NN-EUC suggest that dissimilarity representations distort the neighborhood relations substantially, and (ii) NN-DTW is considered as *exceptionally difficult to beat*. We observed that PCA results in more robust SVM classifiers. We conclude that sophisticated methods defined on mathematically well structured spaces can partially compensate for weaker representations.

Future work aims at exploring dissimilarity representations for time series classification based on different design decisions: (i) choice of elastic distances on time series, (ii) choice of prototype selection or dimension reduction methods, and (iii) choice of learning methods.

Acknowledgements. B. Jain was funded by the DFG Sachbeihilfe JA 2109/4-1.

A   Performance Profiles

Performance profiles have been introduced by Dolan to compare the efficiency of algorithms [7]. Here, we use performance profiles to compare differences in the classification accuracy of a collection of classifiers on a set of classification problems. The comparison is summarized by one curve per classifier, which is easier to read than a table of classification accuracies.

To define a performance profile, we assume that $\mathbb{C}$ is a set of classifiers to be compared and $\mathbb{P}$ is the set of all classification problems. For each classification problem $p \in \mathbb{P}$ and each classifier $c \in \mathbb{C}$, we define

$$\rho_{c,p} = \text{accuracy of classifier } c \in \mathbb{C} \text{ on problem } p \in \mathbb{P}$$

as the performance of classifier c for problem p. In performance profiles, we do not consider the absolute performance of a classifier in terms of its classification accuracy, but its relative performance with respect to the best performing classifier. The classifier with the best performance on problem p has classification accuracy

$$\rho_p^* = \max\left\{\rho_{\kappa,p} : \kappa \in \mathbb{C}\right\}.$$

Then the relative performance of classifier c on problem p is given by

$$r_{c,p} = 1 - \frac{\rho_{c,p}}{\rho_p^*}.$$

The relative performance $r_{c,p}$ takes values from the interval $[0, 1]$. The better the performance of a classifier for a given problem, the lower is its relative performance. Thus, the lower the relative performance, the better the classifier. Moreover, from

$$r_{c,p} \cdot \rho_p^* = \left(1 - \frac{\rho_{c,p}}{\rho_p^*}\right)\rho_p^* = \rho_p^* - \rho_{c,p}$$

follows that $r_{c,p}$ is the factor by which the classification accuracy $\rho_{c,p}$ deviates from the best classification accuracy ρ_p^*.

Finally, the performance profile of classifier $c \in \mathbb{C}$ over all problems $p \in \mathbb{P}$ is an empirical cumulative distribution function

$$P_c(\tau) = \frac{1}{|\mathbb{P}|}\left|\{p \in \mathbb{P} : r_{c,p} \leq \tau\}\right|.$$

It is sufficient to keep three three facts in mind to interpret performance profiles:

1. The value $P_c(0)$ is the fraction of problems on which classifier c is best.
2. $P_c(\tau)$ is the fraction of problems on which the performance of classifier c deviates at most by factor τ from the best performance.
3. $\tau_{\max}$ with $P_c(\tau_{\max}) = 1$ is the maximum factor by which classifier c deviates from the best performance.

References

1. Batista, G.E., Wang, X., Keogh, E.J.: A complexity-invariant distance measure for time series. In: SIAM International Conference on Data Mining, vol. 11, pp. 699–710 (2011)
2. Boser, B.E., Guyon, I., Vapnik, V.: A training algorithm for optimal margin classifiers. In: Proceedings of the Fifth Annual Workshop on Computational Learning Theory, pp. 144–152 (1992)
3. Bunke, H., Riesen, K.: Graph classification based on dissimilarity space embedding. In: da Vitoria Lobo, N., Kasparis, T., Roli, F., Kwok, J.T., Georgiopoulos, M., Anagnostopoulos, G.C., Loog, M. (eds.) Structural, Syntactic, and Statistical Pattern Recognition. LNCS, vol. 5342, pp. 996–1007. Springer, Heidelberg (2008)
4. Cao, L.J., Chua, K.S., Chong, W.K., Lee, H.P., Gu, Q.M.: A comparison of PCA, KPCA and ICA for dimensionality reduction in support vector machine. Neurocomputing **55**(1–2), 321–336 (2003)
5. Chen, Y., Garcia, E., Gupta, M., Rahimi, A., Cazzanti, L.: Similarity-based classification: concepts and algorithms. J. Mach. Learn. Res. **10**, 747–776 (2009)
6. Cortes, C., Vapnik, V.: Support-vector network. Mach. Learn. **20**, 273–297 (1995)
7. Dolan, E.D., Moré, J.J.: Benchmarking optimization software with performance profiles. Math. Program. **91**(2), 201–213 (2002)
8. Duin, R., de Ridder, D., Tax, D.: Experiments with object based discriminant functions; a featureless approach to pattern recognition. Pattern Recogn. Lett. **18**(11–13), 1159–1166 (1997)
9. Duin, R.P.W., Pekalska, E.: The dissimilarity space: bridging structural and statistical pattern recognition. Pattern Recogn. Lett. **33**(7), 807–962 (2012)
10. Fu, T.: A review on time series data mining. Eng. Appl. Artif. Intell. **24**(1), 164–181 (2011)
11. Geibel, P., Jain, B., Wysotzki, F.: SVM learning with the SH inner product. In: European Symposium on Artificial Neural Networks (2004)
12. Geurts, P.: Pattern extraction for time series classification. In: Siebes, A., De Raedt, L. (eds.) PKDD 2001. LNCS (LNAI), vol. 2168, pp. 115–127. Springer, Heidelberg (2001)
13. Graepel, T., Herbrich, R., Bollmann-Sdorra, P., Obermayer, K.: Classification on pairwise proximity data. In: Advances in Neural Information Processing Systems (1999)
14. Graepel, T., Herbrich, R., Schölkopf, B., Smola, A., Bartlett, P., Müller, K.-R., Obermayer, K., Williamson, R.: Classification on proximity data with LP-machines. In: International Conference on Artificial Neural Networks (1999)
15. Gudmundsson, S., Runarsson, T.P., Sigurdsson, S.: Support vector machines and dynamic time warping for time series. In: Joint Conference on Neural Networks (2008)
16. Haasdonk, H., Burkhardt, B.: Invariant kernels for pattern analysis and machine learning. Mach. Learn. **68**, 35–61 (2007)
17. Hochreiter, S., Obermayer, K.: Support vector machines for dyadic data. Neural Comput. **18**(6), 1472–1510 (2006)
18. Jain, B.J., Geibel, P., Wysotzki, F.: SVM learning with the Schur? Hadamard inner product for graphs. Neurocomputing **64**, 93–105 (2005)
19. Jain, B.J., Spiegel, S.: Time series classification in dissimilarity spaces. In: Proceedings of the 1st International Workshop on Advanced Analytics and Learning on Temporal Data (2015)

20. Jain, B.J.: Generalized gradient learning on time series. Mach. Learn. **100**(2), 587–608 (2015)
21. Kate, R.J.: Using dynamic time warping distances as features for improved time series classification. Data Min. Knowl. Discov. **30**(2), 283–312 (2016)
22. Keogh, E., Zhu, Q., Hu, B., Hao, Y., Xi, X., Wei, L., Ratanamahatana, C.A.: The UCR Time Series Classification/Clustering Homepage (2011). www.cs.ucr.edu/~eamonn/time_series_data/
23. Laub, J., Müller, K.R.: Feature discovery in non-metric pairwise data. J. Mach. Learn. Res. **5**, 801–818 (2004)
24. Lin, J., Keogh, E., Wei, L., Lonardi, S.: Experiencing SAX: a novel symbolic representation of time series. Data Min. Knowl. Discov. **15**(2), 107–144 (2007)
25. Lines, J., Bagnall, A.: Time series classification with ensembles of elastic distance measures. Data Min. Knowl. Discov. **29**(3), 565–592 (2015)
26. Livi, L., Rizzi, A., Sadeghian, A.: Optimized dissimilarity space embedding for labeled graphs. Inf. Sci. **266**, 47–64 (2014)
27. Ong, C., Mary, X., Canu, S., Smola, A.J.: Learning with non-positive kernels. In: International Conference on Machine Learning (2004)
28. Pekalska, E., Duin, R.P.W.: The Dissimilarity Representation for Pattern Recognition. World Scientific, River Edge (2005)
29. Pekalska, E., Duin, R.P.W., Paclik, P.: Prototype selection for dissimilarity-based classifiers. Pattern Recogn. **39**(2), 189–208 (2006)
30. Petitjean, F., Ketterlin, A., Gançarski, P.: A global averaging method for dynamic time warping, with applications to clustering. Pattern Recogn. **44**(3), 678–693 (2011)
31. Riesen, K., Neuhaus, M., Bunke, H.: Graph embedding in vector spaces by means of prototype selection. In: Escolano, F., Vento, M. (eds.) GbRPR. LNCS, vol. 4538, pp. 383–393. Springer, Heidelberg (2007)
32. Riesen, K., Bunke, H.: Graph classification based on vector space embedding. Int. J. Pattern Recogn. Artif. Intell. **23**(6), 1053–1081 (2009)
33. Spillmann, B., Neuhaus, M., Bunke, H., Pękalska, E., Duin, R.P.W.: Transforming strings to vector spaces using prototype selection. In: Yeung, D.-Y., Kwok, J.T., Fred, A., Roli, F., de Ridder, D. (eds.) Structural, Syntactic, and Statistical Pattern Recognition. LNCS, vol. 4109, pp. 287–296. Springer, Heidelberg (2006)
34. Subasi, A., Gursoy, M.I.: EEG signal classification using PCA, ICA, LDA and support vector machines. Expert Syst. Appl. **37**(12), 8659–8666 (2010)
35. Xi, X., Keogh, E., Shelton, C., Wei, L., Ratanamahatana, C.A.: Fast time series classification using numerosity reduction. In: International Conference on Machine Learning (2006)
36. Xing, Z., Pei, J., Keogh, E.: A brief survey on sequence classification. ACM SIGKDD Explor. Newslett. **12**(1), 40–48 (2010)

Time Series Classification
and Clustering

Fuzzy Clustering of Series Using Quantile Autocovariances

Borja Lafuente-Rego[✉] and Jose A. Vilar

Research Group on Modeling, Optimization and Statistical Inference (MODES),
Department of Mathematics, Computer Science Faculty,
University of A Coruña, A Coruña, Spain
{borja.lafuente,jose.vilarf}@udc.es

Abstract. Unlike conventional clustering, fuzzy cluster analysis allows data elements to belong to more than one cluster by assigning membership degrees of each data to clusters. This work proposes a fuzzy C–medoids algorithm to cluster time series based on comparing their estimated quantile autocovariance functions. The behaviour of the proposed algorithm is studied on different simulated scenarios and its effectiveness is concluded by comparison with alternative approaches. Finally, an application on real data involving series of hourly electricity demand is developed to illustrate the usefulness of the methodology.

Keywords: Quantile autocovariances · Dissimilarity between time series · Fuzzy clustering · Conditional heteroskedastic processes

1 Introduction

In classical cluster analysis each datum is assigned to exactly one cluster, thus producing a "hard" partition of the data set into several disjoint subsets. This approach can be inadequate in the presence of data objects that are equally distant to two ore more clusters. Fuzzy cluster analysis allows gradual memberships of data objects to clusters, providing versatility to reflect the certainty with which each data is assigned to the different clusters. Overviews of fuzzy clustering methods are provided by [6,7]. Interest in this approach has increased in recent years. Proof of this is the large amount of publications in this field (e.g. [11,12]).

In this paper, a fuzzy C–medoids algorithm to cluster time series using the quantile autocovariance functions is proposed. Motivation behind this approach is twofold. First, quantile autocovariances have shown a high capability to cluster time series generated from a broad range of dependence models [19]. On the other hand, the use of a fuzzy approach for clustering time series is justified in order to gain adaptivity for constructing the centroids and to obtain a better characterization of the temporal pattern of the series (see discussion in [9]). A similar fuzzy analysis was carried out by Maharaj and D'Urso [21] considering different metrics in the frequency domain. Specifically, we have focused on the

© Springer International Publishing Switzerland 2016
A. Douzal-Chouakria et al. (Eds.): AALTD 2015, LNAI 9785, pp. 49–64, 2016.
DOI: 10.1007/978-3-319-44412-3_4

classification of heteroskedastic models, which are of great importance in many applications (e.g. to model many financial time series) and have received relatively little attention in the clustering literature (e.g. [8,10]). To illustrate the merits of the proposed algorithm, an extensive simulation study comparing our fuzzy approach with other fuzzy procedures has been carried out.

The rest of the paper is organized as follows. The dissimilarity measure between series based on estimated quantile autocovariance functions is presented in Sect. 2. The proposed C–medoids fuzzy clustering algorithm is described in Sect. 3, and its behaviour is analysed and compared with other fuzzy alternative procedures in Sect. 4 through a simulation study conducted to classify different structures of conditional heteroskedastic processes. In Sect. 5, an application on real data involving time series of hourly electricity demand in the Spanish market is carried out. Some concluding remarks are summarized in Sect. 6.

2   A Dissimilarity Based on Quantile Autocovariances

Consider a set of p series $S = \left\{ \boldsymbol{X}^{(1)}, \ldots, \boldsymbol{X}^{(p)} \right\}$, with $\boldsymbol{X}^{(j)} = (X_1^{(j)}, \ldots, X_T^{(j)})$ being a T-length partial realization from a real valued process $\{X_t^{(j)},\ t \in \mathbb{Z}\}$. We wish to perform cluster analysis on S in such a way that series with similar generating processes are grouped together. To achieve this goal, we propose to measure dissimilarity between two series by comparing the estimators of their quantile autocovariance functions (QAF), which are formally defined below.

Let $X_1, \ldots, X_T$ an observed stretch of a strictly stationary process $\{X_t;\ t \in \mathbb{Z}\}$. Denote by F the marginal distribution of X_t and by $q_\tau = F^{-1}(\tau)$, $\tau \in [0,1]$, the corresponding quantile function. Fixed $l \in \mathbb{Z}$ and an arbitrary couple of quantile levels $(\tau, \tau') \in [0,1]^2$, consider the cross-covariance of the indicator functions $I(X_t \leq q_\tau)$ and $I(X_{t+l} \leq q_{\tau'})$ given by

$$\gamma_l(\tau, \tau') = \operatorname{cov}\left\{ I(X_t \leq q_\tau), I(X_{t+l} \leq q_{\tau'}) \right\} = \mathbb{P}(X_t \leq q_\tau, X_{t+l} \leq q_{\tau'}) - \tau\,\tau'. \tag{1}$$

Function $\gamma_l(\tau, \tau')$, with $(\tau, \tau') \in [0,1]^2$, is called *quantile autocovariance function of lag l*. Replacing in (1) the theoretical quantiles of the marginal distribution F, q_τ and $q_{\tau'}$, by the corresponding empirical quantiles based on $X_1, \ldots, X_T$, $\hat{q}_\tau$ and $\hat{q}_{\tau'}$, we obtain the estimated quantile autocovariance function given by

$$\hat{\gamma}_l(\tau, \tau') = \frac{1}{T-l} \sum_{t=1}^{T-l} I(X_t \leq \hat{q}_\tau)\, I(X_{t+l} \leq \hat{q}_{\tau'}) - \tau\,\tau'. \tag{2}$$

As the quantile autocovariances are able to account for high level dynamic features, a simple dissimilarity criterion between a pair of series $X_t^{(1)}$ and $X_t^{(2)}$ consists in comparing their estimated quantile autocovariances on a common range of selected quantiles. Thus, for L prefixed lags, $l_1, \ldots, l_L$, and r quantile levels, $0 < \tau_1 < \ldots < \tau_r < 1$, we construct the vectors $\boldsymbol{\Gamma}^{(u)}$, $u = 1, 2$, given by

$$\boldsymbol{\Gamma}^{(u)} = \left(\boldsymbol{\Gamma}_{l_1}^{(u)}, \ldots, \boldsymbol{\Gamma}_{l_L}^{(u)} \right), \quad \text{with} \quad \boldsymbol{\Gamma}_{l_i}^{(u)} = \left(\hat{\gamma}_{l_i}^{(u)}(\tau_j, \tau_k);\ j, k = 1 \ldots, r \right), \tag{3}$$

for $i = 1, \ldots, L$, and $\hat{\gamma}$ given in (2). Then, the distance between $X_t^{(1)}$ and $X_t^{(2)}$ is defined as the squared Euclidean distance between their representations $\boldsymbol{\Gamma}^{(1)}$ and $\boldsymbol{\Gamma}^{(2)}$, i.e.

$$d_{QAF}\left(X_t^{(1)}, X_t^{(2)}\right) = ||\boldsymbol{\Gamma}^{(1)} - \boldsymbol{\Gamma}^{(2)}||_2^2 \qquad (4)$$

Computing d_{QAF} for all pairs of series in S allows us to set a pairwise dissimilarity matrix, which can be taken as starting point of a conventional hierarchical clustering algorithm. Alternatively, a partitioning clustering, such as the k-means algorithm, could be performed averaging the $\boldsymbol{\Gamma}$ representations to determine the centroids. Then, d_{QAF} would be also used to calculate the distances between the series and the centroids involved in the iterative refinement of the cluster solution.

Notice that, in practice, computation of d_{QAF} requires setting a specific number of lags and quantile levels. Our simulation study shown that a small number of quantiles with probability levels regularly spaced on $[0, 1]$ is enough to reach satisfactory results. Furthermore, it was corroborated that using longer sequences of quantiles has a very moderate effect on the clustering accuracy. Anyway, further research is needed to automatically determine the optimal selection of these input parameters.

3   Fuzzy Clustering Based on Quantile Autocovariances

Time series are dynamic objects and therefore different temporal patterns may be necessary to characterize the serial behaviour in different periods of time. In other words, the series are not distributed accurately within a given number of clusters, but they can belong to two or even more clusters. This problem can be adequately treated using a fuzzy clustering procedure, which associates a fuzzy label vector to each element stating its memberships to the set of clusters. In this section we propose a fuzzy C-medoids clustering algorithm for time series by plugging the QAF-dissimilarity introduced in Sect. 2.

Given the set of p time series $S = \left\{ \boldsymbol{X}^{(1)}, \ldots, \boldsymbol{X}^{(p)} \right\}$, consider a vector of estimated quantile autocovariances selected to perform clustering on S, $\boldsymbol{\Gamma} = \left\{ \boldsymbol{\Gamma}^{(1)}, \ldots, \boldsymbol{\Gamma}^{(p)} \right\}$. The fuzzy C-medoids clustering finds the subset of $\boldsymbol{\Gamma}$ of size C, $\tilde{\boldsymbol{\Gamma}} = \left\{ \tilde{\boldsymbol{\Gamma}}^{(1)}, \ldots, \tilde{\boldsymbol{\Gamma}}^{(C)} \right\}$, and the $p \times C$ matrix of fuzzy coefficients $\Omega = (u_{ic})$, $i = 1, \ldots, p, c = 1, \ldots, C$, which lead to solve the minimization problem:

$$\begin{cases} \min_{\tilde{\boldsymbol{\Gamma}}, \Omega} \sum\limits_{i=1}^{p} \sum\limits_{c=1}^{C} u_{ic}^m \left\| \boldsymbol{\Gamma}^{(i)} - \tilde{\boldsymbol{\Gamma}}^{(c)} \right\|_2^2, \\ \text{subject to: } \sum\limits_{c=1}^{C} u_{ic} = 1 \text{ and } u_{ic} \geq 0. \end{cases} \qquad (5)$$

Each $u_{ic} \in [0, 1]$ represents the membership degree of the i-th series to the c-th cluster and the parameter $m > 1$ controls the fuzziness of the partition. As the value of m increases, the boundaries between clusters become softer and therefore the classification is fuzzier. Suitable selection of m is discussed by [7]. If $m = 1$, the hard version of the clustering procedure is obtained, i.e. $u_{ic} \in \{0, 1\}$, that leads to a classical k-means partition of S. The constraints $\sum_{c=1}^{C} u_{ic} = 1$ and $u_{ic} \geq 0$ ensure that no cluster is empty and that all series are included in the cluster partition.

The objective function in (5) cannot be minimized directly, and an iterative algorithm that alternately optimizes the membership degrees and the medoids must be used. At each iteration, local optimal solutions for the membership degrees are first obtained for a set of fixed medoids. This is carried out by solving the constrained optimization problem (5) using the Lagrangian multiplier model. The resulting update formula for the membership degrees takes the form [15].

$$
u_{ic} = \left[\sum_{c'=1}^{C} \left(\frac{\left\| \boldsymbol{\Gamma}^{(i)} - \tilde{\boldsymbol{\Gamma}}^{(c)} \right\|_2^2}{\left\| \boldsymbol{\Gamma}^{(i)} - \tilde{\boldsymbol{\Gamma}}^{(c')} \right\|_2^2} \right)^{\frac{1}{m-1}} \right]^{-1} \quad , \text{ for } i = 1, \ldots, p \text{ and } c = 1, \ldots, C. \quad (6)
$$

Then, the C series, i.e. the realizations $\tilde{\boldsymbol{\Gamma}}^{(c)}$, $c = 1, \ldots, C$, minimizing the objective function in (5) for the fixed membership degrees are selected as new medoids. These two steps are iterated until the optimum or a maximum number of iterations is achieved.

The QAF-based fuzzy C–medoids clustering algorithm (QAF–FCM) is implemented as outlined in Algorithm 1.

Algorithm 1. QAF-based fuzzy C–medoids clustering algorithm (QAF–FCM)

1: Fix C, m and $max.iter$
2: Set $iter = 0$
3: Pick the initial medoids $\tilde{\boldsymbol{\Gamma}} = \left\{ \tilde{\boldsymbol{\Gamma}}^{(1)}, \ldots, \tilde{\boldsymbol{\Gamma}}^{(C)} \right\}$
4: **repeat**
5:     Set $\tilde{\boldsymbol{\Gamma}}_{\text{OLD}} = \tilde{\boldsymbol{\Gamma}}$ {Store the current medoids}
6:     Compute u_{ic}, $i = 1, \ldots, p$, $c = 1, \ldots, C$, using (6)
7:     For each $c \in \{1, \ldots, C\}$, determine the index $j_c \in \{1, \ldots, p\}$ satisfying:

$$
j_c = \underset{1 \leq j \leq p}{\operatorname{argmin}} \sum_{i=1}^{p} u_{ic}^m \left\| \boldsymbol{\Gamma}^{(i)} - \boldsymbol{\Gamma}^{(j)} \right\|_2^2
$$

8:     **return** $\tilde{\boldsymbol{\Gamma}}^{(c)} = \boldsymbol{\Gamma}^{(j_c)}$, for $c = 1, \ldots, C$ {Update the medoids}
9:     $iter \leftarrow iter + 1$
10: **until** $\tilde{\boldsymbol{\Gamma}}_{\text{OLD}} = \tilde{\boldsymbol{\Gamma}}$ or $iter = max.iter$

It is worthy to point out some brief remarks concerning the QAF–FCM algorithm. First, as in the classical fuzzy framework, it cannot be guaranteed that the global optimum will be attained. The algorithm might get stuck in a local minimum, and hence considering several random initializations is advisable in order to reach a stable solution. The numerical experiments described in the following section brought insight into the algorithm performance. For instance, it was observed that a few iterations are enough to attain an optimal solution and the maximum number of iterations was seldom reached. Also, optimal results were attained when the crisp solution from a hierarchical clustering based on the pairwise QAF distances was used as initial set of medoids.

As in any other partitional clustering procedure, the total number of clusters C has to be preset. Numerous methods and internal and external indexes have been proposed for testing the null hypothesis $C = 1$ and estimating the number of clusters in a dataset, however, none of them is completely satisfactory (see overview in [17]). Currently, Hennig and Lin [14] propose to use a parametric bootstrap to approximate the distribution of a prefixed cluster validation index under the null hypothesis of non-clustering structure. Then, the validation index can be used to test homogeneity and furthermore to calibrate its behaviour in order to obtain proper estimates of the underlying number of clusters. Anyway, the problem of determining the number of clusters goes beyond the scope of the present work. Thus, the value of C is assumed to be known in our experiments with simulated data and it is estimated by means of commonly used indexes in the study involving real data.

4   Simulation Study

The proposed fuzzy algorithm was tested against two other fuzzy clustering algorithms via simulation. In particular, the classification of heteroskedastic time series was considered by simulating two different scenarios formed by (i) GARCH(1,1) models and (ii) different structures of conditional heteroskedasticity. The selected generating models at each case are detailed below.

- **Scenario 1:** Consider $X_t = \mu_t + a_t$, with $\mu_t \sim$ AR(1) and $a_t = \sigma_t \epsilon_t$, $\epsilon_t \sim \mathcal{N}(0, 1)$. Then, the following GARCH(1,1) structures for the varying conditional variance are considered:
  M1: $\sigma_t^2 = 0.1 + 0.01a_{t-1}^2 + 0.9\sigma_{t-1}^2$
  M2: $\sigma_t^2 = 0.1 + 0.9a_{t-1}^2 + 0.01\sigma_{t-1}^2$
  M3: $\sigma_t^2 = 0.1 + 0.1a_{t-1}^2 + 0.1\sigma_{t-1}^2$
  M4: $\sigma_t^2 = 0.1 + 0.4a_{t-1}^2 + 0.5\sigma_{t-1}^2$

- **Scenario 2:** Consider $X_t = \mu_t + a_t$, with $\mu_t \sim$ MA(1) and $a_t = \sigma_t \epsilon_t$, $\epsilon_t \sim \mathcal{N}(0, 1)$. Then, the following ARCH(1), GARCH(1,1), GJR-GARCH and EGARCH structures are considered for the varying conditional variance:
  M1: $\sigma_t^2 = 0.1 + 0.8a_{t-1}^2$
  M2: $\sigma_t^2 = 0.1 + 0.1a_{t-1}^2 + 0.8\sigma_{t-1}^2$
  M3: $\sigma_t^2 = 0.1 + (0.25 + 0.3\mathrm{N}_{t-1})a_{t-1}^2 + 0.5\sigma_{t-1}^2$; $\mathrm{N}_{t-1} = \mathrm{I}(a_{t-1} < 0)$
  M4: $\ln(\sigma_t^2) = 0.1 + \epsilon_{t-1} + 0.3\left[|\epsilon_{t-1}| - \mathbb{E}(|\epsilon_{t-1}|)\right] + 0.4\ln(\sigma_{t-1}^2)$

In all cases ϵ_t consisted of independent zero-mean Gaussian variables with unit variance. For each scenario, five series of length $T = 200$ were generated from each model over $N = 100$ trials.

Two fuzzy clustering algorithms specifically designed to deal with GARCH models were used and compared with our proposal. Both algorithms rely on different dissimilarity measures constructed using the AR representation of a GARCH(p,q) process given by

$$\sigma_t^2 = \gamma + \sum_{i=1}^{p} \alpha_i a_{t-i}^2 + \sum_{j=1}^{q} \beta_j \sigma_{t-j}^2 \qquad (7)$$

with $\gamma > 0$, $0 \le \alpha_i < 1$ and $0 \le \beta_j < 1$, for $i = 1,\ldots,p$ and $j = 1,\ldots,q$, and such that $\sum_{i=1}^{p} \alpha_i + \sum_{j=1}^{q} \beta_j < 1$. The dissimilarities are defined as follows.

1. Dissimilarity based on the autoregressive representation of the GARCH models [20,23]. Given $\boldsymbol{X}^{(k)}$ and $\boldsymbol{X}^{(k')}$ in S, we define

$$d_{AR}^2(\boldsymbol{X}^{(k)}, \boldsymbol{X}^{(k')}) = \sum_{r=1}^{R} (\widehat{\pi}_{rk} - \widehat{\pi}_{rk'})^2,$$

with $\widehat{\pi}_{rz}$ an estimator of the r-th coefficient $\pi_r = (\alpha_r + \beta_r) + \sum_{j=1}^{\min(q,r)} \beta_j \pi_{r-j}$, for the series z, $z = k, k'$. Parameter R determines the maximum number of autoregressive coefficients π_r to be considered. A GARCH–based fuzzy C-medoids clustering (GARCH–FCMdC) is proposed in [8] by considering the optimization problem:

$$\begin{cases} \min_{\tilde{\boldsymbol{\Pi}},\Omega} \sum_{i=1}^{p} \sum_{c=1}^{C} u_{ic}^m \sum_{r=1}^{R} \left(\widehat{\pi}_{ri} - \widetilde{\widehat{\pi}}_{rc} \right)^2, \\ \text{subject to: } \sum_{c=1}^{C} u_{ic} = 1 \text{ and } u_{ic} \ge 0, \end{cases} \qquad (8)$$

where $\tilde{\boldsymbol{\Pi}}$ denotes the family of subsets of size C grouping estimated autoregressive vectors for the series in study.

2. The GARCH-based distance measure [4] given by

$$d_{\text{GARCH}}(\boldsymbol{X}^{(k)}, \boldsymbol{X}^{(k')}) = (\boldsymbol{L}_k - \boldsymbol{L}_{k'})' (\boldsymbol{V}_k + \boldsymbol{V}_{k'})^{-1} (\boldsymbol{L}_k - \boldsymbol{L}_{k'}) \qquad (9)$$

with $\boldsymbol{L}_j = \left(\widehat{\alpha}_j, \widehat{\beta}_j \right)$ the vector of estimated parameters, and $\boldsymbol{V}_j$ the estimated covariance matrix for $\boldsymbol{L}_j$, $j = k, k'$. An alternative GARCH-based fuzzy C-medoids clustering (GARCH–FCMdCC) is proposed in [8] by minimizing:

$$\begin{cases} \min_{\boldsymbol{\mathcal{L}},\Omega} \sum_{i=1}^{p} \sum_{c=1}^{C} u_{ic}^m \left[(\boldsymbol{L}_i - \boldsymbol{L}_c)' (\boldsymbol{V}_i + \boldsymbol{V}_c)^{-1} (\boldsymbol{L}_i - \boldsymbol{L}_c) \right], \\ \text{subject to: } \sum_{c=1}^{C} u_{ic} = 1 \text{ and } u_{ic} \ge 0, \end{cases} \qquad (10)$$

where $\boldsymbol{\mathcal{L}}$ denotes the family of subsets of size C grouping estimated $\boldsymbol{L}_i$ vectors for the series in study.

The clustering algorithm was carried out for different values of m in order to assess the influence of the fuzziness parameter. Specifically, a total of $N = 100$ trials were performed for each scenario and three values of the fuzziness parameter, namely $m = \{1.3, 1.5, 2\}$.

At each trial, the quality of the clustering procedure was evaluated comparing the experimental cluster solution with the true cluster partition. For it, each series was assigned to the cluster with the highest membership degree, and then two different agreement measures were used, namely the Gavrilov index [13] and the adjusted Rand index (ARI) [16]. The Gavrilov index simply provides a measure of the number of series sharing a same cluster in both partitions, and hence it is very natural and intuitive. This index is 1 when the two partitions agree perfectly, and returns 0 when they are completely dissimilar. On the other hand, the ARI measures the level of agreement in terms of pairs of series located together in the same or different clusters for both partitions, but in such a way that its expected value equal to zero when the partitions are drawn at random (according to a generalized hypergeometric model) keeping fixed the frequencies of objects. The maximum value of the adjusted Rand index is also 1, but typically takes values substantially lower than other indexes and provides a major sensitivity on the cluster stability. Thus, it is known that higher values of ARI are related with higher values of the other indexes, but very small ARI values suggest a complex database with likely overlapping classes. In sum, although other alternative indexes could have been used (such as Fowlkes-Mallows, Jaccard or Wallace, among others), we think that our choice is proper to reach the goal of comparing the performance of the different clustering procedures.

The mean values and standard deviations of the two indexes based on the 100 trials using both the hard and the fuzzy cluster procedures are provided in Table 1.

Note that the metrics based on quantile autocovariances and the AR representation presented the best results in Scenario 1 with the hard cluster procedure. In the fuzzy clustering, the behavior of d_{GARCH} substantially worsened, while very similar (even somewhat higher) scores were obtained with d_{QAF} and d_{AR}. Although considering different values of m did not have an important effect in this scenario, the best results were attained with $m = 1.3$ for d_{QAF} and d_{AR}, and with $m = 1.5$ for d_{GARCH}. The worst performance corresponded to the GARCH–based dissimilarity for both the hard and the fuzzy versions.

The metric based on quantile autocovariances also obtained the best results in Scenario 2, with indexes of agreement above 0.8 and a slight improvement by using the fuzzy clustering. The GARCH-based metrics, d_{AR} and d_{GARCH} were strongly affected by the model misspecification and clearly produced the worst results regardless of the considered clustering procedure. Again, the value of the fuzziness parameter had very little effect in this scenario. In this case, the best results were reached with $m = 1.5$ for the three metrics.

Another way to test the quality of the clustering procedures is to consider the mean number of clusters correctly identified. Specifically, at the cluster solution obtained for each iteration, we identify: (i) number of correct clusters (CC),

Table 1. Averages and standard deviations (in brackets) of two cluster similarity indexes obtained from 100 trials.

		Scenario 1		Scenario 2	
		Gavrilov	Adj. Rand	Gavrilov	Adj. Rand
Hard cluster					
	d_{AR}	0.709	0.525	0.534	0.208
		(.033)	(.076)	(.075)	(.107)
	d_{GARCH}	0.699	0.457	0.536	0.162
		(.082)	(.130)	(.088)	(.122)
	d_{QAF}	0.784	0.670	0.831	0.714
		(.096)	(.137)	(.099)	(.132)
Fuzzy cluster					
$m = 1.3$	d_{AR}	0.708	0.511	0.544	0.185
		(.036)	(.082)	(.078)	(.111)
	d_{GARCH}	0.531	0.249	0.456	0.077
		(.086)	(.128)	(.068)	(.093)
	d_{QAF}	0.797	0.643	0.849	0.717
		(.127)	(.179)	(.101)	(.152)
$m = 1.5$	d_{AR}	0.705	0.503	0.545	0.188
		(.046)	(.097)	(.075)	(.106)
	d_{GARCH}	0.641	0.338	0.528	0.162
		(.107)	(.162)	(.088)	(.114)
	d_{QAF}	0.795	0.649	0.853	0.717
		(.126)	(.181)	(.100)	(.164)
$m = 2$	d_{AR}	0.706	0.503	0.540	0.145
		(.040)	(.091)	(.087)	(.119)
	d_{GARCH}	0.595	0.290	0.507	0.183
		(.102)	(.139)	(.082)	(.115)
	d_{QAF}	0.783	0.631	0.851	0.708
		(.122)	(.185)	(.101)	(.165)

i.e. clusters exactly formed by the five series generated from the same model; (ii) number of incomplete clusters (IC), i.e. clusters only formed by series with equal underlying model but without including the five series simulated from that model; and (iii) number of mixed clusters (MC), that is clusters grouping series generated from different models. Then, the values CC, IC and MC were averaged over the 100 trials and the attained results are shown in Table 2.

In both scenarios, the highest values of CC were obtained by the fuzzy clustering algorithm based on d_{QAF} and using $m = 1.5$. The other two metrics not

Table 2. Distribution of the number of Correct Clusters (CC), Incomplete Clusters (IC) and Mixed Clusters (MC) obtained from 100 trials.

		Scenario 1			Scenario 2		
		CC	MC	IC	CC	IC	MC
Hard cluster							
	d_{AR}	0.49	1.05	2.46	0.00	0.54	3.46
	d_{GARCH}	0.08	0.12	3.80	0.04	0.31	3.65
	d_{QAF}	1.54	0.76	1.70	1.89	0.53	1.58
Fuzzy cluster							
$m = 1.3$	d_{AR}	0.45	1.08	2.47	0.02	0.49	3.49
	d_{GARCH}	0.02	0.08	3.90	0.00	0.23	3.77
	d_{QAF}	1.53	0.49	1.98	1.93	0.43	1.64
$m = 1.5$	d_{AR}	0.46	0.96	2.58	0.02	0.55	3.43
	d_{GARCH}	0.06	0.09	3.85	0.01	0.30	3.69
	d_{QAF}	1.55	0.53	1.92	1.95	0.41	1.64
$m = 2$	d_{AR}	0.48	1.02	2.50	0.01	0.41	3.58
	d_{GARCH}	0.04	0.12	3.84	0.00	0.32	3.68
	d_{QAF}	1.43	0.62	1.95	1.92	0.39	1.69

even make it to classify well one group, the best results are obtained by the d_{AR} metric and it only classifies well 0.45 clusters in mean.

5   A Case Study

In this section, the proposed fuzzy C–medoids clustering algorithm is used to perform clustering on a set of series of electricity demand. Specifically, our database consists of hourly electricity demand in the Spanish market from 1st January 2011 to 31th December 2012. All data are sourced from the official website of Operador del Mercado Iberico de Energia[1]. Records corresponding to Saturdays and Sundays have been removed from the database because electricity demand is lower in the weekends. Thus we have 24 time series (one for each hour of the day) of length $T = 731$. Graphs of the single series can be seen in Fig. 1.

Since all series are non–stationary in mean, the original series are transformed taking one regular difference. These new series are depicted in Fig. 2.

The clustering purpose is to identify groups of hours showing similar electricity demand patterns. For it, we must be aware of the dynamical character inherent to the objects subjected to cluster. Figure 2 clearly shows that the variance is not constant over time, observing periods of time with different ranges of fluctuation. Since heteroskedasticity is present, the two fuzzy clustering procedures based on GARCH models described in the above section can be a suitable

---

[1] http://www.omel.es/files/flash/ResultadosMercado.swf.

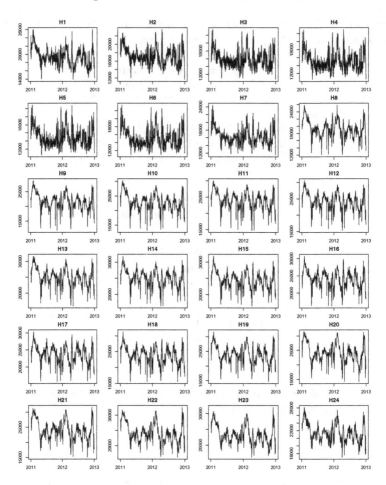

Fig. 1. Daily series (weekends excluded) of electricity demand for each hour of the day from 1st January 2011 to 31th December 2012.

approach in this case. On the other hand, our simulation results also shown the high capability of the quantile autocovariance functions to discriminate between generating heteroskedastic processes. Furthermore, using the d_{QAF}–based approach allows us to overcome the problem of obtaining accurate estimates for the parameters of the underlying heteroskedastic models. Based on these arguments, we decide to perform cluster analysis based on these three clustering procedures. A detailed analysis and comparison of the attained results is shown below.

Just as in simulations, d_{QAF} is constructed by using one lag ($L = 1$, with $l_1 = 1$) and a grid of quantiles formed by all the combinations (q_{τ_i}, q_{τ_j}), with $\tau_i = i/10$, for $i = 1,\ldots,9$. As for the GARCH–based metrics, GARCH(1,1) models were used to estimate the underlying structures, thus providing a suitable trade–off between number of parameters and quality of the estimation measured

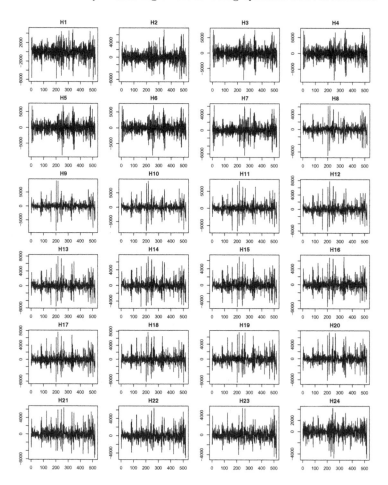

Fig. 2. Daily series (weekends excluded) of electricity demand taking one regular difference.

by the AIC index. In all cases we set a value of the fuzziness parameter $m = 1.5$ in the partitioning algorithm.

A fuzzy extension of the classical silhouette width criterion [5] was used to determine the optimal number of clusters. This fuzzy version takes into consideration the membership degrees matrix and consists in selecting the number of clusters maximizing the so–called Fuzzy Silhoutte Width, FSW, defined by

$$\text{FSW} = \frac{\sum_{i=1}^{p} \left(u_{ir} - u_{iq}\right)^{\alpha} s_i}{\sum_{i=1}^{p} \left(u_{ir} - u_{iq}\right)^{\alpha}}$$

where s_i is the standard silhouette width for the i–th element, u_{ir} and u_{iq} are the first and the second largest elements of the i–th row of the fuzzy partition matrix and $\alpha \geq 0$ is a weighting coefficient. The standard silhouette width, CSW, is

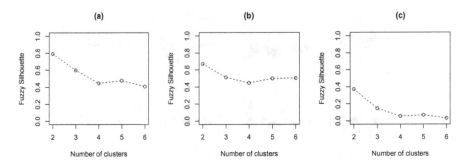

Fig. 3. Fuzzy silhouette width for different cluster partition sizes using QAF FCM (a), GARCH FCMdC (b) and GARCH FCMdCC (c).

Table 3. Membership degrees obtained with QAF–based FCM, GARCH–based FCMdC and GARCH–based FCMdCC, with $m = 1.5$ and considering 2 clusters.

	QAF FCM			GARCH FCMdC			GARCH FCMdCC		
	Membership degrees		Crisp	Membership degrees		Crisp	Membership degrees		Crisp
	C_1	C_2		C_1	C_2		C_1	C_2	
H1	0.63044	0.36956	1	0.00002	0.99998	2	0.00210	0.99790	2
H2	1.00000	0.00000	1	0.00197	0.99803	2	0.00001	0.99999	2
H3	0.98282	0.01718	1	0.92689	0.07311	1	0.00008	0.99992	2
H4	0.94118	0.05882	1	0.99946	0.00054	1	0.00004	0.99996	2
H5	1.00000	0.00000	1	0.99957	0.00043	1	0.00003	0.99997	2
H6	0.99923	0.00077	1	1.00000	0.00000	1	0.00000	1.00000	2
H7	0.98282	0.01718	1	0.99388	0.00612	1	0.00045	0.99955	2
H8	0.00003	0.99997	2	0.00097	0.99903	2	0.93374	0.06626	1
H9	0.00003	0.99997	2	0.00015	0.99985	2	0.99381	0.00619	1
H10	0.00077	0.99923	2	0.00037	0.99963	2	0.98976	0.01024	1
H11	0.00077	0.99923	2	0.00002	0.99998	2	0.21507	0.78493	2
H12	0.00002	0.99998	2	0.00004	0.99996	2	0.16560	0.83440	2
H13	0.00002	0.99998	2	0.99998	0.00002	1	0.00016	0.99984	2
H14	0.00002	0.99998	2	0.93229	0.06771	1	0.00006	0.99994	2
H15	0.00002	0.99998	2	0.99894	0.00106	1	0.00003	0.99997	2
H16	0.00002	0.99998	2	0.97576	0.02424	1	0.00022	0.99978	2
H17	0.00002	0.99998	2	0.04883	0.95117	2	0.00002	0.99998	2
H18	0.00056	0.99944	2	0.00008	0.99992	2	0.03052	0.96948	2
H19	0.00000	1.00000	2	0.00863	0.99137	2	1.00000	0.00000	1
H20	0.00003	0.99997	2	0.00003	0.99997	2	0.01559	0.98441	2
H21	0.00056	0.99944	2	0.22170	0.77830	2	0.00000	1.00000	2
H22	0.01718	0.98282	2	1.00000	0.00000	1	0.00207	0.99793	2
H23	0.00003	0.99997	2	0.01154	0.98846	2	0.00000	1.00000	2
H24	0.99998	0.00002	1	0.00000	1.00000	2	0.00108	0.99892	2

Table 4. Membership degrees obtained with QAF–based FCM with $m = 1.5$ considering 2 and 3 clusters.

	2 Clusters			3 Clusters			
	Membership degrees		Crisp	Membership degrees			Crisp
	C_1	C_2		C_1	C_2	C_3	
H1	0.63044	0.36956	1	1.00000	0.00000	0.00000	1
H2	1.00000	0.00000	1	0.99878	0.00098	0.00024	1
H3	0.98282	0.01718	1	0.99484	0.00395	0.00121	1
H4	0.94118	0.05882	1	0.99229	0.00574	0.00197	1
H5	1.00000	0.00000	1	0.92388	0.06811	0.00801	1
H6	0.99923	0.00077	1	0.30793	0.66185	0.03021	2
H7	0.98282	0.01718	1	0.00000	1.00000	0.00000	2
H8	0.00003	0.99997	2	0.05793	0.09475	0.84733	3
H9	0.00003	0.99997	2	0.00097	0.00294	0.99610	3
H10	0.00077	0.99923	2	0.00045	0.00149	0.99806	3
H11	0.00077	0.99923	2	0.00171	0.00507	0.99323	3
H12	0.00002	0.99998	2	0.00011	0.00049	0.99940	3
H13	0.00002	0.99998	2	0.00027	0.00178	0.99794	3
H14	0.00002	0.99998	2	0.00032	0.00107	0.99861	3
H15	0.00002	0.99998	2	0.00134	0.00940	0.98927	3
H16	0.00002	0.99998	2	0.00088	0.00636	0.99277	3
H17	0.00002	0.99998	2	0.00000	0.00000	1.00000	3
H18	0.00056	0.99944	2	0.00051	0.00498	0.99451	3
H19	0.00000	1.00000	2	0.00002	0.00014	0.99984	3
H20	0.00003	0.99997	2	0.00020	0.00135	0.99846	3
H21	0.00056	0.99944	2	0.00047	0.00384	0.99569	3
H22	0.01718	0.98282	2	0.00136	0.01488	0.98377	3
H23	0.00003	0.99997	2	0.01539	0.13091	0.85370	3
H24	0.99998	0.00002	1	0.00206	0.98054	0.01740	2

obtained by setting $\alpha = 0$ in FSW. As α increases, FSW moves away from CSW. Unlike CSW, which is the arithmetic mean of the individual silhouette widths, FSW provides a weighted average of these coefficients so that objects belonging to overlapping clusters are underweight. Hence, compared to CSW, FSW takes advantage from regarding information contained in the fuzzy partition matrix on degrees to which clusters overlap one another. In terms of the reached value, FSW admits a similar interpretation as CSW, i.e. the higher the value of FSW, the better the assignment of the objects to the clusters. Overall, values above 0.7 suggest a strong cluster structure. The usual value $\alpha = 1$ was used in our application.

Figure 3 suggests the existence of two major groups for the three classification algorithms. The fuzzy algorithm based on the quantile autocovariances dissimilarity produced the highest index with a value 0.789. This index indicates that a strong structure has been found according to arguments given in [18]. Likewise, a reasonable structure is also suggested by the index 0.671 obtained with the GARCH–based FCMdC algorithm, and only the algorithm based on the Caiado distance (GARCH–based FCMdCC) produced a low index of 0.371, which could indicate lack or weakness of an underlying cluster structure.

Table 3 shows the membership degrees obtained with the three methods. The fuzzy algorithm based on d_{QAF} leads to a cluster partition formed by $C_1 = \{H24, H1, H2, H3, H4, H5, H6, H7\}$ and C_2 grouping the remaining series. The cluster C_1 corresponds with the hours of the day where the electricity demand is low, while C_2 identifies the time of the day where the power consumption is greater. With this procedure only $H1$ has an individual fuzzy silhouette index close to zero, the remaining elements have indexes above 0.5. Attending to the partition obtained using d_{AR}, $C_1 = \{H3, H4, H5, H6, H7, H13, H14, H15, H16, H22\}$ and C_2 grouping the rest of the series. This partition presents some individual fuzzy silhouette widths close to 0 (H14 is equal to 0) and could be not properly classified. Finally, it has not been obtained any interesting information when using the d_{GARCH} metric.

Table 4 presents the membership degrees using d_{QAF} for the case with two and three clusters. Since the fuzzy silhouette index for the three–cluster solution is 0.598, which is a very good index, it seems reasonably to analyze this possibility. In this case, the difference with the two–cluster solution is that the cluster C_1 is divided in two subclusters. One formed with the hours of the day with the lowest demand of electricity, and a second cluster with an intermediate electricity consumption, that corresponds with the hours of the day when most of the people is starting to go to bed or starting to wake up ($H6, H7, H24$).

6   Concluding Remarks

In this paper, we focus on the classification of time series featuring a fuzzy clustering algorithm in the framework of a partitioning around medoids. A dissimilarity–based approach is considered. We propose a C–medoids fuzzy clustering algorithm using an innovative dissimilarity measure based on the quantile autocovariances (d_{QAF}).

The simulation study shows that the proposed dissimilarity produces satisfactory results by performing fuzzy cluster analysis. The proposed clustering algorithm was tested against two GARCH–based fuzzy clustering algorithms present in the literature in two different heteroskedastic scenarios. The fuzzy clustering algorithm based on d_{QAF} led to the best results. In fact, apart from d_{QAF}, none of the remaining examined dissimilarities shown acceptable results by clustering heteroskedastic processes, thus emphasizing the usefulness of d_{QAF} in this framework. It is important to remark that the proposed procedure assumes that the time series are strictly stationary. This is a quite usual requirement for many of the metrics introduced in time series clustering, but it is indeed a limitation of the method in practice and further research must be carried out to encompass non–stationarity. Other limitation inherent to the fuzzy paradigm is the need of selecting the fuzziness parameter. An alternative clustering approach free of this requirement is the probabilistic clustering, where each element is assigned to one single cluster according to the probability estimated from the data. Strictly speaking, a probabilistic clustering is neither crisp nor fuzzy, but it is a soft procedure since assignments are determined by an estimated probability. This way, although a fuzzy partition is not generated, the probabilistic models such as mixture models [22] can be useful in situations where clusters overlap. The main problem with these methods is to identify the underlying models, which can be specially challenging with high-dimensional data [3] or in the time series framework. Recent papers by Aielli and Caporin [1,2] provide interesting procedures for clustering univariate and multivariate GARCH models using Gaussian mixture models to represent the probabilistic behaviour of the estimated GARCH parameters. Extension of these procedures to encompass different dependence structures and analysis of their clustering behaviour compared with fuzzy procedures is an interesting issue which deserves further research.

Acknowledgement. The authors wish to thank the two reviewers for their helpful comments and valuable suggestions, which have allowed us to improve the quality of this work. This research was supported by the Spanish grant MTM2014-52876-R from the Ministerio de Economía y Competitividad.

References

1. Aielli, G.P., Caporin, M.: Fast clustering of GARCH processes via Gaussian mixture models. Math. Comput. Simul. **94**, 205–222 (2013)
2. Aielli, G.P., Caporin, M.: Variance clustering improved dynamic conditional correlation MGARCH estimators. Comput. Stat. Data Anal. **76**, 556–576 (2014)
3. Bouveyron, C., Brunet-Saumard, C.: Model-based clustering of high-dimensional data: a review. Comput. Stat. Data Anal. **71**, 52–78 (2014)
4. Caiado, J., Crato, N.: A GARCH-based method for clustering of financial time series: international stock markets evidence. MPRA paper, University Library of Munich, Germany (2007). http://EconPapers.repec.org/RePEc:pra:mprapa:2074
5. Campelloi, R., Hruschka, E.: A fuzzy extension of the sihouette width criterion for cluster analysis. Fuzzy Sets Syst. **157**, 2858–2875 (2006)
6. Döring, C., Lesot, M.J., Kruse, R.: Data analysis with fuzzy clustering methods. Comput. Stat. Data Anal. **51**(1), 192–214 (2006)
7. D'Urso, P.: Fuzzy clustering. In: Hennig, C., Meila, M., Murtagh, F., Rocci, R. (eds.) Handbook of Cluster Analysis, pp. 545–574. Chapman & Hall (2015, in press)
8. D'Urso, P., Cappelli, C., Lallo, D.D., Massari, R.: Clustering of financial time series. Phys. A **392**(9), 2114–2129 (2013)
9. D'Urso, P., Maharaj, E.A.: Autocorrelation-based fuzzy clustering of time series. Fuzzy Sets Syst. **160**(24), 3565–3589 (2009)
10. D'Urso, P., De Giovanni, L., Massari, R.: GARCH-based robust clustering of time series. Fuzzy Sets Syst. (2015)

11. D'Urso, P., De Giovanni, L., Massari, R.: Time series clustering by a robust autoregressive metric with application to air pollution. Chemometr. Intell. Lab. Syst. **141**(15), 107–124 (2015)
12. D'Urso, P., De Giovanni, L., Massari, R., Lallo, D.D.: Noise fuzzy clustering of time series by the autoregressive metric. Metron **71**(3), 217–243 (2013)
13. Gavrilov, M., Anguelov, D., Indyk, P., Motwani, R.: Mining the stock market (extended abstract): which measure is best? In: Proceedings of the Sixth ACM SIGKDD International Conference on Knowledge Discovery and Data Mining, KDD 2000, pp. 487–496. ACM, New York (2000)
14. Hennig, C., Lin, C.J.: Flexible parametric bootstrap for testing homogeneity against clustering and assessing the number of clusters. Stat. Comput. **25**(4), 821–833 (2015)
15. Höppner, F., Klawonn, F., Kruse, R., Runkler, T.: Fuzzy Cluster Analysis: Methods for Classification, Data Analysis and Image Recognition. Wiley, Chichester (1999)
16. Hubert, L., Arabie, P.: Comparing partitions. J. Classif. **2**(1), 193–218 (1985)
17. Jain, A.K., Dubes, R.C.: Algorithms for Clustering Data. Prentice-Hall Inc., Upper Saddle River (1988)
18. Kaufman, L., Rousseeuw, P.J.: Finding Groups in Data: An Introduction to Cluster Analysis, 9th edn. Wiley, New York (1990)
19. Lafuente-Rego, B., Vilar, J.A.: Clustering of time series using quantile autocovariances. Adv. Data Anal. Classif. 1–25 (2015)
20. Maharaj, E.A.: Clusters of time series. J. Classif. **17**(2), 297–314 (2000)
21. Maharaj, E.A., D'Urso, P.: Fuzzy clustering of time series in the frequency domain. Inf. Sci. **181**(7), 1187–1211 (2011)
22. McLachlan, G.J., Basford, K.E.: Mixture Models: Inference and Applications to Clustering. Marcel Dekker Inc., New York/Basel (1988)
23. Piccolo, D.: A distance measure for classifying ARIMA models. J. Time Series Anal. **11**(2), 153–164 (1990)

A Reservoir Computing Approach for Balance Assessment

Claudio Gallicchio[1]([⊠]), Alessio Micheli[1], Luca Pedrelli[1], Luigi Fortunati[2], Federico Vozzi[3], and Oberdan Parodi[3]

[1] Department of Computer Science, University of Pisa,
Largo B. Pontecorvo 3, Pisa, Italy
{gallicch,micheli,luca.pedrelli}@di.unipi.it
[2] Istituto di Scienze e Tecnologie dell'Informazione "A. Faedo" - Consiglio Nazionale delle Ricerche - ISTI-CNR Pisa, via Moruzzi 1, Pisa, Italy
luigi.fortunati@isti.cnr.it
[3] Istituto di Fisiologia Clinica - Consiglio Nazionale delle Ricerche - IFC-CNR Pisa, via Moruzzi 1, Pisa, Italy
vozzi@ifc.cnr.it, oberdan.parodi@virgilio.it

Abstract. A relevant aspect in the field of health monitoring is represented by the evaluation of balance stability in the elderly. The Berg Balance Scale (BBS) represents a golden standard test for clinical assessment of balance stability. Recently, the Wii Balance Board has been successfully validated as an effective tool for the analysis of static balance-related features such as the duration or the speed of assessment of patient's center of pressure. In this paper we propose an innovative unobtrusive approach for automatic evaluation of balance assessment, by analyzing the whole temporal information generated by the balance board. In particular, using Recurrent Neural Networks implemented according to the Reservoir Computing paradigm, we propose to estimate the BBS score of a patient from the temporal data gathered during the execution on the balance board of one simple BBS exercise. The experimental assessment of the proposed approach on real-world data shows promising results.

Keywords: Reservoir computing · Echo state network · Learning with temporal data · Balance assessment

1 Introduction

Physical activity, health and quality of life are closely interconnected: the human body is designed to move and therefore needs a regular physical activity in order to function optimally and avoid illness. It has been observed in literature that a sedentary lifestyle is a risk factor for the development of many chronic illnesses. The common physiological aging causes a decrease of global functional abilities: one of the most important is balance disorder [31]. The control of balance is complex, with a strong integration and coordination of multiple body elements including visual, auditor and motor systems [19]. Repeated falling are major cause of

© Springer International Publishing Switzerland 2016
A. Douzal-Chouakria et al. (Eds.): AALTD 2015, LNAI 9785, pp. 65–77, 2016.
DOI: 10.1007/978-3-319-44412-3_5

injuries with frequent hospitalization and consequent health care system costs. A comprehensive clinical assessment of balance is important for both diagnostic and therapeutic reasons in clinical practice [11,34]. In this context, the *Berg Balance Scale* (BBS) test is considered the gold standard for balance functional assessment [27], with small intra-inter rater feasibility and good internal validity. The work of Berg et al. [10] assessed the validity of the BBS by examining how scale scores are related to clinical judgments, laboratory measures of postural sway and external criteria reflecting balancing ability. Furthermore, scores could predict falls in the elderly and how they are related to motor and functional performance in stroke patients. The Berg's utility includes grading different patients' balance abilities, monitoring functional balance over time and evaluating patients responses to different protocols of treatment [35]. Based on a test of 14 exercises/items, the BBS test is performance-based and has a scale of 0–4 (clinician assigned) score for each item (higher score for more independent performance), with a maximum overall score of 56. Within the scopes of the DOREMI European project (GA 611650) [7], a technological platform to support and motivate elderly people to perform physical activity is under development, aiming at reducing sedentariness, cognitive decline and malnutrition, promoting an improvement of quality of life and social inclusion. This hardware and software-based platform is able to monitor users' physical activity levels, integrating these information with nutritional parameters. One of the elements of the DOREMI platform is a balance board, based on the use of *Nintendo Wii Balance Board*, which is able to gather information pertaining to users' weight distribution at the four corners of the board. Such tool allows to design an automatic system aiming at performing balance assessment through the daily repetition of one simple BBS exercise. This type of analysis, done by users at medical facilities or, remotely, at their own houses, can help clinicians in the evaluation of older people equilibrium and in the control of its evolution. The use of the Wii Balance Board is motivated by the fact that it represents a low-cost and portable tool, which has recently been successfully adopted for problems related to standing posture correction [29] and for training standing balance in the elderly [36]. Moreover, the Wii Balance Board has been validated in comparison with gold standard force platforms [26] in its reliability to track users' balance parameters, such as the center of pressure path length and velocity [13]. However, it is worth to observe that the whole signal time-series generated by the Wii Balance Board potentially contains a richer information than such static parameters.

In this paper we propose to analyze the data generated by the Wii Balance Board by using Recurrent Neural Networks (RNNs) [23], which represent a class of learning models particularly suitable and widely used for processing and catching dynamic knowledge from noisy temporal data. Within the class of RNNs, we take into consideration the Reservoir Computing (RC) paradigm [24,33] and specifically the Echo State Network (ESN) model [16,20,21], which constitute a state-of-the-art approach for efficiently learning in temporal domains, supported by theoretical investigations [16,32] and with hundreds of successful experimental studies reported in literature [25,33]. Recently, ESNs have proved to be particularly suitable for processing heterogeneous noisy temporal information generated by sensors, resulting in successful real-world applications in the areas of Ambient Assisted Living [3,6,8,9,12,15] and Human Activity Recognition [28]. Moreover, the successful results achieved by the RUBICON Project [1,2,4,5,14] represent a further experimental background to the appropriateness of the RC approach in such application areas. In particular, we take into consideration the problem of estimating the BBS score of a patient using in input the temporal information generated by the execution of one simple BBS exercise on the Wii Balance Board. This approach potentially allows to avoid the need to repeat the execution of all the 14 BBS exercises for new patients. An alternative approach is described in [30], and tries to estimate the BBS score of a patient using data extracted from a tri-axial accelerometer placed on the lower back of the user during the execution of several items of the BBS. Such approach, however, adopts a solution which results to be more intrusive for the patient and does not explicitly takes into account the temporal dimension of the gathered input data. At the best of our knowledge, our work represents the first attempt at estimating the BBS score directly from the temporal data generated while the patient performs a simple balance exercise in a non-intrusive way using an external device.

2   Balance Assessment Using Reservoir Computing

A measurement campaign has been conducted on 21 volunteers, aged between 65 and 80 years. We measured the weight signal produced at the 4 corners of the Wii Balance Board (i.e. front left, front right, back right, back left) sampled at 5 Hz during the execution of the exercise # 10 in the BBS test, i.e. *turn to look behind*, selected in order to be of simple execution and of short duration ($\approx$10 s). To take into account for possible variations in the exercise execution, for each patient we recorded data gathered from the execution of a number of maximum 10 repetitions of the exercise. As a result of this process, we obtained a *Balance dataset* for the definition of a regression task on sequences, containing couples of the type $(\mathbf{s}, y_{tg})$, where $\mathbf{s}$ is the 4-dimensional input sequence of users' weight values recorded by the Wii Balance Board during the exercise execution and y_{tg} is the target BBS score (over all the 14 exercises) of the corresponding patient, representing the ground-truth information evaluated by a clinician during the measurement campaign. Examples of the gathered input signals are reported in Fig. 1, illustrating the temporal evolution of the weight values at the four corners of the Wii Balance Board during 3 exercise repetitions by the same user, therefore corresponding to the same ground-truth BBS score. Figure 1 shows the typical noisy signal and the resulting difficulties in the identification by inspection of a common pattern associated to specific values of the BBS score. Overall, the Balance dataset contains a total number of 172 sequences. The length of the collected sequences varies in the range 30–96 time steps, with an average length of $\approx$50, corresponding to a duration of $\approx$10 s. All the input sequences in the dataset were individually normalized to zero mean and unitary standard deviation.

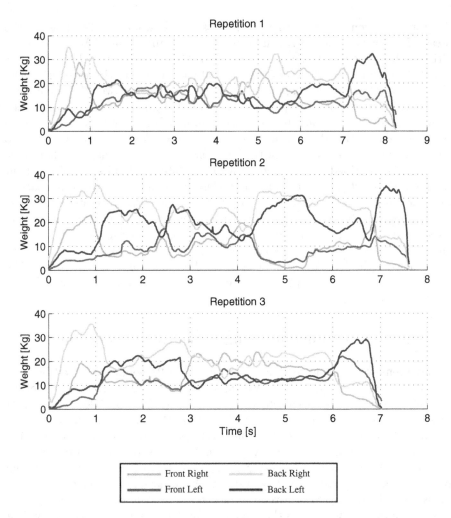

Fig. 1. Streams of weight values recorded at the four corners (front right, front left, back right, back left) of the Wii Balance Board during the execution of the exercise # 10 of the BBS test. Plots in the figure correspond to different repetitions of the execution by the same user, with a ground-truth BBS score of 53.

The Mean Absolute Error (MAE) of the BBS score estimation provided by the learning models has been adopted for performance assessment of the proposed approach. In this regard, it is worth noticing that the Balance dataset contains an outlier patient with BBS score of 24, which has been discarded for performance evaluation.

We model the dynamics of the temporal data involved by the balance estimation task by using ESNs. In particular, we take into consideration the Leaky Integration ESN (LI-ESN) model [22], a variant of the standard ESN that has

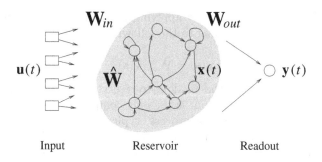

Fig. 2. Architecture of a LI-ESN with $N_R = 4$ input units, $N_R = 7$ reservoir units and $N_Y = 1$ readout unit.

proved to be especially suitable for dealing with the characteristics of the temporal data generated from sensors [15]. LI-ESNs implement discrete time dynamical systems, and consist of two main components, a dynamical *reservoir*, which realizes a recurrent encoding of the input history and provides the system with a memory of the past [16], and a static *readout* which computes the output. More in detail, a LI-ESN is composed of an input layer with N_U units, a recurrent non-linear reservoir layer with N_R sparsely connected units, and a linear readout layer with N_Y units. The general architecture of a LI-ESN is illustrated in Fig. 2.

Given the input at time step t, $\mathbf{u}(t) \in \mathbb{R}^{N_U}$, the reservoir of the LI-ESN computes a state $\mathbf{x}(t) \in \mathbb{R}^{N_R}$ according to the following state transition function

$$\mathbf{x}(t) = (1 - a)\mathbf{x}(t - 1) + af(\mathbf{W}_{in}\mathbf{u}(t) + \hat{\mathbf{W}}\mathbf{x}(t - 1)) \tag{1}$$

where $\mathbf{W}_{in} \in \mathbb{R}^{N_R \times N_U}$ is the input-to-reservoir weight matrix (possibly including a bias term), $\hat{\mathbf{W}} \in \mathbb{R}^{N_R \times N_R}$ is the recurrent reservoir weight matrix, f is the element-wise applied activation function, which typically is a non-linearity of a sigmoidal type (in this paper we use $tanh$), and $a \in [0, 1]$ is the *leaking rate* parameter that controls the speed of the reservoir dynamics in reaction to the input [22,24]. Note that when $a = 1$, Eq. 1 reduces to the standard ESN state transition function. For regression tasks in which an output value is required in correspondence of an entire input sequence, such is the case of the application considered in this paper, the use of a *mean state mapping* function has proved to be effective in several application contexts [17,18]. Accordingly, given an input sequence of length n, $\mathbf{s} = [\mathbf{u}(1), \ldots, \mathbf{u}(n)]$, the state activation is averaged over all the steps of the input sequence, as follows

$$\chi(\mathbf{s}) = \frac{1}{n} \sum_{t=1}^{n} \mathbf{x}(t) \tag{2}$$

where $\chi(\mathbf{s}) \in \mathbb{R}^{N_R}$ denotes the output of the state mapping function.

The output of the LI-ESN is computed by the readout through a linear combination of the reservoir state. In this case, for each input sequence $\mathbf{s}$, an output $\mathbf{y}(\mathbf{s}) \in \mathbb{R}^{N_Y}$ is computed by applying the readout to the output of the state mapping function, according to the following equation:

$$\mathbf{y}(\mathbf{s}) = \mathbf{W}_{out}\chi(\mathbf{s}) \tag{3}$$

where $\mathbf{W}_{out} \in \mathbb{R}^{N_Y \times N_R}$ is the readout-to-reservoir weight matrix (possibly including a bias term). The readout is the only component of the LI-ESN architecture that undergoes a training process, typically by the means of efficient linear methods, e.g. pseudo-inversion and ridge regression [24]. The reservoir is left untrained after initialization under the constraints of the *echo state property* (ESP) [16,20,21]. Conditions for the ESP are given in [20,21], while a sufficient condition is often considered too restrictive for practical applications, a reservoir initialization condition related to the spectral radius of $\tilde{\mathbf{W}} = (1 - a)\mathbf{I} + a\hat{\mathbf{W}}$ is often used in literature and is adopted in this paper, namely

$$\rho(\tilde{\mathbf{W}}) < 1. \tag{4}$$

A simple process to meet the ESP consists in randomly initializing the values in $\hat{\mathbf{W}}$ from a uniform distribution, and then re-scaling them such that Eq. 4 is satisfied. The weight values in $\mathbf{W}_{in}$ are typically randomly chosen from a uniform distribution over $[-scale_{in}, scale_{in}]$, where $scale_{in}$ is an input scaling parameter. For further details concerning reservoir initialization, characterization of state dynamics and readout training the reader is referred to [16,24].

3   Experimental Results

The experimental analysis presented in this paper is focused on assessing the generalization performance of the proposed LI-ESN approach for automatic balance estimation. Secondly, we also consider the empirical evaluation of the trade-off between the number of exercise repetitions per patient needed for training and the predictive performance that can correspondingly be obtained. This latter point aims at eventually reducing the patients' effort for future data gathering campaigns. Accordingly, two experimental settings were used, as detailed in the following.

In the first experimental setting, we considered LI-ESNs with 10% of reservoir units connectivity, spectral radius $\rho = 0.99$ and variable values for the reservoir dimension N_R, input scaling parameter $scale_{in}$ and leaky parameter a. For each reservoir hyper-parametrization, we independently generated 5 reservoir guesses, averaging the results over such guesses. For readout training we used ridge regression, taking into consideration different values of the regularization parameter λ_r. The predictive performance of LI-ESNs was evaluated by means of a 7-fold cross validation, splitting the available data according to a 3 persons-out approach. Note that such approach is of particular relevance for the aims of performance evaluation in real-world conditions usage, in which the system is applied to estimate the BBS score of patients that are completely unknown during training. The reservoir hyper-parametrization and readout regularization

Table 1. Range of hyper-parameters values considered for the LI-ESN model selection.

Hyper-parameter	Values considered for model selection
Reservoir dimension N_R	$10, 20, 50, 100, 200$
Input scaling $scale_{in}$	$0.1, 0.5, 1$
Leaky parameter a	$0.1, 0.3, 0.5, 0.7, 1.0$
Readout regularization λ_r	$0.001, 0.01, 0.1, 1, 10$

Table 2. MAE (expressed in points of the Berg Balance Scale test) achieved by LI-ESNs on training, validation and test sets, averaged over the folds considered for performance assessment on the balance estimation task.

MAE Training	MAE Validation	MAE Test
$3.65(\pm0.06)$	$4.26(\pm0.11)$	$4.44(\pm0.25)$

were selected, from the ranges reported in Table 1, on a validation set by an extra level of 6-fold cross validation on each training fold. Table 2 shows the obtained averaged training, validation and test performance. As can be observed, LI-ESNs resulted in a very good predictive performance, with a test MAE of 4.44 ± 0.25 points of the BBS test. Such performance appears promising also considering the tolerance in the ground-truth data due to human observations. The goodness of the achieved generalization performance is also illustrated in Fig. 3, which compares the BBS scores estimations provided by the LI-ESNs on the test set with the corresponding clinician assigned ground-truth values.

In comparison with literature results, it is worth noticing that the performance achieved by our approach outperforms the result reported in [30], which achieves in the best condition a MAE error value of 4.63 (with standard deviation of the error of 3.89) for patients within a corresponding age range. Such an approach uses a k-NN algorithm on data gathered from a tri-axial accelerometer placed on the users' lower back during the execution of 3 exercises of the BBS test, and in [30] it is assessed on a specifically collected dataset, different from the one considered in our work. Thereby, to further assess the relevance of the results achieved by LI-ESNs with respect to the state-of-the-art, we directly compared them with those obtained by considering an approach similar to the method proposed in [30], applied to the same Balance dataset described in this paper. To this aim, each patients data were normalized to the average length of the sequences by means of either interpolation or decimation. After that, the 4 input streams from the Wii Balance Board sensors were concatenated to form a 1-dimensional time-series for each exercise repetition. This procedure enabled the comparison of sequences using a distance measure. As in [30], k-NN has been implemented by using Euclidean distance, correlation coefficient and Tanimoto coefficient, and considering values of k in the range $k \in \{3, 5, 7, 10\}$. As for the LI-ESNs experiments, the predictive performance of k-NN was evaluated by adopting a 7-fold

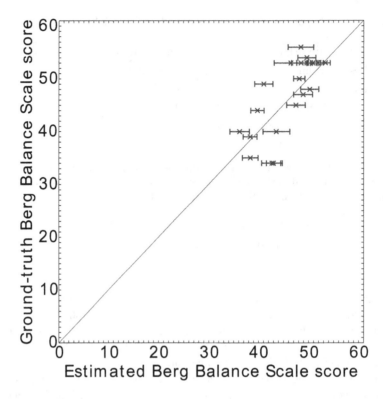

Fig. 3. Comparison among the LI-ESN estimations of the Berg Balance Scale scores for patients' data evaluated in the test set and corresponding ground-truth (clinician-measured) scores. Each point in the plot corresponds to a patient, whereas the error bar accounts for the variability of the estimation among the different exercise repetitions for the same patient.

cross validation scheme, whereas the distance measure for the k-NN method and the value of k were selected on a validation set by an extra level of 6-fold cross validation. After model selection, the best configuration was obtained in correspondence of the Tanimoto coefficient and the value of $k = 3$ (which also corresponds to the best configuration in [30], on the dataset therein considered), leading to a MAE of 1.94($\pm$2.76), 4.61($\pm$3.61) and 7.03($\pm$4.47) BBS points on the training, validation and test set of our Balance dataset, respectively. In comparison to these results, it is possible to observe (see Table 2) that our proposed LI-ESN approach provides better accuracy both for validation and test sets, with a better generalization performance quantifiable in a test error reduction of $\approx$37 % with respect to the one achieved with the method in [30], at the same time showing a favorable ratio among training, validation and test errors.

The second experimental setting aimed at evaluating how the performance of the proposed LI-ESN approach scales with the number of available training data for each patient. To this purpose we used the same 3-persons out 7-fold cross

Table 3. MAE (expressed in points of the Berg Balance Scale test) achieved by LI-ESNs on training and validation and sets, for decreasing number of training sequences available for each patient.

Number of training sequences per patient	MAE Training	MAE Validation
10	3.61($\pm$0.09)	4.41($\pm$0.07)
9	3.59($\pm$0.04)	4.44($\pm$0.07)
8	3.66($\pm$0.06)	4.50($\pm$0.07)
7	3.58($\pm$0.07)	4.40($\pm$0.07)
6	3.69($\pm$0.06)	4.47($\pm$0.06)
5	3.77($\pm$0.03)	4.40($\pm$0.07)
4	3.81($\pm$0.03)	4.42($\pm$0.05)
3	3.88($\pm$0.07)	4.47($\pm$0.07)
2	4.05($\pm$0.12)	4.61($\pm$0.13)
1	4.29($\pm$0.07)	4.93($\pm$0.15)

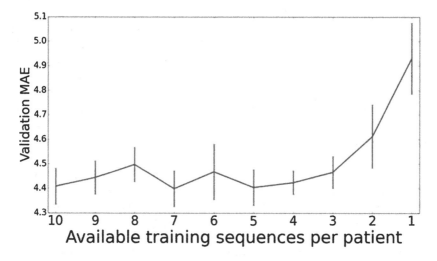

Fig. 4. Validation MAE (and standard deviation) achieved by LI-ESNs on the Balance dataset for decreasing number of training sequences available for each patient.

validation scheme used in the first experimental setting, progressively reducing the number of training sequences considered for each patient from 10 to 1. For this second experimental setting, we restricted to the case of LI-ESNs with $N_R = 100$ reservoir units, whereas all the others reservoir hyper-parameters and readout regularization values were selected (for each fold) on the validation set, considering the same range of values as in the case of the first experimental setting. Detailed results achieved on training and validation sets are reported in Table 3, whereas the trend of performance degradation on the validation set with decreasing number of training sequences available per patient is graphically illustrated in Fig. 4. Results show that the validation performance is approximately stable for a number of training sequences per patient in the range of 10-4, with MAE on the training and validation sets generally not larger than ≈3.8 and ≈4.4 points, respectively. On the other hand, when less than 4 training sequences per patient are used the performance rapidly worsens, up to a MAE of 4.29 and 4.93 points on the training and validation sets, respectively.

4   Conclusions

In this paper, we have proposed an RC-based approach for assessing the balance abilities of elderly people from temporal data recorded by a Wii Balance Board during the execution of one simple BBS exercise. The proposed system has the major advantage of allowing an automatic evaluation the BBS score using only 1 out of the 14 BBS exercises. The experimental analysis on a real-world dataset showed that our approach is able to achieve a very good predictive performance, up to 4.44 BBS points of discrepancy on the test set with respect to the clinician assigned gold standard. Such result is of particular value also considering both the use of a single BBS item for the score estimation and the tolerance that is typical of any subjective assessment scale. Overall, the possibility to infer the BBS scores with a good performance from the temporal data recorded in correspondence of a single BBS exercise shows the potentiality of our idea of exploiting the entire curve of the signal stream as a rich source of information for the evaluation of balance assessment. Moreover, we also addressed the problem of evaluating the trade-off between the number of repetitions of the BBS exercise for each patient, required for training the RC networks, and the predictive performance correspondingly obtained. Such investigation showed that a moderate number of repetitions in the training set turned out to be already sufficient in order to obtain a good performance. Note that this aspect is of particular interest under the point of view of trying to minimize the effort needed for the collection of an adequate and sufficiently sampled dataset for balance estimation, as indeed the repeated execution of BBS exercises by elderly people could be onerous. Finally, the results showed in this work have a potential utility by themselves, for the development of a balance estimation tool, moreover they will be eventually exploited within the purposes of the DOREMI project as a part of a larger health monitoring system aiming at improving elderly quality of life and orchestrating healthy active aging.

Acknowledgments. The work was funded by a grant from DOREMI project (FP7-ICT-2013, GA no. 611650). The authors would like to acknowledge Dr. Sara Lanzisera, Dr. Cristina Laddaga (ASL5, Pisa), Dr. Andrea Bemi (Istituto Superiore di Istruzione C. Piaggia, Viareggio), Dr. Franca Giugni (CNR-IFC), Dr. Filippo Palumbo and Dr. Erina Ferro (CNR-ISTI) for their valuable inputs, support and effort during the preparation and execution of the tests. Finally, the authors would also like to acknowledge all the volunteer participants to the measurement campaign for their support and active participation in these activities.

References

1. Amato, G., Bacciu, D., Broxvall, M., Chessa, S., Coleman, S., Di Rocco, M., Dragone, M., Gallicchio, C., Gennaro, C., McGinnity, T.M., Lozano, H., Micheli, A., Ray, A., Renteira, A., Saffiotti, A., Swords, D., Vairo, C., Vance, P.: Robotic ubiquitous cognitive ecology for smart homes. J. Intell. Robot. Syst. **80**, 1–25 (2015)
2. Amato, G., Broxvall, M., Chessa, S., Dragone, M., Gennaro, C., López, R., Maguire, L., Mcginnity, T., Micheli, A., Renteria, A., O'Hare, G., Pecora, F.: Robotic ubiquitous cognitive network. In: Novais, P., Hallenborg, K., Tapia, D.I., Corchado Rodríguez, J.M. (eds.) Ambient Intelligence - Software and Applications. AISC, vol. 153, pp. 191–195. Springer, Heidelberg (2012)
3. Bacciu, D., Barsocchi, P., Chessa, S., Gallicchio, C., Micheli, A.: An experimental characterization of reservoir computing in ambient assisted living applications. Neural Comput. Appl. **24**(6), 1451–1464 (2014)
4. Bacciu, D., Broxvall, M., Coleman, S., Dragone, M., Gallicchio, C., Gennaro, C., Guzmán, R., López, R., Lozano-Peiteado, H., Ray, A., Renteira, A., Saffiotti, A., Vairo, C.: Self-sustaining learning for robotic ecologies. In: SENSORNETS, pp. 99–103 (2012)
5. Bacciu, D., Chessa, S., Gallicchio, C., Lenzi, A., Micheli, A., Pelagatti, S.: A general purpose distributed learning model for robotic ecologies. Robot Control. **10–1**, 435–440 (2012)
6. Bacciu, D., Chessa, S., Gallicchio, C., Micheli, A., Barsocchi, P.: An experimental evaluation of reservoir computation for ambient assisted living. In: Apolloni, B., Bassis, S., Esposito, A., Morabito, F.C. (eds.) Neural Nets and Surroundings. SIST, vol. 19, pp. 41–50. Springer, Heidelberg (2013)
7. Bacciu, D., et al.: Smart environments and context-awareness for lifestyle management in a healthy active ageing framework. In: Pereira, F., Machado, P., Costa, E., Cardoso, A. (eds.) EPIA 2015. LNCS, vol. 9273, pp. 54–66. Springer, Heidelberg (2015)
8. Bacciu, D., Gallicchio, C., Micheli, A., Chessa, S., Barsocchi, P.: Predicting user movements in heterogeneous indoor environments by reservoir computing. In: Bhatt, M., Guesgen, H.W., Augusto, J.C. (eds.) Proceedings of the IJCAI Workshop on Space, Time and Ambient Intelligence (STAMI 2011), pp. 1–6 (2011)
9. Barsocchi, P., Chessa, S., Micheli, A., Gallicchio, C.: Forecast-driven enhancement of received signal strength (RSS)-based localization systems. ISPRS Int. J. Geo-Inf. **2**(4), 978–995 (2013)
10. Berg, K.O., Wood-Dauphinee, S.L., Williams, J.I., Maki, B.: Measuring balance in the elderly: validation of an instrument. Can. J. Public Health (Revue canadienne de sante publique) **83**, S7–S11 (1991)
11. Bloem, B.R., Visser, J.E., Allum, J.H.: Movement Disorders - Handbook of Clinical Neurophysiology. Elsevier, Amsterdam (2009)
12. Chessa, S., Gallicchio, C., Guzman, R., Micheli, A.: Robot localization by echo state networks using RSS. In: Bassis, S., Esposito, A., Morabito, F.C. (eds.) Recent Advances of Neural Networks Models and Applications. SIST, vol. 26, pp. 147–154. Springer, Heidelberg (2014)
13. Clark, R.A., Bryant, A.L., Pua, Y., McCrory, P., Bennell, K., Hunt, M.: Validity and reliability of the Nintendo Wii Balance Board for assessment of standing balance. Gait Posture **31**(3), 307–310 (2010)

14. Dragone, M., Amato, G., Bacciu, D., Chessa, S., Coleman, S., Di Rocco, M., Gallic-chio, C., Gennaro, C., Lozano-Peiteado, H., Maguire, L., McGinnity, T., Micheli, A., OHare, G.M., Renteria, A., Saffiotti, A., Vairo, C., Vance, P.: A cognitive robotic ecology approach to self-configuring and evolving AAL systems. Eng. Appl. Artif. Intell. **45**, 269–280 (2015)

15. Gallicchio, C., Micheli, A., Barsocchi, P., Chessa, S.: User movements forecasting by reservoir computing using signal streams produced by mote-class sensors. In: Del Ser, J., Jorswieck, E.A., Miguez, J., Matinmikko, M., Palomar, D.P., Salcedo-Sanz, S., Gil-Lopez, S. (eds.) Mobilight 2011. LNICST, vol. 81, pp. 151–168. Springer, Heidelberg (2012)

16. Gallicchio, C., Micheli, A.: Architectural and Markovian factors of echo state networks. Neural Netw. **24**(5), 440–456 (2011)

17. Gallicchio, C., Micheli, A.: Tree echo state networks. Neurocomputing **101**, 319–337 (2013)

18. Gallicchio, C., Micheli, A.: A preliminary application of echo state networks to emotion recognition. In: Proceedings of EVALITA 2014, pp. 116–119 (2014)

19. Horak, F.B., Wrisley, D.M., Frank, J.: The balance evaluation systems test (BESTest) to differentiate balance deficits. Phys. Ther. **89**(5), 484–498 (2003)

20. Jaeger, H.: The "echo state" approach to analysing and training recurrent neural networks. Technical report, GMD - German National Research Institute for Computer Science (2001)

21. Jaeger, H., Haas, H.: Harnessing nonlinearity: predicting chaotic systems and saving energy in wireless communication. Science **304**(5667), 78–80 (2004)

22. Jaeger, H., Lukoševičius, M., Popovici, D., Siewert, U.: Optimization and applications of echo state networks with leaky-integrator neurons. Neural Netw. **20**(3), 335–352 (2007)

23. Kolen, J., Kremer, S. (eds.): A Field Guide to Dynamical Recurrent Networks. IEEE Press, New York (2001)

24. Lukoševičius, M., Jaeger, H.: Reservoir computing approaches to recurrent neural network training. Comput. Sci. Rev. **3**(3), 127–149 (2009)

25. Lukoševičius, M., Jaeger, H., Schrauwen, B.: Reservoir computing trends. KI-Künstliche Intelligenz **26**(4), 365–371 (2012)

26. Maki, B.E., Holliday, P.J., Topper, A.K.: A prospective study of postural balance and risk of falling in an ambulatory and independent elderly population. J. Gerontol. **49**(2), M72–M84 (1994)

27. Mancini, M., Horak, F.: The relevance of clinical balance assessment tools to differentiate balance deficits. Eur. J. Phys. Rehab. Med. **46**(2), 239–248 (2010)

28. Palumbo, F., Barsocchi, P., Gallicchio, C., Chessa, S., Micheli, A.: Multisensor data fusion for activity recognition based on reservoir computing. In: Botía, J.A., Álvarez-García, J.A., Fujinami, K., Barsocchi, P., Riedel, T. (eds.) EvAAL 2013. CCIS, vol. 386, pp. 24–35. Springer, Heidelberg (2013)

29. Shih, C.H., Shih, C.T., Chu, C.L.: Assisting people with multiple disabilities actively correct abnormal standing posture with a Nintendo Wii Balance Board through controlling environmental stimulation. Res. Dev. Disabil. **31**(4), 936–942 (2010)

30. Simila, H., Mantyjarvi, J., Merilahti, J., Lindholm, M., Ermes, M.: Accelerometry-based Berg balance scale score estimation. IEEE J. Biomed. Health Inform. **18**(4), 1114–1121 (2014)

31. Tinetti, M.E.: Performance-oriented assessment of mobility problems in elderly patients. J. Am. Geriatr. Soc. **34**(2), 119–126 (1986)

32. Tiño, P., Hammer, B., Bodén, M.: Markovian bias of neural-based architectures with feedback connections. In: Hammer, B., Hitzler, P. (eds.) Perspectives of Neural-Symbolic Integration, vol. 77, pp. 95–133. Springer, Heidelberg (2007)
33. Verstraeten, D., Schrauwen, B., D'Haene, M., Stroobandt, D.: An experimental unification of reservoir computing methods. Neural Netw. **20**(3), 391–403 (2007)
34. Visser, J.E., Carpenter, M.G., van der Kooij, H., Bloem, B.R.: The clinical utility of posturography. Clin. Neurophysiol. **119**(11), 2424–2436 (2008)
35. Wood-Dauphinee, S.L., Berg, K.O., Bravo, G.: The balance scale: responding to clinically meaningful changes. Can. J. Rehab. **10**, 35–50 (1997)
36. Young, W., Ferguson, S., Brault, S., Craig, C.: Assessing and training standing balance in older adults: a novel approach using the Nintendo Wii Balance Board. Gait Posture **33**(2), 303–305 (2011)

Learning Structures in Earth Observation Data with Gaussian Processes

Fernando Mateo, Jordi Muñoz-Marí, Valero Laparra, Jochem Verrelst, and Gustau Camps-Valls[✉]

Image Processing Laboratory, University of Valencia,
C/Catedrático José Beltrán 2, 46980 Paterna, Spain
{fmateo,jordi,lapeva,jverrelst,gcamps}@uv.es
http://isp.uv.es/

Abstract. Gaussian Processes (GPs) has experienced tremendous success in geoscience in general and for bio-geophysical parameter retrieval in the last years. GPs constitute a solid Bayesian framework to formulate many function approximation problems consistently. This paper reviews the main theoretical GP developments in the field. We review new algorithms that respect the signal and noise characteristics, that provide feature rankings automatically, and that allow applicability of associated uncertainty intervals to transport GP models in space and time. All these developments are illustrated in the field of geoscience and remote sensing at a local and global scales through a set of illustrative examples.

Keywords: Kernel methods · Gaussian Process Regression (GPR) · Bio-geophysical parameter estimation

1 Introduction

Spatio-temporally explicit, quantitative retrieval methods of Earth surface and atmosphere characteristics are a requirement in a variety of Earth observation applications. Optical sensors mounted on-board Earth observation (EO) satellites are being endowed with high temporal, spectral and spatial resolutions, and thus enable the retrieval and monitoring of climate and bio-geophysical variables [9,25]. With the super-spectral Copernicus Sentinel-2 (S2) [10] and the forthcoming Sentinel-3 missions [8], among other planned space missions, an unprecedented data stream for land, ocean and atmosphere monitoring will soon become available to a diverse user community. This vast data streams require enhanced processing techniques. Statistical inference methods play an important role in this area of research. Understanding is more challenging than predicting, and thus statistical models should not only be accurate but also capture plausible physical relations and explain the problem at hand.

Over the last few decades a wide diversity of bio-geophysical retrieval methods have been developed, but only a few of them made it into operational processing

Electronic supplementary material The online version of this chapter (doi:10.1007/978-3-319-44412-3_6) contains supplementary material, which is available to authorized users.

© Springer International Publishing Switzerland 2016
A. Douzal-Chouakria et al. (Eds.): AALTD 2015, LNAI 9785, pp. 78–94, 2016.
DOI: 10.1007/978-3-319-44412-3_6

chains. Essentially, we may find two main approaches to the inverse problem of estimating biophysical parameters from spectra: *parametric physically-based models* and *non-parametric statistical models*. Lately, machine learning has attained outstanding results in the estimation of climate variables and related bio-geophysical parameters at local and global scales [7]. For example, current operational vegetation products, like leaf area index (LAI), are typically produced with neural networks [2], Gross Primary Production (GPP) as the largest global CO_2 flux driving several ecosystem functions is estimated using ensembles of random forests and neural networks [3,15], biomass has been estimated with stepwise multiple regression [24], PCA and piecewise linear regression for sun-induced fluorescence (SIF) estimation [12], support vector regression showed high efficiency in modelling LAI, fractional vegetation cover (fCOVER), evapotranspiration [11,35], relevance vector machines were successful in ocean chlorophyll estimation [5], and recently, Gaussian Processes (GPs) [21] provided excellent results in vegetation properties estimation [22,30–32]. The family of Bayesian non-parametrics, and of Gaussian processes in particular [21], have been payed wide attention in the last years in remote sensing data analysis. We will review the main developments in GPs for EO data analysis in this paper.

The remainder of the paper is organized in two main parts: Sect. 2 reviews the main notation and theory of GP regression. Section 3 presents some of the most recent advances of GP models applied to remote sensing data processing. Section 4 presents ways to extract knowledge from those GP models. We conclude in Sect. 5 with a discussion about the upcoming challenges and research directions.

2   Gaussian Process Regression

2.1   Gaussian Processes: A Gentle Introduction

Gaussian processes (GPs) are state-of-the-art tools for discriminative machine learning. They can be interpreted as a family of kernel methods with the additional advantage of providing a full conditional statistical description for the predicted variable. Standard regression approximates observations (often referred to as *outputs*) $\{y_n\}_{n=1}^N$ as the sum of some unknown latent function $f(\mathbf{x})$ of the inputs $\{\mathbf{x}_n \in \mathbb{R}^D\}_{n=1}^N$ plus *constant power (homoscedastic)* Gaussian noise, i.e.

$$y_n = f(\mathbf{x}_n) + \varepsilon_n, \quad \varepsilon_n \sim \mathcal{N}(0, \sigma^2). \tag{1}$$

GP regression proceeds in a Bayesian, non-parametric way, to fit the observed data. A zero mean[1] GP prior is placed on the latent function $f(\mathbf{x})$ and a Gaussian prior is used for each latent noise term ε_n, $f(\mathbf{x}) \sim \mathcal{GP}(\mathbf{0}, k_{\boldsymbol{\theta}}(\mathbf{x}, \mathbf{x}'))$, where $k_{\boldsymbol{\theta}}(\mathbf{x}, \mathbf{x}')$ is a covariance function parametrized by $\boldsymbol{\theta}$ and σ^2 is a hyperparameter that specifies the noise power. Essentially, a GP is a stochastic process whose marginals are distributed as a multivariate Gaussian. In particular, given the priors $\mathcal{GP}$, samples drawn from $f(\mathbf{x})$ at the set of locations $\{\mathbf{x}_n\}_{n=1}^N$ follow a

---

[1] It is customary to subtract the sample mean to data $\{y_n\}_{n=1}^N$, and then to assume a zero mean model.

Table 1. Some kernel functions used in the literature.

Kernel function	Expression
Linear	$k(\mathbf{x}, \mathbf{x}') = \mathbf{x}^\top \mathbf{x}' + c$
Polynomial	$k(\mathbf{x}, \mathbf{x}') = (\alpha \mathbf{x}^\top \mathbf{x}' + c)^d$
Gaussian	$k(\mathbf{x}, \mathbf{x}') = \exp(-\|\mathbf{x} - \mathbf{x}'\|^2/(2\sigma^2))$
Exponential	$k(\mathbf{x}, \mathbf{x}') = \exp(-\|\mathbf{x} - \mathbf{x}'\|/(2\sigma^2))$
Rational Quadratic	$k(\mathbf{x}, \mathbf{x}') = 1 - (\|\mathbf{x} - \mathbf{x}'\|^2)/(\|\mathbf{x} - \mathbf{x}'\|^2 + c)$
Multiquadric	$k(\mathbf{x}, \mathbf{x}') = \sqrt{\|\mathbf{x} - \mathbf{x}'\|^2 + c^2}$
Inv. Multiquad	$k(\mathbf{x}, \mathbf{x}') = 1/(\sqrt{\|\mathbf{x} - \mathbf{x}'\|^2 + \theta^2})$
Power	$k(\mathbf{x}, \mathbf{x}') = -\|\mathbf{x} - \mathbf{x}'\|^d$
Log	$k(\mathbf{x}, \mathbf{x}') = -\log(\|\mathbf{x} - \mathbf{x}'\|^d + 1)$

joint multivariate Gaussian with zero mean and covariance (sometimes referred as to *kernel*) matrix $\mathbf{K_{ff}}$ with $[\mathbf{K_{ff}}]_{ij} = k_{\boldsymbol{\theta}}(\mathbf{x}_i, \mathbf{x}_j)$.

If we consider a test location $\mathbf{x}_*$ with corresponding output y_*, priors $\mathcal{GP}$ induce a prior distribution between the observations $\mathbf{y} \equiv \{y_n\}_{n=1}^N$ and y_*. Collecting available data in $\mathcal{D} \equiv \{\mathbf{x}_n, y_n | n = 1, \ldots N\}$, it is possible to analytically compute the posterior distribution over the unknown output y_*:

$$p(y_*|\mathbf{x}_*, \mathcal{D}) = \mathcal{N}(y_*|\mu_{\mathrm{GP}*}, \sigma^2_{\mathrm{GP}*}) \tag{2}$$

$$\mu_{\mathrm{GP}*} = \mathbf{k}_{\mathbf{f}*}^\top (\mathbf{K_{ff}} + \sigma^2 \mathbf{I}_n)^{-1} \mathbf{y} = \mathbf{k}_{\mathbf{f}*}^\top \boldsymbol{\alpha} \tag{3}$$

$$\sigma^2_{\mathrm{GP}*} = \sigma^2 + k_{**} - \mathbf{k}_{\mathbf{f}*}^\top (\mathbf{K_{ff}} + \sigma^2 \mathbf{I}_n)^{-1} \mathbf{k}_{\mathbf{f}*}. \tag{4}$$

which is computable in $\mathcal{O}(n^3)$ time (this cost arises from the inversion of the $n \times n$ matrix $(\mathbf{K_{ff}} + \sigma^2 \mathbf{I})$, see [21]. In addition to the computational cost, GPs require large memory since in naive implementations one has to store the training kernel matrix, which amounts to $\mathcal{O}(n^2)$.

2.2   On the Model Selection

The corresponding hyperparameters $\{\boldsymbol{\theta}, \sigma_n\}$ are typically selected by Type-II Maximum Likelihood, using the marginal likelihood (also called evidence) of the observations, which is also analytical (explicitly conditioning on $\boldsymbol{\theta}$ and σ_n):

$$\log p(\mathbf{y}|\boldsymbol{\theta}, \sigma_n) = \log \mathcal{N}(\mathbf{y}|\mathbf{0}, \mathbf{K_{ff}} + \sigma_n^2 \mathbf{I}). \tag{5}$$

When the derivatives of (5) are also analytical, which is often the case, conjugated gradient ascend is typically used for optimization.

2.3   On the Covariance Function

The core of a kernel method like GPs is the appropriate definition of the covariance (or kernel) function. A standard, widely used covariance function is the squared exponential, $k(\mathbf{x}_i, \mathbf{x}_j) = \exp(-\|\mathbf{x}_i - \mathbf{x}_j\|^2/(2\sigma^2))$, which captures sample similarity well in most of the (unstructured) problems, and only one hyperparameter σ needs to be tuned.

In the context of GPs, kernels with more hyperparameters can be efficiently inferred. This is an opportunity to exploit asymmetries in the feature space by including a parameter per feature, as in the very common anisotropic squared exponential (SE) kernel function:

$$k(\mathbf{x}_i, \mathbf{x}_j) = \nu \exp\left(-\sum_{f=1}^{F} \frac{(\mathbf{x}_i^f - \mathbf{x}_j^f)^2}{2\sigma_f^2}\right) + \sigma_n^2 \delta_{ij},$$

where ν is a scaling factor, σ_n is the standard deviation of the (estimated) noise, and a σ_f is the length-scale per input features, $f = 1, \ldots, F$. This is a very flexible covariance function that typically suffices to tackle most of the problems. Table 1 summarizes the most common kernel functions in standard applications with kernel methods.

2.4 Gaussian Processes Exemplified

Let us illustrate the solution of GP regression (GPR) in a toy example. In Fig. 1 we include an illustrative example with 6 training points in the range between -2 and $+2$. We firstly depict several random functions drawn from the GP prior and then we include functions drawn from the posterior. We have chosen an isotropic Gaussian kernel and $\sigma_\nu = 0.1$. We have plotted the mean function plus/minus two standard deviations (corresponding to a 95 % confidence interval). Typically, the hyperparameters are unknown, as well as the mean, covariance and likelihood functions. We assumed a Squared Exponential (SE) covariance function and learned the optimal hyperparameters by minimizing the negative log marginal likelihood (NLML) w.r.t. the hyperparameters. We observe three different

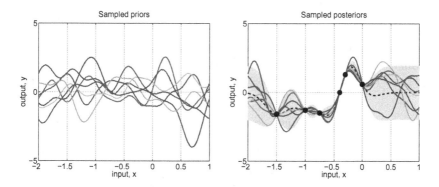

Fig. 1. Example of a Gaussian process. Left: some functions drawn at random from the GP prior. Right: some random functions drawn from the posterior, i.e. the prior conditioned on 6 noise-free observations indicated in big black dots. The shaded area represents the point-wise mean plus and minus two times the standard deviation for each input value (corresponding to the 95 confidence region). It can be noted that the confidence intervals become large for regions far from the observations.

regions in the figure. Below $x = -1.5$, we do not have samples and the GPR provides the solution given by the prior (zero mean and ± 2). At the center, where most of the data points lie, we have a very accurate view of the latent function with small error bars (close to $\pm 2\sigma_\nu$). For $x > 0$, we do not have training samples neither so we have same behaviour. GPs typically provide an accurate solution where the data lies and high error bars where we do not have available information and, consequently, we presume that the prediction in that area is not accurate. This is why in regions of the input space without points the confidence intervals are wide resembling the prior distribution.

3   Advances in Gaussian Process Regression

In this section, we review some recent advances in GPR especially suited for remote sensing data analysis. We will review the main aspects to design covariance functions that capture non-stationarities and multiscale time relations in EO data, as well as GPs that can learn arbitrary transformations of the observed variable and noise models.

3.1   Structured, Non-stationary and Multiscale

Commonly used kernels families include the squared exponential (SE), periodic (Per), linear (Lin), and rational quadratic (RQ), cf. Table 1. Illustration of the base kernel and drawings from the GP prior is shown in Fig. 2. These base kernels can be actually combined following simple operations: summation, multiplication or convolution. This way one may build sophisticated covariances from simpler ones. Note that the same essential property of kernel methods apply here: a valid covariance function must be positive semidefinite. In general, the design of the kernel should rely on the information that we have for each estimation problem and should be designed to get the most accurate solution with the least amount of samples.

In Fig. 2, all the base kernels are one-dimensional. Nevertheless, kernels over multidimensional inputs can be actually constructed by adding and multiplying kernels over individual dimensions: (a) linear, (b) squared exponential (or RBF),

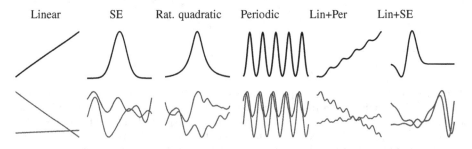

| Linear | SE | Rat. quadratic | Periodic | Lin+Per | Lin+SE |

Fig. 2. Base kernels (top) and two random draws from a GP with each respective kernel and combination of kernels (bottom).

(c) rational quadratic, and (d) periodic. See Table 1 for the explicit functional form of each kernel. Some simple kernel combinations are represented in the two last columns of the figure: a linear plus periodic covariances may capture structures that are periodic with trend (e), while a linear plus squared exponential covariances can accommodate structures with increasing variation (f). By summing kernels, we can model the data as a superposition of independent functions, possibly representing different structures in the data. For example, in multitemporal image analysis, one could for instance dedicate a kernel for the time domain (perhaps trying to capture trends and seasonal effects) and another kernel function for the spatial domain (equivalently capturing spatial patterns and auto-correlations). In time series models, sums of kernels can express superposition of different processes, possibly operating at different scales: very often changes in geophysical variables through time occur at different temporal resolutions (hours, days, etc.), and this can be incorporated in the prior covariance with those simple operations. In multiple dimensions, summing kernels gives additive structure over different dimensions, similar to generalized additive models [13]. Alternatively, multiplying kernels allows us to account for interactions between different input dimensions or different notions of similarity. In the following section, we show how to design kernels that incorporate particular time resolutions, trends and periodicities.

3.2   Time-based Covariance for GPR

Signals to be processed typically show particular characteristics, with time-dependent cycles and trends. One could include time t_i as an additional feature in the definition of the input samples. This *stacked approach* [4] essentially relies on a covariance function $k(\mathbf{z}_i, \mathbf{z}_j)$, where $\mathbf{z}_i = [t_i, \mathbf{x}_i]^\top$. The shortcoming is that the time relations are naively left to the nonlinear regression algorithm, and hence no explicit time structure model is assumed. To cope with this, one can use a linear combination (or composite) of different kernels: one dedicated to capture the different temporal characteristics, and the other to the feature-based relations.

The issue here is how to design kernels capable of dealing with non-stationary processes. A possible approach is to use a *stationary* covariance operating on the variable of interest after being mapped with a nonlinear function engineered to discount such undesired variations. This approach was used in [23] to model *spatial patterns* of solar radiation with GPR. It is also possible to adopt a squared exponential (SE) as stationary covariance acting on the *time* variable mapped to a two-dimensional *periodic space* $\mathbf{z}(t) = [\cos(t), \sin(t)]^\top$, as explained in [21],

$$k(t_i, t_j) = \exp\left(-\frac{\|\mathbf{z}(t_i) - \mathbf{z}(t_j)\|^2}{2\sigma_t^2}\right), \tag{6}$$

which gives rise to the following periodic covariance function

$$k(t_i, t_j) = \exp\left(-\frac{2\sin^2[(t_i - t_j)/2]}{\sigma_t^2}\right), \tag{7}$$

where σ_t is a hyper-parameter characterizing the periodic scale and needs to be inferred. It is not clear, though, that the seasonal trend is exactly periodic, so we modify this equation by taking the product with a squared exponential component, to allow a decay away from exact periodicity:

$$k_2(t_i, t_j) = \gamma \exp\left(-\frac{2\sin^2[\pi(t_i - t_j)]}{\sigma_t^2} - \frac{(t_i - t_j)^2}{2\sigma_d^2} \right), \tag{8}$$

where γ gives the magnitude, σ_t the smoothness of the periodic component, σ_d represents the *decay-time* for the periodic component, and the period has been fixed to one year. Therefore, our final covariance is expressed as

$$k([\mathbf{x}_i, t_i], [\mathbf{x}_j, t_j]) = k_1(\mathbf{x}_i, \mathbf{x}_j) + k_2(t_i, t_j), \tag{9}$$

which is parameterized by only three more hyperparameters collected in $\boldsymbol{\theta} = \{\nu, \sigma_1, \ldots, \sigma_F, \sigma_n, \sigma_t, \sigma_d, \gamma\}$. Note that this kernel function allows us to incorporate time easily, but the relations between time t_i and signal $\mathbf{x}_i$ samples is missing. Some approximations to deal with this issue exist in the literature, such as cross-kernel composition [4,6] or latent force models [1].

We show the advantage of encoding such prior knowledge and structure in the relevant problem of solar irradiation prediction using GPR. Noting the non-stationary temporal behaviour of the signal, we develop a particular time-based composite covariance to account for the relevant seasonal signal variations. Data from the AEMET radiometric observatory of Murcia (Southern Spain, 38.0° N, 1.2° W) were used. Table 2 reports the obtained results with GPR models and several statistical regression methods: regularized linear regression (RLR), support vector regression (SVR), relevance vector machine (RVM) and GPR. All methods were run with and without using two additional dummy time features containing the year and day-of-year (DOY). We will indicate the former case with a subscript, like e.g. SVR_t. First, including time information improves all baseline models. Second, the best overall results are obtained by the GPR models, when including time information or not. Third, in particular, the proposed temporal GPR (TGPR) outperforms the rest in accuracy (root-mean-square error, RMSE, and mean absolute error, MAE) and goodness-of-fit (R), and closely follows the elastic net in bias (ME). TGPR performs better than GPR and GPR_t in all quality measures.

3.3 Heteroscedastic GPR: Learning the Noise Model

The standard GPR is essentially homoscedastic, i.e., assumes constant noise power σ^2 for all observations. This assumption can be too restrictive for some problems. Heteroscedastic GPs, on the other hand, let noise power vary smoothly throughout input space, by changing the prior over ε_n to $\varepsilon_n \sim \mathcal{N}(0, e^{g(\mathbf{x}_n)})$, and placing a GP prior over $g(\mathbf{x}) \sim \mathcal{GP}(\mu_0 \mathbf{1}, k_{\boldsymbol{\theta}_g}(\mathbf{x}, \mathbf{x}'))$. Note that the exponential is needed[2] in order to describe the non-negative variance. The hyperparameters of the covariance functions of both GPs are collected in $\boldsymbol{\theta}_f$ and $\boldsymbol{\theta}_g$, accounting for the signal and the noise relations, respectively.

---

[2] Of course, other transformations are possible, just not as convenient.

Table 2. Results for the estimation of the daily solar irradiation of linear and nonlinear regression models. Subscript METHOD$_t$ indicates that the METHOD includes time as input variable. Best results are highlighted in bold, the second best in italics.

METHOD	ME	RMSE	MAE	R
RLR	0.27	4.42	3.51	0.76
RLR$_t$	0.25	4.33	3.42	0.78
SVR [26]	0.54	4.40	3.35	0.77
SVR$_t$	0.42	4.23	3.12	0.79
RVM [28]	0.19	4.06	3.25	0.80
RVM$_t$	0.14	3.71	3.11	0.81
GPR [21]	0.14	3.22	2.47	*0.88*
GPR$_t$	*0.13*	*3.15*	*2.27*	*0.88*
TGPR	**0.11**	**3.14**	**2.19**	**0.90**

Relaxing the homoscedasticity assumption into heteroscedasticity yields a richer, more flexible model that contains the standard GP as a particular case corresponding to a constant $g(\mathbf{x})$. Unfortunately, this also hampers analytical tractability, so approximate methods must be used to obtain posterior distributions for $f(\mathbf{x})$ and $g(\mathbf{x})$, which are in turn required to compute the predictive distribution over y_*.

As an alternative to the costly classic heteroscedastic GP approaches, variational techniques allow to approximate intractable integrals arising in Bayesian inference and machine learning. A sophisticated variational approximation called *Marginalized Variational (MV)* approximation was introduced in [16]. The MV approximation renders (approximate) Bayesian inference in the heteroscedastic GP model both fast and accurate. We will refer to this variational approximation for heteroscedastic GP regression as VHGPR. A simple comparison between the homoscedastic canonical GP and the VHGPR model is shown in Fig. 3.

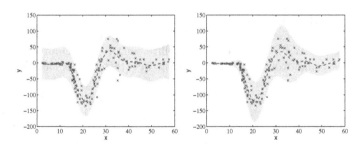

Fig. 3. Predictive mean and variance of the standard GP (left) and the heteroscedastic GP (right). It is noticeable that in the low noise regime the VHGP produces tighter confidence intervals as expected, while high noise variance associated to high signal variance (middle of the observed signal) the predictive variance is more reasonable too.

3.4   Warped GPR: Learning the Output Transformation

Very often, in practical applications, one transforms the observed variable to better pose the problem. Actually, it is a standard practice to 'linearize' or 'uniformize' the distribution of the observations (which is commonly skewed due to the sampling strategies in *in situ* data collection) by applying non-linear link functions like the logarithmic, the exponential or the logistic functions.

Warped GPR [27] essentially warps observations **y** through a nonlinear parametric function g to a latent space $z_i = g(y_i) = g(f(\mathbf{x}_i) + \varepsilon_i)$, where f is a possibly noisy latent function with d inputs, and g is a function with scalar inputs parametrized by ψ. The function g must be *monotonic*, otherwise the probability measure will not be conserved in the transformation, and the distribution over the targets may not be valid [27]. It can be shown that replacing y_i by z_i into the standard GP model leads to an extended problem that can be solved by taking derivatives of the negative log likelihood function in (5), but now with respect to both $\boldsymbol{\theta}$ and ψ parameter vectors.

For both the GPR and WGPR models we need to define the covariance (kernel, or Gram) function $k(\cdot,)$, which should capture the similarity between samples. We used the standard Automatic Relevance Determination (ARD) covariance [21]. Model hyperparameters are collectively grouped in $\boldsymbol{\theta} = \{\nu, \sigma_n, \sigma_1, \ldots, \sigma_d\}$. In addition, for the WGPR we need to define a parametric smooth and monotonic form for g, which can be defined as:

$$g(y_i; \psi) = \sum_{\ell=1}^{L} a_\ell \tanh(b_\ell\, y_i + c_\ell), \qquad a_\ell,\ b_\ell \geq 0,$$

where $\psi = \{\mathbf{a}, \mathbf{b}, \mathbf{c}\}$. Recently, flexible non-parametric functions have replaced such parametric forms [18], thus placing another prior for $g(\mathbf{x}) \sim \mathcal{GP}(f, c(f, f'))$, whose model is learned via variational inference.

For illustration purposes, we focus on the estimation of chlorophyll-a concentrations from remote sensing upwelling radiance just above the ocean surface. We used the SeaBAM dataset [19,20], which gathers 919 *in situ* pigment measurements around the United States and Europe. The dataset contains coincident *in situ* chlorophyll concentration and remote sensing reflectance measurements (Rrs(λ), [sr^{-1}]) at some wavelengths (412, 443, 490, 510 and 555 nm) that are present in the SeaWiFS ocean colour satellite sensor. The chlorophyll concentration values range from 0.019 to 32.79 mg/m^3 (revealing a clear exponential distribution).

Table 3 shows different scores–bias (ME), accuracy (RMSE, MAE) and goodness-of-fit (R)–between the observed and predicted variable when using the raw data (no *ad hoc* transform at all) and the empirically adjusted transform. Results are shown for three flavours of GPs: the standard GPR [21], the variational heteroscedastic GP (VHGPR) [17], and the proposed warped GP regression (WGPR) [18,27] for different rates of training samples. Empirically-based warping slightly improves the results over working with raw data for the same number of training samples, but this requires prior knowledge about the problem, time and efforts to fit an appropriate function. On the other hand, WGPR outperforms the rest of GPs in all comparisons over standard GPR and

Table 3. Results using both raw and empirically-transformed observation variables.

	ME	RMSE	MAE	R
Raw				
GPR	0.02	1.74	0.33	0.82
VHGPR	0.29	2.51	0.46	0.65
WGPR	0.08	1.71	0.30	0.83
Empirically-based				
GPR	0.15	1.69	0.29	0.86
VHGPR	0.15	1.70	0.29	0.85
WGPR	0.17	1.75	0.30	0.86

VHGPR ($\sim +1 - 10\%$). Finally, WGPR nicely compensates the lack of prior knowledge about the (possibly skewed) distribution of the observation variable.

3.5   Source Code and Toolboxes

The most widely known sites to obtain free source code on GP modeling are GPML[3] and GPstuff[4]. The former website centralizes the main activities in GP modeling and provides up-to-date resources concerned with probabilistic modeling, inference and learning based on GPs, while the latter is a versatile collection of GP models and computational tools required for inference, sparse approximations and model assessment methods. We also recommend to the interested reader in regression in general, our MATLAB SimpleR[5] toolbox that contains many regression tools organized in families: tree-based, bagging and boosting, neural nets, kernel regression methods, and several Bayesian nonparametric models like GPs.

4   Analysis of Gaussian Process Models

An interesting possibility in GP models is to extract knowledge from the trained model. We will show in what follows two different approaches: (1) feature ranking exploiting the automatic relevance determination (ARD) covariance and (2) uncertainty estimation looking at the predictive variance estimates.

4.1   Ranking Features Through the ARD Covariance

One of the advantages of GPs is that during the development of the GP model the predictive power of each single band is evaluated for the parameter of interest through calculation of the ARD. Specifically, band ranking through σ_b may reveal

---

[3] http://www.gaussianprocess.org/.
[4] http://becs.aalto.fi/en/research/bayes/gpstuff/.
[5] http://isp.uv.es/soft.htm.

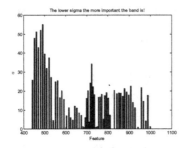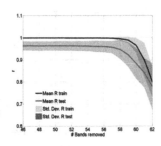

Fig. 4. Estimated σ_b values for one GP model using 62 CHRIS bands (left). The lower the σ_b the more important the band is for regression. *Chl* r and standard deviation (SD) of training and validation for GP fittings using backward elimination (right).

the bands that contribute the most to the development of a GP model. An example of the σ_b's for one GP model trained with field leaf chlorophyll content (*Chl*) data and with 62 CHRIS bands is shown in Fig. 4 (left). The band with highest σ_b is the least contributing to the model. It can be noted that a relatively few bands (about 8) were evaluated as crucial for *Chl* estimation, while the majority of bands were evaluated as less contributing.

This does not necessarily mean that other bands are obstructing optimized accuracies. Only when less than 4 bands were left accuracies started to degrade rapidly Fig. 4 (right). The figure suggests that the most relevant spectral region is to be found between 550 and 1000 nm. Most contributing bands were positioned around the red edge, at 680 and 730 nm respectively, but not all bands within the red edge were evaluated as relevant. This is due to when having a large number of bands available then neighbouring bands do not provide much additional information and can thus be considered as redundant.

Consequently, the σ_b proved to be a valuable tool to detect most sensitive bands of a sensor towards a biophysical parameter. A more systematic analysis was applied by sorting the bands on their relevance and counting the band rankings over 50 repetitions. In [32] the four most relevant bands were tracked for *Chl*, LAI and fCOVER and for different Sentinel-2 settings. It demonstrated the potential of Sentinel-2, with its new band in the red-edge, for vegetation properties estimation. Also in [34] σ_b were used to analyze band sensitivity of Sentinel-2 towards LAI. A similar approach was pursued on analyzing leaf *Chl* based on tracking the most sensitive spectral regions of sun-induced fluorescence data [29], as displayed in Fig. 5.

4.2 Uncertainty Intervals

In this section, we use GP models for retrieval and portability in space and time. For this, we will exploit the associated predictive variance (i.e. uncertainty interval) provided by GP models. Consequently, retrievals with high uncertainties refer to pixel spectral information that deviates from what has been represented during the training phase. In turn, low uncertainties refer to pixels that were well represented in the training phase. The quantification of variable-associated

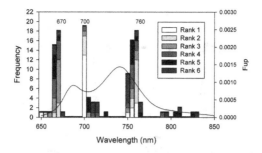

Fig. 5. Frequency plots of the top eight ranked bands with lowest σ_b values in 20 runs of GPR prediction of Chl based on upward fluorescence (F_{up}) emission. An emission curve is given as illustration.

uncertainties is a strong requirement when remote sensing products are ingested in higher level processing, e.g. to estimate ecosystem respiration, photosynthetic activity, or carbon sequestration [14].

The application of GPs for the estimation of biophysical parameters was initially demonstrated in [30]. A locally collected field dataset called SPARC-2003 at Barrax (Spain) was used for training and validation of GPs for the vegetation parameters of LAI, Chl and fCOVER. Sufficiently high validation accuracies were obtained ($R^2 > 0.86$) for processing a CHRIS image into these parameters, as shown in Fig. 6. Within the uncertainty maps, areas with reliable retrievals are clearly distinguished from areas with unreliable retrievals. Low uncertainties were found on irrigated areas and harvested fields. High uncertainties were found on areas with remarkably different spectra, such as bright, whitish calcareous soils, or harvested fields. This indicates that the input spectrum deviates from what has been presented during the training stage, thereby imposing uncertainties to the retrieval.

GP models were subsequently applied to the SPARC dataset that was re-sampled to different Sentinel-2 band settings and then uncertainties were inspected [32]. On the whole, adding spectral information led to reduction of uncertainties and thus more meaningful biophysical parameter maps. The locally-trained GP models were applied to simulated Sentinel-2 images in a follow-up study [33]. Time series over the local Barrax site as well images across the world were processed. Also the role of an extended training dataset by adding spectra of non-vegetated surfaces were evaluated. Subsequently the uncertainty values were analyzed. By using the extended training dataset not only further improved performances but also allowed a decrease in theoretical uncertainties. The GP models were successfully applied to simulated Sentinel-2 images covering various sites; associated relative uncertainties were on the same order as those generated by the reference image.

As a final example, uncertainty estimates were exploited to assess the robustness of the retrievals at multiple spatial scales. In [31], retrievals from hyperspectral airborne and spaceborne data over the Barrax area were compared. Based on the spareborne SPARC-2003 dataset, GP developed a model that was excellently validated (r^2: 0.96). The SPARC-trained GP model was subsequently applied to

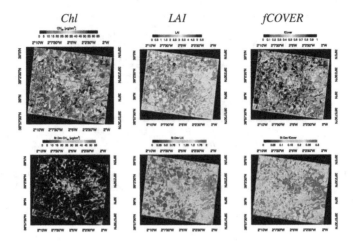

Fig. 6. Prediction maps (top) and associated uncertainty intervals (bottom), generated with GP and four bands of the CHRIS 12-07-2003 nadir image.

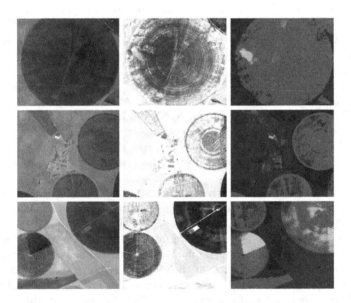

Fig. 7. Three examples [top, middle, bottom] of CASI RGB snapshots [left], *Chl* estimates [middle], and related uncertainty intervals [right].

airborne CASI flightlines (Barrax, 2009) to generate *Chl* maps. The accompanying uncertainty maps provided insight in the robustness of the retrievals. In general similar uncertainties were achieved by both sensors, which is encouraging for upscaling estimates from field to landscape scale. The high spatial resolution of CASI in combination with the uncertainties allows us to observe the spatial patterns of retrievals in more detail. Some examples of mean estimates and associated uncertainties are shown in Fig. 7.

5   Conclusions and Further Work

This paper provided a comprehensive survey to the field of Gaussian Processes (GPs) in the context of remote sensing data analysis for Earth observation applications, and in particular for biophysical parameter estimation. We summarized the main properties of GPs and the advantages over other methods for estimation: essentially GPs can provide competitive predictive power, give error-bars for the estimations, allows to design and optimize sensible kernel functions, and also to analyze the encoded knowledge in the model via automatic relevance determination kernel functions.

GP models offer as well a solid Bayesian framework to formulate new algorithms well-suited to the signal characteristics. We have seen for example that by incorporating proper priors, we can encompass signal-dependent noise, and infer parametric forms of warping the observations as an alternative to either *ad hoc* filtering. On the downside, we need to mention the scalability issue: essentially, the optimization of GP models require computing determinants and invert matrices of size $n \times n$, which runs cubically in computational time and quadratically in memory storage. In the last years, however, great advances have appeared in machine learning and now it is possible to train GPs with several thousands of points.

All the developments were illustrated at a local scales through a full set of illustrative examples in the field of geosciences and remote sensing. In particular, we treated important problems of ocean and land sciences: from accurate estimation of oceanic chlorophyll content and pigments, to vegetation properties from multi- and hyperspectral sensors.

Acknowledgments. The authors wish to deeply acknowledge the collaboration, comments and fruitful discussions with many researchers during the last decade on GP models for remote sensing and geoscience applications: Miguel Lázaro-Gredilla (Vicarious), Robert Jenssen (Univ. Tromsø, Norway), Martin Jung (MPI, Jena, Germany), and Sancho Salcedo-Saez (Univ. Alcalá, Madrid, Spain).

This paper has been partially supported by the Spanish Ministry of Economy and Competitiveness under projects TIN2012-38102-C03-01 and ESP2013-48458-C4-1-P, and by the European Research Council (ERC) consolidator grant entitled SEDAL with grant agreement 647423. AG is thankful to Marie Curie International Incoming Fellowship for supporting this work.

References

1. Álvarez, M.A., Luengo, D., Lawrence, N.D.: Linear latent force models using Gaussian processes. IEEE Trans. Pattern Anal. Mach. Intell. **35**(11), 2693–2705 (2013). http://dx.doi.org/10.1109/TPAMI.2013.86
2. Baret, F., Weiss, M., Lacaze, R., Camacho, F., Makhmara, H., Pacholcyzk, P., Smets, B.: Geov1: LAI and FAPAR essential climate variables and FCOVER global time series capitalizing over existing products. Part1: principles of development and production. Rem. Sens. Environ. **137**, 299–309 (2013)

3. Beer, C., Reichstein, M., Tomelleri, E., Ciais, P., Jung, M., Carvalhais, N., Rödenbeck, C., Arain, M.A., Baldocchi, D., Bonan, G.B., Bondeau, A., Cescatti, A., Lasslop, G., Lindroth, A., Lomas, M., Luyssaert, S., Margolis, H., Oleson, K.W., Roupsard, O., Veenendaal, E., Viovy, N., Williams, C., Woodward, F.I., Papale, D.: Terrestrial gross carbon dioxide uptake: global distribution and covariation with climate. Science **329**(834), 834–838 (2010)
4. Camps-Valls, G., Gómez-Chova, L., Muñoz-Marí, J., Vila-Francés, J., Calpe-Maravilla, J.: Composite kernels for hyperspectral image classification. IEEE Geosci. Remote Sens. Lett. **3**(1), 93–97 (2006)
5. Camps-Valls, G., Gómez-Chova, L., Vila-Francés, J., Amorós-López, J., Muñoz-Marí, J., Calpe-Maravilla, J.: Retrieval of oceanic chlorophyll concentration with relevance vector machines. Rem. Sens. Environ. **105**(1), 23–33 (2006)
6. Camps-Valls, G., Martínez-Ramón, M., Rojo-Álvarez, J.L., Muñoz-Marí, J.: Non-linear system identification with composite relevance vector machines. IEEE Signal Process. Lett. **14**(4), 279–282 (2007)
7. Camps-Valls, G., Tuia, D., Gómez-Chova, L., Malo, J. (eds.): Remote Sensing Image Processing. Morgan & Claypool, San Rafael (2011)
8. Donlon, C., Berruti, B., Buongiorno, A., Ferreira, M.H., Féménias, P., Frerick, J., Goryl, P., Klein, U., Laur, H., Mavrocordatos, C., Nieke, J., Rebhan, H., Seitz, B., Stroede, J., Sciarra, R.: The global monitoring for environment and security (GMES) Sentinel-3 mission. Rem. Sens. Environ. **120**, 37–57 (2012)
9. Dorigo, W.A., Zurita-Milla, R., Wit, A.J.W., Brazile, J., Singh, R., Schaepman, M.E.: A review on reflective remote sensing and data assimilation techniques for enhanced agroecosystem modeling. Int. J. Appl. Earth Obs. Geoinf. **9**(2), 165–193 (2007)
10. Drusch, M., Bello, U., Carlier, S., Colin, O., Fernandez, V., Gascon, F., Hoersch, B., Isola, C., Laberinti, P., Martimort, P., Meygret, A., Spoto, F., Sy, O., Marchese, F., Bargellini, P.: Sentinel-2: ESA's Optical high-resolution mission for GMES operational services. Rem. Sens. Environ. **120**, 25–36 (2012)
11. Durbha, S., King, R., Younan, N.: Support vector machines regression for retrieval of leaf area index from multiangle imaging spectroradiometer. Rem. Sens. Environ. **107**(1–2), 348–361 (2007)
12. Guanter, L., Zhang, Y., Jung, M., Joiner, J., Voigt, M., Berry, J.A., Frankenberg, C., Huete, A., Zarco-Tejada, P., Lee, J.E., Moran, M.S., Ponce-Campos, G., Beer, C., Camps-Valls, G., Buchmann, N., Gianelle, D., Klumpp, K., Cescatti, A., Baker, J.M., Griffis, T.J.: Global and time-resolved monitoring of crop photosynthesis with chlorophyll fluorescence. Proc. Natl. Acad. Sci. PNAS **111**, E1327–E1333 (2014)
13. Hastie, T., Tibshirani, R., Friedman, J.H.: The Elements of Statistical Learning: Data Mining, Inference, and Prediction, 2nd edn. Springer, New York (2009)
14. Jagermeyr, J., Gerten, D., Lucht, W., Hostert, P., Migliavacca, M., Nemani, R.: A high-resolution approach to estimating ecosystem respiration at continental scales using operational satellite data. Glob. Change Biol. **20**(4), 1191–1210 (2014)
15. Jung, M., Reichstein, M., Margolis, H.A., Cescatti, A., Richardson, A.D., Arain, M.A., Arneth, A., Bernhofer, C., Bonal, D., Chen, J., Gianelle, D., Gobron, N., Kiely, G., Kutsch, W., Lasslop, G., Law, B.E., Lindroth, A., Merbold, L., Montagnani, L., Moors, E.J., Papale, D., Sottocornola, M., Vaccari, F., Williams, C.: Global patterns of land-atmosphere fluxes of carbon dioxide, latent heat, and sensible heat derived from eddy covariance, satellite, and meteorological observations. J. Geophys. Res. Biogeosciences **116**(G3), 1–16 (2011)
16. Lázaro-Gredilla, M., Titsias, M.K.: Variational heteroscedastic Gaussian process regression. In: 28th International Conference on Machine Learning, ICML 2011, pp. 841–848. ACM, Bellevue (2011)

17. Lázaro-Gredilla, M., Titsias, M.K., Verrelst, J., Camps-Valls, G.: Retrieval of biophysical parameters with heteroscedastic Gaussian processes. IEEE Geosci. Rem. Sens. Lett. **11**(4), 838–842 (2014)
18. Lázaro-Gredilla, M.: Bayesian warped Gaussian processes. In: NIPS, pp. 1628–1636 (2012)
19. Maritorena, S., O'Reilly, J.: OC2v2: Update on the Initial Operational SeaWiFS Chlorophyll Algorithm, vol. 11, pp. 3–8. Wiley (2000). NASA Goddard Space Flight Center, Greenbelt, Maryland, USA
20. O'Reilly, J.E., Maritorena, S., Mitchell, B.G., Siegel, D.A., Carder, K., Garver, S.A., Kahru, M., McClain, C.: Ocean color chlorophyll algorithms for SeaWiFS. J. Geophys. Res. **103**(C11), 24937–24953 (1998)
21. Rasmussen, C.E., Williams, C.K.I.: Gaussian Processes for Machine Learning. The MIT Press, New York (2006)
22. Roelofsen, H., Kooistra, L., Van Bodegom, P., Verrelst, J., Krol, J., Witte, J.C.: Mapping a priori defined plant associations using remotely sensed vegetation characteristics. Rem. Sens. Environ. **140**, 639–651 (2014)
23. Sampson, P., Guttorp, P.: Nonparametric estimation of nonstationary spatial covariance structure. J. Am. Stat. Assoc. Publ. **87**(417), 108–119 (1992)
24. Sarker, L.R., Nichol, J.E.: Improved forest biomass estimates using ALOS AVNIR-2 texture indices. Rem. Sens. Environ. **115**(4), 968–977 (2011)
25. Schaepman, M., Ustin, S., Plaza, A., Painter, T., Verrelst, J., Liang, S.: Earth system science related imaging spectroscopy - an assessment. Rem. Sens. Environ. **113**(1), S123–S137 (2009)
26. Smola, A.J., Schölkopf, B.: A tutorial on support vector regression. Stat. Comput. **14**, 199–222 (2004)
27. Snelson, E., Rasmussen, C., Ghahramani, Z.: Warped Gaussian processes. In: Advances in Neural Information Processing Systems NIPS. MIT Press (2004)
28. Tipping, M.E.: The relevance vector machine. In: Solla, S.A., Leen, T.K., Müller, K.R. (eds.) Advances in Neural Information Processing Systems 12. MIT Press, Cambridge (2000)
29. Wittenberghe, S., Verrelst, J., Rivera, J., Alonso, L., Moreno, J., Samson, R.: Gaussian processes retrieval of leaf parameters from a multi-species reflectance, absorbance and fluorescence dataset. J. Photochem. Photobiol. B Biol. **134**, 37–48 (2014)
30. Verrelst, J., Alonso, L., Camps-Valls, G., Delegido, J., Moreno, J.: Retrieval of vegetation biophysical parameters using Gaussian process techniques. IEEE Trans. Geosci. Rem. Sens. **50**(5 PART 2), 1832–1843 (2012)
31. Verrelst, J., Alonso, L., Rivera Caicedo, J., Moreno, J., Camps-Valls, G.: Gaussian process retrieval of chlorophyll content from imaging spectroscopy data. IEEE J. Sel. Topics Appl. Earth Obs. Rem. Sens. **6**(2), 867–874 (2013)
32. Verrelst, J., Muñoz, J., Alonso, L., Delegido, J., Rivera, J., Moreno, J., Camps-Valls, G.: Machine learning regression algorithms for biophysical parameter retrieval: opportunities for Sentinel-2 and -3. Rem. Sens. Environ. **118**, 127–139 (2012)
33. Verrelst, J., Rivera, J., Moreno, J., Camps-Valls, G.: Gaussian processes uncertainty estimates in experimental Sentinel-2 LAI and leaf chlorophyll content retrieval. ISPRS J. Photogrammetry Rem. Sens. **86**, 157–167 (2013)

34. Verrelst, J., Rivera, J., Veroustraete, F., Muñoz-Marí, J., Clevers, J., Camps-Valls, G., Moreno, J.: Experimental Sentinel-2 LAI estimation using parametric, non-parametric and physical retrieval methods - A comparison. ISPRS J. Photogrammetry Rem. Sens. **108**, 260–272 (2015)
35. Yang, F., White, M., Michaelis, A., Ichii, K., Hashimoto, H., Votava, P., Zhu, A.X., Nemani, R.: Prediction of continental-scale evapotranspiration by combining MODIS and AmeriFlux data through support vector machine. IEEE Trans. Geosci. Rem. Sens. **44**(11), 3452–3461 (2006)

Monitoring Short Term Changes of Infectious Diseases in Uganda with Gaussian Processes

Ricardo Andrade-Pacheco[1]([⊠]), Martin Mubangizi[3,4], John Quinn[3,4], and Neil Lawrence[2]

[1] Global Health Group MEI, University of California San Francisco,
San Francisco, USA
`Ricardo.AndradePacheco@ucsf.edu`
[2] Department of Computer Science, University of Sheffield, Sheffield, UK
[3] College of Computing and Information Science,
Makerere University, Kampala, Uganda
[4] UN Global Pulse, Pulse Lab Kampala, Kampala, Uganda

Abstract. A method to monitor infectious diseases based on health records is proposed. Infectious diseases, specially Malaria, are a constant threat for Ugandan public health. The method is applied to health facility records of Malaria in Uganda. The first challenge to overcome is the noise introduced by missing reports of the health facilities. We use Gaussian processes with vector-valued kernels to estimate the missing values in the time series. Later on, for aggregate data at a District level, we use a combination of kernels to decompose the case-counts time series into short and long term components. This method allows not only to remove the effect of specific components, but to study the components of interest with more detail. The short term variations of an infection are divided into four cyclical stages. The progress of an infection across the population can be easily analysed and compared between different Districts. The graphical tool provided can help quick response planning and resources allocation.

Keywords: Gaussian processes · Infectious diseases · Kernel functions · Time series

1 Introduction

Infectious diseases are a burden for Ugandan public health [32]. Just Malaria is one of the leading causes of morbidity and mortality in the country. Potential outbreaks of other diseases like Cholera, Dysentery or Typhoid, while smaller in number of cases, represent a constant threat for the population. Different intervention plans can implemented to prevent and treat these diseases [4]. Their success will depend on how well they can be anticipated and how fast the population can react to them. Hence, decision-making for public health has to be grounded on sound and reliable information. This makes of mathematical modeling a strong ally for planning and decision-making. In this regard, we propose

© Springer International Publishing Switzerland 2016
A. Douzal-Chouakria et al. (Eds.): AALTD 2015, LNAI 9785, pp. 95–110, 2016.
DOI: 10.1007/978-3-319-44412-3_7

that characterising the short term changes of the number of disease cases is an alternative worth exploring for monitoring the disease health of a population.

The Health Management Information System (HMIS), operated by the Ministry of Health, handles its information in a centralized database. Every week, all the health facilities across the country are expected to communicate their data to the central system. This information can be later accessed and analysed. However, this process is not perfect and missing weekly records are a common occurrence in the central database. Missing values obscure the trend of the disease case-counts at the health facilities. This effect is propagated when analysing aggregate data. Under-reporting is prone to create artificial trends, when studying data at a Sub-county or District levels. Unfortunately, the quantification of this error is not straightforward, as this requires to identify which health facilities are missing at each time point and then quantify the aggregated effect.

A common approach for time series analysis is to decompose the observed variation into specific patterns such as *trends, cyclic effects* or *irregular fluctuations* [3,5,12]. Reproducing Kernel Hilbert Spaces, and in particular Gaussian process (GP) models, are a natural approach for analysing functions that represent time series [18,19]. GPs provide a robust framework for non-parametric probabilistic modeling [31]. The use of covariance kernels enables to analyse nonlinear patterns by embedding an inference problem into an abstract space with a *convenient structure* [23]. By combining different covariance kernels (via additions, multiplications or convolutions) into a single one, a GP is able to describe more complex functions. Each of the individual kernels contributes by encoding a specific set of properties or pattern of the resulting function [8].

In this work, we present a model for estimating missing case-counts records and a monitoring system for infectious diseases based on Gaussian processes. First we focus on a methodology for data imputation. The approach followed is to share information across health facilities. Once the missing values have been estimated, our approach seeks to isolate the relevant components of the time series to study the short term variations of the disease. The output of this model is a graphical tool that classifies the evolution of an infection in the population into four stages of simple interpretation.

This paper is organized as follows. In Sect. 2, we present some examples and explain the theory behind the methods used. In Sect. 3, we apply these methods to HMIS data of Malaria cases. First, we describe the model used for data imputation. Later,we expose the characterization of the short term variations in which the monitoring system is based. In Sect. 4, we apply our methods to a simulated dataset. We show how close our estimates are to the ground truth and illustrate the performance of the method of infection stage detection. In Sect. 5, we discuss our findings and mention some of the challenges we have faced when using this methodology to diseases different from Malaria.

2   Methods Used

Say we are interested in learning the functional relation between inputs and output, based on a set of observations $\{(\mathbf{x}_i, y_i)\}_{i=1}^n$. GP models introduce an additional *latent variable* $f_\mathbf{x}$, whose covariance kernel K is a function of the input values. Usually, y_i is considered a distorted version of the latent variable.

2.1   Coregionalized Gaussian Processes

To deal with multiple outputs, GP models resort to generalizations of kernel functions to the vector-valued case [1]. In time series literature, vector-valued functions are commonly treated in the family of VAR models [20], while in geo-statistics literature *co-Kriging* generalizations are used [14,17]. These approaches are equivalent. Let $h_\mathbf{x} = (f_\mathbf{x}^1, \ldots, f_\mathbf{x}^d)^\top$ be a vector-valued GP, its corresponding covariance matrix is given by

$$\left[\mathrm{cov}(h_\mathbf{x}, h_\mathbf{z})_{ij} \right] = \left[\mathrm{cov}(f_\mathbf{x}^i, f_\mathbf{z}^j) \right]. \tag{1}$$

The diagonal elements of the correlation matrix $\left[\mathrm{cov}(h_\mathbf{x}, h_\mathbf{z})_{ii} \right]$ are just the covariance functions of the real-valued GP elements. The non-diagonal elements represent the *cross-covariance functions* between components [2,15,16]. Vector-valued kernels can be defined as a sum of products between kernels for the input space $\mathbb{R}^q$ and kernels for the index set of output components $\mathcal{J} = \{1, \ldots, d\}$ [1]. When using such construction, the kernels are regarded as *separable kernels*. Let $K : \mathbb{R}^q \times \mathbb{R}^q \to \mathbb{R}$ and $B : \mathcal{J} \times \mathcal{J} \to \mathbb{R}$ be kernels for the input space and for the index set, respectively. Then a separable vector-valued kernel $\Gamma : \mathbb{R}^q \times \mathbb{R}^q \to \mathbb{R}^{d \times d}$ can be formulated as

$$\Gamma(\mathbf{x}, \mathbf{z}) = \left[K(\mathbf{x}, \mathbf{z}) \times B(i, j) \right] \tag{2}$$

where

$$\mathbf{B} = \left[B(i, j) \right], \tag{3}$$

for $i, j \in \mathcal{J}$. In this formulation, kernel K has the same interpretation as any kernel on the input space of real-valued functions. In contrast, kernel B (and therefore the matrix $\mathbf{B}$) is interpreted as an encoder of the interactions among outputs (tasks). In geostatistics, a multivariate spatial dependence assumed to have an structure as in Eq. (2) is said to be *intrinsically coregionalized* [11]. In such context, $\mathbf{B}$ is also known as *coregionalization matrix*.

An illustration of a GP for multiple outputs is presented in Fig. 1. In the example, we have two outputs, each one generated from a cosine wave with a drift plus random noise. Observations were randomly generated, but tests sets were chosen so that there was no overlap in the input space. For output one the test set are points in $[75, 100]$ and for output two the test set are points in $[0, 30]$. A couple of standard GP models fit adequately each output in the training region. In this case, we used a Matérn-$\frac{3}{2}$ plus a linear kernel. In the test set region, the model becomes more uncertain about the target values. The linear trend has been learnt adequately, but the Matérn kernel cannot predict

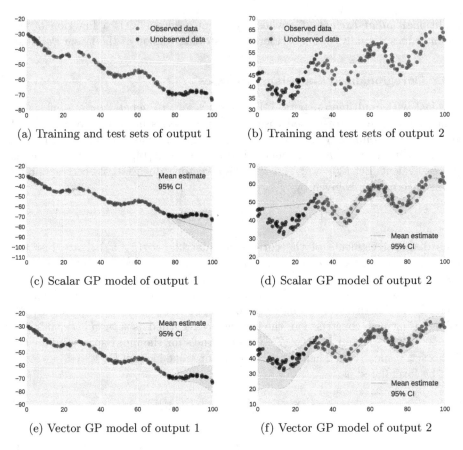

(a) Training and test sets of output 1   (b) Training and test sets of output 2

(c) Scalar GP model of output 1   (d) Scalar GP model of output 2

(e) Vector GP model of output 1   (f) Vector GP model of output 2

Fig. 1. Scalar-valued GP vs vector-valued GP. Panels (a) and (b) show realizations of two different outputs. For each output, Panels (c) and (d) show the mean estimates and credible intervals after fitting a different scalar-valued GP to each of them. Panels (e) and (f) show the corresponding mean estimates and credible intervals from a single vector-valued GP model.

the oscillations around it since it has no means to encode this information[1]. When using a vector-valued kernel (again a Matérn-$\frac{3}{2}$ plus a linear kernel), the resulting model is still not able to learn the periodic pattern. However, it is able to encode a functional relation between the outputs. Therefore, for making predictions, the model takes into account the information learnt from the other output.

---

[1] Such a task would require the use of a periodic kernel, which is able to learn a sinusoidal pattern. A periodic kernel does not impose any additional complication for learning the model. Nevertheless, we decided no to use it to show the capabilities of the vector-valued kernel regression.

2.2 Signal Decomposition with GP

Suppose we have data generated from the combination of two independent signals. This example is illustrated in Fig. 2. Usually, we are not able to observe the signals separately. Moreover, the combined signal they yield is corrupted by noise in the data collected (see Fig. 2b). For the sake of this example, suppose that the two signals represent a long term trend (the smooth signal) and a seasonal component (the sinusoidal signal). For an observer, the oscillations of the seasonal component masks the behaviour of the long term trend. At some point, however, the observer might want to know whether the trend is increasing or decreasing. Similarly, there might be interest in studying only the seasonal component isolated from the trend. For example, in economics and finance, business recession and expansion periods are determined by studying the cyclic component of a set of indicators [28]. The cyclic component tells if an indicator is above or below the trend, and its differences tell if it is increasing or decreasing. We propose a similar approach for monitoring disease incidence time series, but in our case, we will use a non-parametric approach. To extract the original signals, the observed data can be modeled using a GP with a combination of kernels (e.g., two RBF kernels), one having a shorter lengthscale than the other. Figures 2c and d show a model of the combined and independent signals. Rather than using simple differences, we use the derivative of the time series. The derivative can be computed as linear functional of the underlying GP [22]. The time series and its derivative can be represented using a vector-valued setting. If $h_\mathbf{x} = (f_\mathbf{x}, \partial f_\mathbf{x}/\partial x_i)^\top$, the corresponding kernel is defined as

$$\Gamma(\mathbf{x}_i, \mathbf{x}_j) = \begin{bmatrix} K(\mathbf{x}_i, \mathbf{x}_j) & \frac{\partial}{\partial x_j} K(\mathbf{x}_i, \mathbf{x}_j) \\ \frac{\partial}{\partial x_i} K(\mathbf{x}_i, \mathbf{x}_j) & \frac{\partial^2}{\partial x_i x_j} K(\mathbf{x}_i, \mathbf{x}_j) \end{bmatrix}. \tag{4}$$

In most multi-output problems, observations of the different outputs are needed to learn their relation. Here, the relation between $f_\mathbf{x}$ and its derivative is known beforehand through the derivative of K. Thus $\partial f_\mathbf{x}/\partial x_i$ can be learnt by relying entirely on $f_\mathbf{x}$. It is worth mentioning that this approach allows also to quantify the uncertainty of the rate of change of the time series.

For the signals described above, Figs. 2e and f show the corresponding derivatives computed using a kernel of the form of Eq. (4). The derivatives of the long term trend are computed with high confidence, while the derivatives of the seasonal component have more uncertainty. The last is due to the magnitude of the seasonal component relative to the noise magnitude.

3 Application to HMIS Data

3.1 Coregionalization of Health Facilities Data

Assuming some smoothness across time, missing observations of disease case-counts can be estimated through the interpolation of the reported values. Gaussian processes are a powerful interpolation tool easy to implement for this

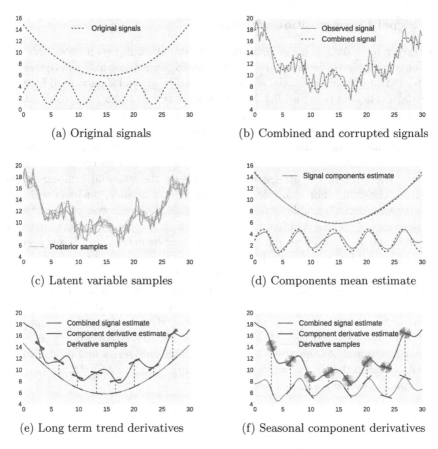

Fig. 2. Series decomposition. Panel (a) shows two independent signals. Panel (b) shows the combination of both signals and a distorted signal after adding some noise. Panel (c) shows some samples of a model describing the combined signal. Panel (d) compares the mean estimate of each component with the original signals. Panels (e) and (f) show the derivatives of the signal components (for comparison, the estimate of the individual signals are shown below the composed signal).

task. This approach can be improved if we consider information form nearby health facilities. For example, usually, after a wet season in a specific region, an increase in the number of Malaria cases or outbreaks for other diseases are expected[2]. This effect should be similar in all health facilities within the region[3].

---

[2] An alternative is to include information about weather conditions in the estimates. That approach deserves a much broader discussion and falls out of the scope of this work.

[3] Being more specific, the effect should be similar in those health facilities that are dedicated to treat the disease in question.

Hence, even if a particular facility is not reporting, the surrounding facilities can give us a clue about the changes in the number of cases it is experiencing.

We are not attempting any sort of spatial smoothing of the number of infections (however, the methodological framework we are using can be applied for spatial modeling as well [6,7]). Here we are modeling the time series of each health facility and learning the correlation with the surrounding facilities. Just in the case that there is a correlation, the information from the neighbor facilities will be used in the model predictions. Because vector-valued kernels have a complexity of $\mathcal{O}((\sum n_d)^3)$, where n_d is the number of observations of output d, we are limited in the number of health facilities that we can model together. Even sparse GP approximations [21,24,26] would not be of much help if we attempted a joint model of all the health facilities[4]. We decided to model only those health facilities that were in the same Sub-county, and whenever this was a very large number, like can happen in Kampala (above two hundred), we clustered the facilities based on their spatial location[5] and modeled each cluster by separate. As a base model, we used a GP model with no correlation, where the variation is explained only by a mean model[6]. The base case was contrasted with a model that uses a bias kernel plus a Matérn-$\frac{3}{2}$ kernel to explain the evolution of the case-counts in a health facility across time. As a third case, we considered a model that also incorporates a vector-valued Matérn-$\frac{3}{2}$, and thus takes into consideration information from the neighborhood of health facilities. The latter is the most flexible model. The combination of three kernels allows the resulting GP to represent more complicated functions than the first two models. In addition, the model is expected to perform even better whenever it finds a strong correlation between the health facilities, as it is able to share information across them. The correlation between a pair of health facilities i and j can be computed as

$$\rho = \frac{B(i,j)}{\sqrt{B(i,i)B(j,j)}}. \tag{5}$$

In Table 1, we compare an implementation of the models described above in the Sub-counties of Hoima District. We used information of 52 weeks and only modeled health facilities with at least 8 observations in that period. The criteria for the comparison was leave-one-out cross-validation [29,30]. In some cases, the vector-valued model is out-performed by the second model. This suggests an inappropiate fit, since the second model is a constrained version of the vector-valued one. After some analysis, we found that this happens when spurious correlations between the health facilities are learnt. Then, rather than improving the model, the vector-valued kernel is introducing noise by sharing information across facilities. This occurs specially when some facilities have very few data

---

[4] The number of health facilities was around four thousand in the sample of information used.

[5] We did not have the spatial location for some health facilities. These facilities were assigned randomly to different clusters.

[6] This model was implemented by using a GP with a bias kernel.

Table 1. Leave-one-out cross-validation. Three models for the health facilities of each sub-county in Hoima where compared. M1 is a mean model of the number of cases in each health facility. M2 uses a kernel with exponential smoothing across time, but no correlation between health facilities is considered. M3 uses a two kernels for exponential smoothing, one of them allowing a correlation between health facilities.

Sub-county	Health facilities	M1	M2	M3
Kigorobya	5	−136.56	−59.42	−85.33
Bugambe	3	−62.17	−21.34	−9.54
Busiisi Dv	2	−53.84	−19.77	−46.01
Buhimba	6	−217.61	−159.47	−142.70
Kyangwali	6	−115.83	−147.59	−17.29
Kahoora Dv	8	−139.86	−106.03	−101.43
Kabwoya	5	−155.18	−53.61	−120.85
Kitoba	4	−145.29	−79.96	−51.40
Buhanika	1	−38.14	−16.60	−
Buseruka	3	−71.91	−30.60	−5.67
Mparo Dv	2	−51.81	−24.75	−19.50
Kyabigambire	5	−172.19	−63.25	−12.72
Kiziranfumbi	4	−121.67	−47.32	−60.63
Bujumbura Dv	2	−69.08	−45.91	−58.60

points[7], so that there is no strong evidence in favor or against any correlation. The numeric optimization can then converge to any value even if it is not realistic. The last, makes evident a risk associated to vector-valued kernels when not fitted adequately. The use of prior distributions on the coregionalization parameters might help in this regard. But then these priors require to be carefully defined.

Figure 3 shows the coregionalization matrices of the models of Buhimba and Kyangwali Sub-counties. To ease the interpretation, the values presented are correlations computed as in Eq. (5).

3.2   Aggregate Missing Data Estimation

From the perspective of public administration, it is frequently needed to present data in terms of administrative units. In this case, this means analysing aggregate data at a Sub-county or District level. A problem that arises when aggregating raw data is to define a criteria to handle non-reported values. Figure 4a shows the data reported of three health facilities in Hoima District. Although the three facilities have reported almost every week, all of them have some blanks. In fact, it is in the least of the cases when none of the facilities fail to report on the

---

[7] Even when we limited the study to health facilities with at least 8 observations, some health facilities did not have enough information to fit a model adequately.

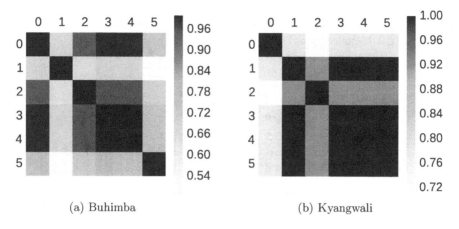

(a) Buhimba   (b) Kyangwali

Fig. 3. Correlation matrices across health facilities. Panel (a) shows the correlation across 6 facilities in Buhimba Sub-county. Panel (b) shows the correlation across 6 facilities in Kyangwali Sub-county.

same week. Hence, the aggregate data (treating missing values as zero) is biased almost everywhere. Interpolating the missing values for each health facility as explained in the previous subsection is an easy task. It makes sense to use a coregionalized model as the time series shows a similar pattern. Since we are making estimates at health facility level, we can provide aggregate estimates at any level requested. The uncertainty characterization of the aggregates is more complex. Once we have learnt a model for each health facility in the country, we can generate samples at all the missing points and obtain samples of all the Sub-counties and Districts. Figure 4b shows the aggregate data of Hoima District. The raw data is shown at the bottom of the stacked bars and the imputed data is shown at the top. We also show the 95 % credible interval (red lines).

3.3   Monitoring Short Term Changes with GP

We can analyse the time series of the disease counts according the long and short term variations. The long term variations would correspond to an average case-counts of the disease across some period. For an endemic disease like Malaria, the short term variations could be a seasonal effect [10], while for epidemic diseases like Dysentery or Cholera, a short term variation could describe an outbreak. Quick response actions, such as distribution of medicine and allocation of patients to health centres, have to take place in this time regime to be effective.

The characterization of the long and short term components can be done through GP modeling, as exposed in Sect. 2.2. The oscillations around the long term trend are described by the short term signal component. The derivative of this signal, tells the rate at which it is changing, and thus the direction (increasing or decreasing). Based on the motion around the trend we can identify four

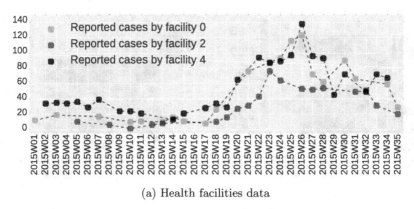

(a) Health facilities data

(b) Aggregate data

Fig. 4. Hoima District data. Panel (a) shows the raw data of three health facilities of Buhimba Sub-county. Panel (b) shows the aggregate raw data and the aggregate imputed data of Hoima District. (Color figure online)

stages the time series of the disease cases goes through: expansion and contractions above or below the long term trend. A diagram of these stages is presented in Fig. 5.

We are interested in implementing this methodology to aggregate data at District and Sub-county levels. Before doing so, we need to consider that our *new* aggregate data is a probabilistic estimate. We have to take into account the uncertainty associated to each data point imputation. This can be done assigning a different noise term to each observation. Some heteroscedastic models learn a functional form of the noise term across the input space [9,13,27,33]. However, our problem is easier. The noise we are assuming is unstructured and it is associated to the uncertainty we have already measured (see Sect. 3.2).

An example of this approach is illustrated in Fig. 6. In the top panel (Fig. 6a), the aggregate estimate of Malaria cases in Kasese District is shown. Each of the bullets A-D, in Fig. 6a, correspond to a different stage according to the diagram in Fig. 5. The infection stages can be represented in a cyclic diagram as

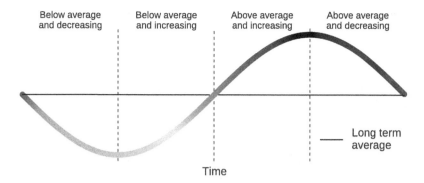

Fig. 5. Infection stages according to the short term variations around the trend. The multicolored line represents the number of disease cases across time, while the red line represents the long term trend. The first section of the diagram corresponds to a number of disease cases below the long term average and decreasing. The second section corresponds to an increasing number of cases, but still below the trend. The third section corresponds to an increasing number of cases above the trend. The last section corresponds to a reduction in the number of cases, but still above the long term average. (Color figure online)

shown in the bottom panel (Fig. 6b). Each quadrant represents a different stage. The infection goes through them in a counter clockwise motion. The values of the short term variation and its rate of change are scaled by their standard deviations. The white region at the center represents the cases when the ratio signal vs noise is not strong enough to describe short term behaviour of the series. The black line represents motion of the number of disease cases (this is the red line in Fig. 6a) through the four stages. For a better comparison of both panels in the figure, the bullets A-D are also marked in the diagram (white bullets).

This tracking system is independent of the order of magnitude of the disease counts, and therefore can be used to compare the infection stage in different regions. It is easy to identify Districts where the disease is being controlled or where the infection is progressing fast. In Fig. 7, we show the monitoring system on the whole country at four different weeks.

4   Application to Simulated Data

Since we ignore the actual values of the missing points in the HMIS database, it is not possible to tell how accurate the estimates of the previous Section are. In this Section, we illustrate the performance of the methodology proposed with simulated data. We generated 4 time series and randomly removed some of their points. Then we applied our methodology sequentially. We added observations one at a time, and for every new time point added we estimated the missing values and predicted the disease stage. In Sect. 3, due to the limited amount of data used, the methodology was not implemented in sequence. However, the disease stage detection should be implemented this way to be useful.

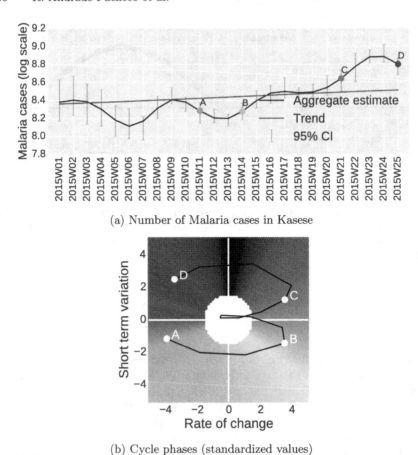

(a) Number of Malaria cases in Kasese

(b) Cycle phases (standardized values)

Fig. 6. Infection phases in Kasese District. Panel (a) shows the case-counts time series. Panel (b) shows a cyclic diagram of the different infection stages. (Color figure online)

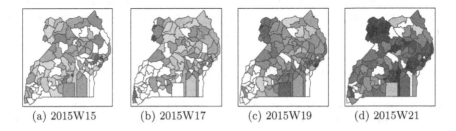

(a) 2015W15   (b) 2015W17   (c) 2015W19   (d) 2015W21

Fig. 7. Monitoring system of Malaria across all Districts. Panels show different weeks.

In Fig. 8a, we show the simulated data. For each time series, the bullets represent the reported values and the lines represent the complete data, which is usually unknown. Figure 8b shows a comparison of the complete aggregate data

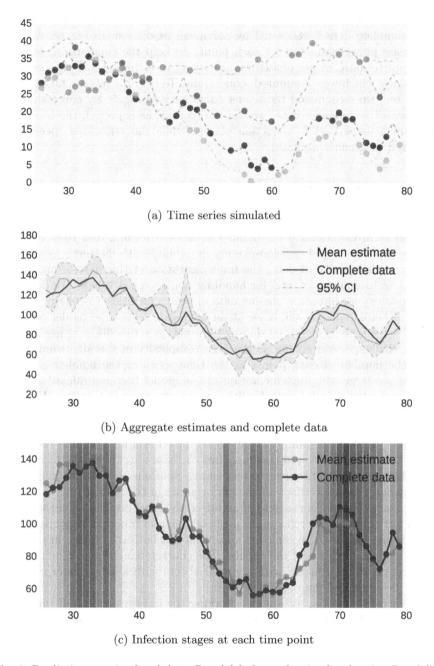

(a) Time series simulated

(b) Aggregate estimates and complete data

(c) Infection stages at each time point

Fig. 8. Predictions on simulated data. Panel (a) shows the simulated series. Panel (b) shows the aggregate estimates and the aggregate complete data. Panel (c) shows the disease stage identified for each time point. (Color figure online)

and the estimates with a coregionalization model. We can see that the actual values lie within the 95 % credible intervals of the estimates, and that the trend of the complete data is recovered by our mean prediction. In Fig. 8c, we show the disease phase estimated for each point. To help the comparison, we show the complete data, whose phases we are trying to estimate, and the predicted data values, which were computed sequentially. To help the interpretation of the colors used, we recommend the reader to go back to Fig. 5. By contrasting the colors with the complete data, we can notice that, as expected, the blue-green spectrum is associated to reduction phases, while the yellow-red spectrum is associated to expansion phases.

5   Final Discussion

We proposed a monitoring system of infection diseases based on the analysis of the short term variations in the number of cases. We think that such approach could help planning and decision-making in public health matters.

Due to the quality of data, the implementation of this monitoring system required us to define a criteria for handling non reported values. We described a methodology for imputing missing data of health facilities. Correcting data at this level helps reducing the noise at an aggregate level. The model proposed estimates the missing values by sharing information across different health facilities. A challenge to overcome is the high complexity of the algorithm. When either the number of data points in the time series or the number of health facilities are large, the implementation of the model becomes infeasible. Here, we only modeled jointly health facilities within the same Sub-county. However, infectious diseases are phenomena that goes beyond such administrative borders. While there is no need to model all the health facilities of the country at the same time, it is still pending to define a better criteria for grouping the health facilities. Our results showed the importance of assessing the model fit and specially the coregionalization parameters learnt. Spurious correlations might arise and this has a negative effect on the performance of the model.

We characterized the progress of an infection across population through four stages. For this task we relied on a probabilistic and functional approach. The method used is able to account for uncertainty in both the change in the case-counts and the direction of the change. The characterization and monitoring of the infection status is aided with a graphical tool with a simple interpretation. Results on simulated data are encouraging.

Apart from Malaria, we are also working the implementation of this monitoring system for some epidemic diseases like Cholera, Dysentery and Typhoid. This has brought new challenges we did not face with the Malaria case. Here we will just mention briefly some of them. First of all, the order of magnitude of the number of cases is smaller and data are more scarce for these diseases. Data imputation is harder, as in this regime (very low counts) non reported values could be an implicit report of zero cases. Interpolation becomes more difficult when there are very few data points, and as we mentioned above, this also makes more difficult to learn the coregionalization parameters. The characterization of the infection stage of these diseases also has some additional challenges. Because reported values are more scarce, the aggregate estimates have a higher uncertainty than in the Malaria case. The ratio signal vs noise tends to be small and then the infection stage is not easily identified. More work needs to be done for successfully applying this methodology to these diseases.

To carry on this work, we were granted access to HMIS data. The model was implemented as a prototype, and although the specific code is not public at the moment, methods rely largely on the toolbox *GPy* [25]. We expect that an analysis from this perspective can add situational awareness and contribute to interventions planning and resources allocation when facing infectious diseases.

References

1. Álvarez, M., Rosasco, L., Lawrence, N.D.: Kernels for vector-valued functions: a review. Found. Trends Mach. Learn. **4**(3), 195–266 (2012)
2. Baldassarre, L., Rosasco, L., Barla, A., Verri, A.: Multi-output learning via spectral filtering. Mach. Learn. **87**(3), 259–301 (2012)
3. Baxter, M., King, R.G.: Measuring business cycles: approximate band-pass filters for economic time series. Rev. Econ. Stat. **81**(4), 575–593 (1999)
4. Bhatt, S., Weiss, D., Cameron, E., Bisanzio, D., Mappin, B., Dalrymple, U., Battle, K., Moyes, C., Henry, A., Eckhoff, P., et al.: The effect of malaria control on plasmodium falciparum in Africa between 2000 and 2015. Nature **526**(7572), 207–211 (2015)
5. Cleveland, W.P., Tiao, G.C.: Decomposition of seasonal time series: a model for the census X-11 program. J. Am. Stat. Assoc. **71**(355), 581–587 (1976)
6. Diggle, P.J., Moraga, P., Rowlingson, B., Taylor, B.M., et al.: Spatial and spatio-temporal log-Gaussian Cox processes: extending the geostatistical paradigm. Stat. Sci. **28**(4), 542–563 (2013)
7. Diggle, P.J., Tawn, J., Moyeed, R.: Model-based geostatistics. J. Roy. Stat. Soc. Ser. C (Appl. Stat.) **47**(3), 299–350 (1998)
8. Durrande, N., Hensman, J., Rattray, M., Lawrence, N.D.: Gaussian process models for periodicity detection (2013). arXiv:1303.7090
9. Goldberg, P.W., Williams, C.K.I., Bishop, C.M.: Regression with input-dependent noise: a Gaussian process treatment. In: Jordan, M.I., Kearns, M.J., Solla, S.A. (eds.) Advances in Neural Information Processing Systems, vol. 10, pp. 493–499. MIT Press, Cambridge (1998)
10. Hay, S.I., Snow, R.W., Rogers, D.J.: From predicting mosquito habitat to malaria seasons using remotely sensed data: practice, problems and perspectives. Parasitol. Today **14**(8), 306–313 (1998)
11. Helterbrand, J.D., Cressie, N.: Universal cokriging under intrinsic coregionalization. Math. Geol. **26**(2), 205–226 (1994)
12. Hyvärinen, A., Oja, E.: Independent component analysis: algorithms and applications. Neural Netw. **13**(4), 411–430 (2000)
13. Lázaro-Gredilla, M., Titsias, M.: Variational heteroscedastic Gaussian process regression. In: Getoor, L., Scheffer, T. (eds.) Proceedings of the International Conference in Machine Learning, vol. 28, pp. 841–848. Morgan Kaufmann, San Francisco (2011)

14. Matheron, G.: Pour une analyse krigeante de donnés régionalisées. Technical report, École des Mines de Paris, Fontainebleau, France (1982)
15. Micchelli, C.A., Pontil, M.: Kernels for multi-task learning. In: Advances in Neural Information Processing Systems (NIPS). MIT Press (2004)
16. Micchelli, C.A., Pontil, M.: On learning vector-valued functions. Neural Comput. **17**, 177–204 (2005)
17. Myers, D.E.: Matrix formulation of co-kriging. J. Int. Assoc. Math. Geol. **14**(3), 249–257 (1982)
18. Parzen, E.: An approach to time series analysis. Ann. Math. Stat. **32**, 951–989 (1961)
19. Parzen, E.: Statistical inference on time series by RKHS methods. In: Pyke, R. (ed.) 12th Biennial Seminar, pp. 1–37. Canadian Mathematical Congress (1970)
20. Quenouille, H.: The Analysis of Multiple Time-Series (Griffin's Statistical Monographs & Courses). Griffin, London (1957)
21. Quiñonero Candela, J., Rasmussen, C.E.: A unifying view of sparse approximate Gaussian process regression. J. Mach. Learn. Res. **6**, 1939–1959 (2005)
22. Särkkä, S.: Linear operators and stochastic partial differential equations in Gaussian process regression. In: Honkela, T. (ed.) ICANN 2011, Part II. LNCS, vol. 6792, pp. 151–158. Springer, Heidelberg (2011)
23. Shawe-Taylor, J., Cristianini, N.: Kernel Methods for Pattern Analysis. Cambridge University Press, Cambridge (2004)
24. Snelson, E., Ghahramani, Z.: Sparse Gaussian processes using pseudo-inputs. In: Weiss, Y., Schölkopf, B., Platt, J.C. (eds.) Advances in Neural Information Processing Systems, vol. 18. MIT Press, Cambridge (2006)
25. The GPy authors. GPy: A Gaussian process framework in Python, 2012–2015. http://github.com/SheffieldML/GPy
26. Titsias, M.K.: Variational learning of inducing variables in sparse Gaussian processes. In: van Dyk, D., Welling, M. (eds.) Proceedings of the Twelfth International Workshop on Artificial Intelligence and Statistics, JMLR W & CP, Clearwater Beach, FL, 16–18 April 2009, vol. 5, pp. 567–574 (2009)
27. Tolvanen, V., Jylanki, P., Vehtari, A.: Expectation propagation for nonstationary heteroscedastic Gaussian process regression. In: IEEE International Workshop on Machine Learning for Signal Processing (MLSP), pp. 1–6. IEEE (2014)
28. van Ruth, F., Schouten, B., Wekker, R.: The statistics Netherlands business cycle tracer. Methodological aspects; concept, cycle computation and indicator selection. Technical report, Statistics Netherlands (2005)
29. Vehtari, A., Ojanen, J., et al.: A survey of Bayesian predictive methods for model assessment, selection and comparison. Stat. Surv. **6**, 142–228 (2012)
30. Vehtari, A., Tolvanen, V., Mononen, T., Winther, O.: Bayesian leave-one-out cross-validation approximations for Gaussian latent variable models (2014). arXiv:1412.7461
31. Williams, C.K.I., Rasmussen, C.E.: Gaussian Processes for Machine Learning. MIT Press, Cambridge (2006)
32. World Health Organization. World health statistics. Technical report. WHO Press, Geneva (2015)
33. Wu, Y., Hernández-Lobato, J.M., Ghahramani, Z.: Gaussian process volatility model. In: Ghahramani, Z., Welling, M., Cortes, C., Lawrence, N.D., Weinberger, K.Q. (eds.) Advances in Neural Information Processing Systems, Cambridge, MA, vol. 27, pp. 1044–1052 (2014)

Estimating Dynamic Graphical Models from Multivariate Time-Series Data: Recent Methods and Results

Alex J. Gibberd[1,2(✉)] and James D.B. Nelson[1]

[1] Department of Statistical Science, University College London,
Gower Street, London WC1E 6BT, UK
`alexander.gibberd.12@ucl.ac.uk`
[2] Department of Security and Crime Science,
University College London, London, UK

Abstract. Dynamic graphical models aim to describe the time-varying dependency structure of multiple time-series. In this article we review research focusing on the formulation and estimation of such models. The bulk of work in graphical structurelearning problems has focused in the stationary i.i.d setting, we present a brief overview of this work before introducing some dynamic extensions. In particular we focuson two classes of dynamic graphical model; continuous (smooth) models which are estimated via localised kernels, and piecewise models utilising regularisation based estimation. We give an overview of theoretical and empirical results regarding these models, before demonstrating their qualitative difference in the context of a real-world financial time-series dataset. We conclude with a discussion of the state of the field and future research directions.

Keywords: Graphical model · Sparsity · Changepoint · Time-series · Dynamics · Regularization

1 Introduction

Undirected graphical models (UGM) provide a popular way to describe and examine relationships between sets of variables in multivariate data sets [21, 26]. Estimation of sparse graphical models where only a subset of variables are conditionally dependent are often more robust than their completely dense counterparts. This robustness provides statistical benefits through reduced variance in estimator uncertainty, but comes at the cost of us imposing a prior (the sparsity pattern) and therefore bias on the model. This is the typical bias/variance trade-off associated with statistical estimation.

In some applications, where we believe we already have good knowledge of what dependencies should be in place, one can encode this into a model a-priori.

D.B. Nelson—This work is funded by the Defence Science Technology Laboratory (Dstl) National PhD Scheme.

© Springer International Publishing Switzerland 2016
A. Douzal-Chouakria et al. (Eds.): AALTD 2015, LNAI 9785, pp. 111–128, 2016.
DOI: 10.1007/978-3-319-44412-3_8

In such cases our prior biases can help us provide useful predictive inferences. Such methods are popular in tasks such as risk-modeling and fraud/fault detection [9], as they give practitioners an easy way to encode and visualise their expert knowledge within a statistical model. However, in many (perhaps more) cases we don't really have a good idea of what these dependencies may be in advance, common examples can be found in the study of gene-regulation activity [1,27], electrical brain activity [17,32], Fx/equity trading [38], or computer network traffic [16]. In the situation where we don't have such strong prior knowledge over the sparsity pattern, we can attempt to infer not just an appropriate parameter values, but also select a subset of the parameters (i.e. the graph structure) that well approximate a generative distribution and its dependency structure.

Classically, performing model selection in graphical models has focused in situations where the data is drawn independently and identically [3,14,24]. However, when we think about this assumption in the context of systems we observe, it seems unlikely to hold true. In many situations we might expect dependencies to vary over time, performing static inference in such settings runs risk of drawing false conclusions and missing out interesting dynamic properties of the system. In this paper we review a few recent approaches that relax the identically distributed assumption and result in what we refer to as *dynamic graphical models*. In particular, we focus on dynamic Gaussian Graphical models that can be thought of as a sub class of time-varying coefficient models of Hastie et al. [20].

In Sects. 2 and 3 we introduce definitions and estimation methods for a class of Gaussian graphical models in the static (identically distributed) case. Section 4 introduces extensions to dynamic settings, where we suggest three different classes of dynamic Gaussian Graphical models. We discuss how previous work in dynamic graphs can be placed within these different model frameworks. Section 5 discusses different estimation approaches and results for identifying dynamic graph structure and estimating changepoints. In Sect. 6 we compare two approaches to piecewise-constant graphical modeling with an example application looking at dependency in financial markets. We conclude with a discussion on limitations of the current methods and potential future directions.

2   Gaussian Graphical Models

In this paper we primarily concern ourselves with undirected graphical models $G(V, E)$, where $V = \{1, \ldots, P\}$ denotes a set of indexed vertices relating to variables and E a set of edges indicating conditional dependencies. Specifically, in this work, we consider the set of parametric Gaussian Graphical Models (GGM), whereby the joint distribution follows a multivariate normal distribution such that random vectors are drawn from the P-variate normal[1]:

$$(Y_1, \ldots, Y_P)^\top \sim \mathcal{N}_P(\boldsymbol{\mu}, \boldsymbol{\Sigma}). \tag{1}$$

---

[1] For simplicity, in this paper we assume the mean parameter is zero $\boldsymbol{\mu} = \mathbf{0}$.

The Gaussian nature of such models allows them to model linear dependencies between continuous valued variables. For reference, we also note that graphical models can be constructed for discrete, categorical, and mixed variables [28,30,43] but these are not so well developed in the dynamic settings that we later consider.

To make a statement about the conditional independence properties and relate this to the edge set E, one must look at the partial correlation between variables. The partial covariance is defined as the covariance between two variables conditioned on the rest:

$$\mathrm{ParCov}(Y_i, Y_j, V\backslash\{i,j\}) := \mathrm{Cov}(Y_i|Y_{V\backslash\{i,j\}}, Y_j|Y_{V\backslash\{i,j\}}),$$

where in this case $Y_{V\backslash\{i,j\}}$ is the set of all variables excluding the i,jth elements.

A special property of the Gaussian distribution is that the global and local Markov properties are equivalent (see Lauritzen [26] for proof). In particular, the pairwise independence relation $Y_i \perp Y_j|Y_{V\backslash\{i,j\}}$ implies a set wise relation $Y_A \perp Y_B|Y_S$, where (A, B, S) are disjoint subsets of V, such that the set S separates A from B, i.e. every path from a vertex in A to B must pass through S. This property allows one to show that a pairwise independence $Y_i \perp Y_j|Y_{V\backslash\{i,j\}}$ for an edge (i,j) implies it's exclusion from the set E. In the Gaussian case the pairwise partial-covariance is encoded through entries in the precision matrix $\Theta = \Sigma^{-1}$, whereby $\mathrm{ParCov}(Y_i, Y_j, V\backslash\{i,j\}) = 0 \iff \Theta_{i,j} = 0$. The main corollary of this result is that if we can estimate accurately from data this precision matrix (in particular the pattern of zeros) then we may infer GGM structure and highlight some dependencies between variables.

3   Model Selection

In the previous section we defined GGM in the static setting, in particular we noted the relationship between the parameters of the Gaussian distribution Σ (and the precision matrix Θ) and the edge structure in the graphical model $(G, \mathcal{N}_P(0, \Sigma))$. In this section we discuss how one can practically and robustly estimate the sparsity structure within the precision matrix.

3.1   An Estimation Framework

From a statistical estimation viewpoint, the significance of a model component can often be viewed in terms of a model selection problem. Generally, one may construct an estimate of model fit (a lower score implies better fit) $L(M, \theta, Y)$, relating a given model $M \in \mathcal{M}$ and parameters $\theta \in \mathcal{P}(M)$ to some observed data Y. Additionally, to account for differences in perceived model complexity one should penalise this by a measure of complexity $R(M, \theta)$ (larger is more *complex*). An optimal model and identification of parameters may be found through balancing the two terms, i.e.:

$$(\hat{M}, \hat{\theta}) = \operatorname*{arg\,min}_{M \in \mathcal{M}, \theta \in \mathcal{P}(M)} \left[L(M, \theta, Y) + R(M, \theta) \right]. \tag{2}$$

In statistics such a formulation is referred to as an M-estimator [33], however, such frameworks are popular across all walks of science [6], for example; maximum-likelihood (ML), least-squares, robust (Huber loss), penalised ML estimators can all be discussed in this context. The principle idea is to suggest a mathematical (and therefore can be communicated objectively) statement to the effect of Occam's Razor, whereby given similar model-fit, one should prefer the simpler model. Depending on the specification of the functions $L(\cdot)$ and $R(\cdot)$ and associated model/parameter spaces, the problem in (2) can be either very easy or difficult (for example, are the functions smooth, convex, etc.).

3.2   Maximum Likelihood Estimation

In the GGM case, learning appropriate structure for the graphical model can be linked with the general framework of (2) through a ML or Maximum a-posteriori (MAP) paradigm. Assuming N observations $\boldsymbol{Y} \in \mathbb{R}^{P \times N}$ drawn as i.i.d samples the model fit function $L()$ can be related to the likelihood specified by the multivariate Gaussian. Typically, one prefers to work with the log-likelihood, which if we assume $\boldsymbol{\mu} = \boldsymbol{0}$ is given by:

$$\log(P(\boldsymbol{Y}|\boldsymbol{\Theta}))/N = \frac{1}{2}\log\det(\boldsymbol{\Theta}) - \frac{1}{2}\text{trace}(\hat{\boldsymbol{S}}\boldsymbol{\Theta}) - \frac{P}{2}\ln(\pi),$$

where $\hat{\boldsymbol{S}} = \boldsymbol{Y}\boldsymbol{Y}^{\top}/N$ is often referred to as the empirical covariance matrix. Setting the loss function as $L(\cdot) = -\log\det(\boldsymbol{\Theta}) + \text{trace}(\hat{\boldsymbol{S}}\boldsymbol{\Theta})$ gives (in the setting where $N > P$) a well-behaved smooth, convex function describing how well the distribution parameterised by $\boldsymbol{\Sigma}$ describes the data $\boldsymbol{Y}$. If one considers Eq. (2) with the function $R() = 0$, i.e. no complexity penalty, then the resultant problem gives a ML estimate for the precision matrix:

$$\hat{\boldsymbol{\Theta}}_{\text{ML}} := \arg\min_{\boldsymbol{\Theta} \in \mathbb{R}^{P \times P}} \left[-\log\det(\boldsymbol{\Theta}) + \text{trace}(\hat{\boldsymbol{S}}\boldsymbol{\Theta}) \right]. \tag{3}$$

We note some properties of this estimate:

- In general the estimator will be dense (not many zeros) and therefore the inferred GGM will be close to being complete.
- The estimator exhibits large variance when $N \approx P$ and is very sensitive to changes in observations leading to poor generalisation performance.
- In the high-dimensional setting $(P > N)$, the sample estimator is rank deficient $(\text{rank}(\hat{\boldsymbol{S}}) < P)$ and there is no unique inverse for $\hat{\boldsymbol{S}}$. This setting is extremely important in dynamic graph estimation (see Sect. 4).

3.3   Sparsity Assumptions

In order to avoid estimating a complete GGM graph where all nodes are connected to each other, one must actively select edges according to some criteria. In the asymptotic setting where $N \gg P$ one can test for the significance of edges by considering the asymptotic distribution of the empirical partial correlation coefficients

$(\hat{\rho}_{ij} = -\hat{\Theta}_{ij}/\hat{\Theta}_{ii}^{1/2}\hat{\Theta}_{jj}^{1/2})$ [11]. However, such a procedure cannot be performed in the high-dimensional setting as it requires that the empirical estimates be positive semi-definite. Additionally, one runs into the usual problems associated with multiple hypothesis testing, resulting in computational issues where for exact testing one is required to perform a combinatorially expensive search.

BIC, AIC, ℓ_0-Regularisation, Hard-Thresholding. An alternative approach to testing is to utilise some prior knowledge about the number of edges in the graph. If we assume a flat prior on the model[2] $\mathcal{M}$ and parameters $\boldsymbol{\Theta}(\mathcal{M})$, maximising the approximate posterior probability over models $P(\mathcal{M}|\boldsymbol{Y})$, then leads to the Bayesian information criterion for GGM [13]:

$$\mathrm{BIC}(\hat{\boldsymbol{\Theta}}_{\mathrm{ML}}) = N(-\log\det(\hat{\boldsymbol{\Theta}}_{\mathrm{ML}}) + \mathrm{trace}(\hat{\boldsymbol{S}}\hat{\boldsymbol{\Theta}}_{\mathrm{ML}})) + \hat{s}\log(N), \qquad (4)$$

where $\hat{s}$ is given by the number of unique non-zeros within the ML estimated precision matrix $\hat{\boldsymbol{\Theta}}_{\mathrm{ML}}$. Unfortunately, interpreting such a criteria under the framework in Eq. (2), we find the complexity penalty $R() = \hat{s}\log(N)$ is non-convex, $\hat{s} \propto \|\boldsymbol{\Theta}\|_0 = |\{\Theta_{i,j} \neq 0|\forall i \neq j\}|$ basically counts the number of estimated edges. In order to arrive at a global minima an exhaustive search over the model space of all possible graphs $\mathcal{O}(2^{P^2})$ is required.

Graphical Lasso, ℓ_1-Regularisation, Soft-Thresholding. In order to avoid performing such an exhaustive search over the model space, one can choose to place a different prior on the model, but one that still encourages a parsimonious graphical representation. A popular approach [14,24,41,48] adapted from the linear regression setting is to place a Laplace type prior on the precision matrix entries in an effort to directly shrink off-diagonal values. Whilst one could choose to perform full Bayesian inference for the posterior $P(\boldsymbol{\Theta}|\boldsymbol{Y}, \gamma)$ as examined by Wang et al. [41], a computationally less demanding approach is to perform MAP estimation resulting in the *graphical lasso* problem [14]:

$$\hat{\boldsymbol{\Theta}}_{GL} := \arg\min_{\boldsymbol{\Theta}\succ 0}\left[-\log\det(\boldsymbol{\Theta}) + \mathrm{trace}(\hat{\boldsymbol{S}}\boldsymbol{\Theta}) + \lambda\|\boldsymbol{\Theta}\|_1\right], \qquad (5)$$

where $\|\boldsymbol{\Theta}\|_1 = \sum_{i\neq j}|\Theta_{i,j}|$ is the ℓ_1 norm of $\boldsymbol{\Theta}$. The graphical lasso can yet again be interpreted within the general M-estimation framework, except this time with $R() = \lambda\|\boldsymbol{\Theta}\|_1$. Unlike when using BIC, this complexity penalty is now convex, we can now reliably find a global minima given an appropriate regularising constant λ. There are many efficient optimisation techniques developed to deal with such problems [3,46], additionally, due to the convexity of the problem it is easier to theoretically analyse estimator properties [33].

Neighborhood Selection. Rather than performing inference over all elements of the precision matrix at once, an alternative is to attempt to split the problem up and study the edges connecting each node separately. The *neighbourhood selection*

---

[2] Note: the model here refers to the sparsity pattern, rather than the fact that the distribution is Gaussian.

process involves fitting a regression model of each variables on the others and then iterating across nodes. Indexing the variable of interest by a and the set without a denoted $\backslash a$, then a sparse set of estimates (based on the lasso [39]):

$$\hat{\boldsymbol{\theta}}^a := \arg \min_{\boldsymbol{\theta} \in \mathbb{R}^{P-1}} (N^{-1}\|\boldsymbol{Y}_a - \boldsymbol{Y}_{\backslash a}\boldsymbol{\theta}\|_2^2 + \lambda\|\boldsymbol{\theta}\|_1), \tag{6}$$

can be used to recover the conditional dependency relations corresponding to the ath row-vector in the precision matrix $\boldsymbol{\Theta}$, in the static case such a procedure is shown to be consistent for recovering the support of the precision matrix [31].

It is beyond the scope of this paper to fully review such high-dimensional estimation procedures and results, however, it should be noted that there is a rich literature on this subject. In particular, whilst the precision matrix encodes the dependency structure of a GGM, generalisations to different distributions can be made by altering the loss function (as in the neighborhood selection case). Some notable examples include incorporating losses for binary variables via an Ising model [34], count variables with a multivariate Poisson [43], or to a non-parametric setting via a non-paranormal (c.f. copula) model [24]. Further to the above regularised approaches, one may also consider explicitly constrained approaches, for example the CLIME estimator of Cai et al. [7].

3.4   Theoretical Results for Sparse Precision Estimation

There are several works that discuss the robustness of the graphical lasso formulation in Eq. (5). These concern both the rate of convergence to the true precision matrix for parameter consistency and its support. If an estimator can recover the true graph structure then it is said to be *sparsistent*.

As with other high-dimensional statistical estimation problems, in order to derive bounds for sparsistent recovery one must make sure some assumptions on the problem design. Such conditions are often referred to as *incoherence* or *irrepresentability* conditions. In the graphical structure learning setting these relate to limiting correlation between edges. We give an example of such a condition below which looks at the curvature of the loss function about the true precision matrix $\boldsymbol{\Theta}^*$. In the multivariate Gaussian case the Hessian $\boldsymbol{\Gamma}^* = \nabla_{\boldsymbol{\Theta}}^2 L(\boldsymbol{\Theta})|_{\boldsymbol{\Theta}^*}$ relates to the Fisher information matrix, such that $\Gamma_{(j,k)(l,m)}^* = \mathrm{Cov}(Y_j Y_k, Y_l Y_m)$. Written in this form we can understand the Fisher matrix as relating to the covariance between *edge variables* defined as $Z_{(i,j)} = Y_i Y_j - \mathbb{E}[Y_i Y_j]$, where $i, j \in \{1, \ldots, P\}$.

Definition 1. *Incoherence Condition* (Ravikumar 2011) [35]. *Let S denote the set of components relating to true edges in the graph and S^c its compliment. For example, $\boldsymbol{\Gamma}_{SS}^*$ refers to the sub matrix of the Fisher matrix relating to elements in the true graph. The incoherence condition states that there exists some $\alpha \in (0, 1]$ such that*

$$\max_{e \in S^c}\|\boldsymbol{\Gamma}_{eS}^*(\boldsymbol{\Gamma}_{SS}^*)^{-1}\|_1 \leq (1 - \alpha),$$

or in the multivariate Gaussian case: $\max_{e \in S^c}\|\mathbb{E}[Z_e Z_S^\top]\mathbb{E}[Z_S Z_S^\top]^{-1}\|_1 \leq (1 - \alpha)$.

Unlike conventional asymptotic results, in the high-dimensional case one must work in a doubly asymptotic framework, where both P and N tend to infinity. The result below is typical for high-dimensional graph selection problems. For similar related results see; Rothman et al. [36], Ravikumar et al. [34] who also consider a binary Ising model, and Lam et al. [25] who consider a non-convex penalty function.

Theorem 1. *Consistency of ℓ_1 Log-Det Estimation* (Ravikumar 2011) [35].

If Y_i maintains exponential tail functions for rescaled $Y_i/\sqrt{\Sigma_{ii}^*}$, the graph has s true edges, and a sample size of $N = \Omega(d^2 \log P)$, where d is the maximum node degree, then under suitable regularisation conditions the precision matrix is bounded as:

$$\|\hat{\Theta} - \Theta^*\|_F = \mathcal{O}\left(\sqrt{\frac{s + P \log P}{N}}\right), \tag{7}$$

with probability $1 - 1/P^{\tau-2} \to 1$, where $\tau > 2$.

Furthermore, with an additional condition restricting how the smallest element of $\min_{i,j} |\Theta_{i,j}^*|$ scales as a function of (P, d, N) and $N = \Omega(\tau d^2 \log P)$ one obtains a sparsistency result. The log-det problem is model selection consistent $\mathcal{M}(\hat{\Theta}; \Theta^*) := \{\text{sign}(\hat{\Theta}_{ij}) = \text{sign}(\Theta_{ij}^*) \, \forall (i,j) \in E_{\Theta^*}\}$, such that:

$$\mathbb{P}[\mathcal{M}(\hat{\Theta}; \Theta^*)] \geq 1 - 1/P^\tau \to 1. \tag{8}$$

In the above theoretical work the parameter τ reflects the rate of convergence in probability, it effects the appropriate setting of both the regularsation constant λ and sample size required for the claims. A high τ results in high probability claims, but also an increased lower bound on the sample size.

4   Dynamic Graph Models

In this section we extend the static GGM definition to a dynamic setting whereby the joint distribution and graphical model is permitted to change as a function of time. As previously mentioned there are many other forms of *dynamic graphical models*, however, in the interests of space and for clarity of discussion we focus our efforts here on a class of time-varying GGM. In particular we consider different ways in which such graph structure may be permitted to vary over time.

Consider a P-variate time-series data $Y \in \mathbb{R}^{P \times T}$ as before, however, we now permit the generative distribution to be a function of time, i.e.:

$$(Y_1^t, \ldots Y_P^t)^\top \sim \mathcal{N}(\mathbf{0}, \Sigma^t) \quad \text{for } t = 1, \ldots, T. \tag{9}$$

The challenge is now to learn a GGM via the precision matrix $\Theta^t := (\Sigma^t)^{-1}$ for each time point. Clearly such a model is far more flexible than the identically distributed version, instead of $\mathcal{O}(P^2)$ parameters we now have $\mathcal{O}(P^2 T)$. The model is now non-parametric in the sense that potential complexity can scale with the amount of data we have available. Our aim is to harness this additional flexibility to identify potential changes within the graphical models which may shed insight onto dynamics of the data-generating system. In order to gain consistent structure estimation for (9) we must impose some added constraints. Specifically, we discuss methods for imposing different smoothness constraints on the set $\{\boldsymbol{\Sigma}^t\}_{t=1}^T$ in order to track; (1) continuous, (2) edge-wise, and (3) graph-wise changes in the underlying dependency structures.

4.1 Continuous Evolution

Initial work by Zhou et al. [48] focused in the setting where graphs continuously and smoothly evolve over time. Rather than use the discrete parameterisation of Eq. (9) they parameterise the model in rescaled time $u = 0, 1/T, 2/T, \dots, 1$ as:

$$(Y_1^u, \dots, Y_P^u)^\top \sim \mathcal{N}_P(\mathbf{0}, \boldsymbol{\Sigma}(u)). \tag{10}$$

In this model, the covariance (and therefore precision matrix) are assumed to be continuously smooth functions such that there exists constants $C_0 > 0$, C such that $\max_{i,j} \sup_u |\Sigma_{ij}'(u)| \leq C_0$ and $\max_{i,j} \sup_u |\Sigma_{i,j}''(u)| \leq C$ (Fig. 1).

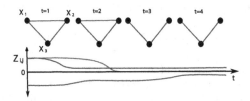

Fig. 1. Example of continuously smooth edge variation in a graphical model.

4.2 Edge-Piecewise Dynamics

There are many situations where we might expect continuous smoothness assumptions to be broken. Recent research [18,23,32] has focused on how one can incorporate different smoothness assumptions when estimating dynamic GGM. Rather than adopt a continuously varying graphical model we now let it be piecewise constant, with changes in structure described at a set of K changepoints $\mathcal{T} = \{\tau_1, \dots, \tau_K\}$, $\tau_i \in \{1, \dots, T\}$. When considering piecewise dynamics, especially in the multivariate setting, there are a variety of smoothness measures that one could adopt. Our discussion here focuses on two broad classes of *edge-wise*, and *graph-wise* smoothness.

  In the edge-wise case, we consider a smoothness relating to the number of jumps or changepoints in the edge structure (i.e. entries in the precision matrix $\boldsymbol{\Theta}^t := (\boldsymbol{\Sigma}^t)^{-1}$). We add the smoothness constraint to Eq. (9), such that:

$$(Y_1^t, \dots Y_P^t)^\top \sim \mathcal{N}(\mathbf{0}, \boldsymbol{\Sigma}^t), \quad \text{such that} \sum_{t=2}^{T-1} \|\boldsymbol{\Theta}^t - \boldsymbol{\Theta}^{t-1}\|_0 = 2K. \tag{11}$$

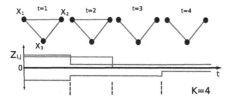 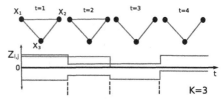

(a) Piecewise-edge variation in a graphical model, multiple edges can change at each time-point but they are counted as separate changepoints.

(b) Graph-wise counting of changepoints, multiple edges can change and still only count as one changepoint.

Fig. 2. Dynamic graphical models with changepoints.

In the above, the ℓ_0 norm counts the number of non-zero elements of the differenced precision matrices, i.e. $\|X\|_0 = |\{X_{i,j} \neq 0 \,\forall i \neq j\}|$. Such a constraint counts changes on each edge of the graphical model separately, hence the factor of 2 accounting for symmetry in the matrices. The works of Ahmed et al. [1] and Monti et al. [32] can be considered in this setting, and to some extent the work of Danaher et al. [10] and Yang et al. [44] who consider smoothing between blocks of observations (Fig. 2a).

4.3   Graph-Piecewise Dynamics

A slightly different variant of the piecewise constant GGM model is to count changepoints not at an edge-wise level, but across the graph and thus covariance/precision matrix as a whole. The joint distribution across data streams is now assumed to be constant between changepoints such that

$$P(Y^t) = P(Y^{t'}) \quad \text{for all } t, t' \in \{\tau_k, \tau_k + 1, \dots, \tau_{k+1}\}, \tag{12}$$

for changepoints $k = 0, \dots, K^3$. If we keep the Gaussian assumption of Eq. (9), then estimation relates to finding a set of $K + 1$ graphical models describing the distribution between changepoints.

Such a definition extends the usual definition of a changepoint [29,45] to multivariate distributions, it is expected that the number of changepoints should be small relative to the total period of measurement, i.e. $K \ll T$ and as such these points may identify *interesting* points in a time-series. We here consider counting non-zero values of a norm over differenced precision matrices:

$$(Y_1^t, \dots Y_P^t)^\top \sim \mathcal{N}(\mathbf{0}, \Sigma^t), \quad \text{such that } \sum_{t=2}^{T} \mathbf{1}(\|\Theta^t - \Theta^{t-1}\|) = K, \tag{13}$$

where $\mathbf{1}(\cdot)$ represents the indicator function. The differences between Eqs. (11) and (13) appear subtle, but correspond to dynamic models with slightly different

---

3 Note: we set the first changepoint (denoted by $k = 0$) at $\tau_0 = 1$ and the last $K + 1$st changepoint is located at $\tau_{K+1} = T$.

properties. In contrast to (11) we note the Eq. (13) only counts one changepoint when multiple edges (off-axis elements of $\Theta_{i,j}$) change together (Fig. 2b). If we impose such a structural constraint across the whole graph we should expect to see more edges change simultaneously for each changepoint. Such a model is studied in several works as a constrained optimisation problem [18,23,37], a Dynamic programming problem [2], and in a Bayesian setting by Xuan et al. [42].

5   Dynamic GGM Estimation

In this section we turn our attention to estimation of dynamic graphical models with the previously discussed smoothness requirements. The techniques here draw on the literature for i.i.d graphical models discussed in Sect. 3, but also on literature for univariate changepoint detection [29,47] and multivariate smoothing [4]. In this section we aim to give a brief overview of past work, and discuss some theoretical results and empirical properties of the different approaches.

For brevity, we omit a detailed discussion of Bayesian approaches to dynamic graph identification, however, the reader is directed to the work of Xuan et al. [42] and Tallih et al. [38] if interested in this direction. Both these works consider a block like model, as in Eq. (13). Xuan et al. [42] suggest an approximate inference scheme where the model space (over graphs) is formed using the graphical lasso on a set of overlapping windows before performing segmentation. Tallih et al. [38] consider a slightly different model, whereby they sample the graph space by introducing a procedure which iteratively adds or removes an edge at a time. Such sampling procedures are effective for small numbers of variables, however, typically these do not scale well to very large problems. For reference, in the static setting one can compare the Bayesian [41] and point estimate [14] versions of graphical lasso.

5.1   Local Kernel/Window Estimation

The continuously varying Gaussian graphical model was first considered by Zhou et al. [48]. To enable temporal sensitivity they suggest to estimate precision matrices through a graphical lasso objective (5), except with the empirical covariance replaced by the localised kernel version:

$$\hat{S}(t) = \sum_s w_{st} y_s y_s^\top / \sum_s w_{st}, \qquad (14)$$

where $w_{st} = K(|s - t|/h_T)$ are weights derived from a symmetric non-negative kernel (typically one may use a box-car/Gaussian function) with bandwidth h_T. The idea is that by replacing $\hat{S}$ with $\hat{S}(t)$ in the graphical lasso problem it is possible to obtain a temporally localized estimate of the graph via $\hat{\Theta}(t)_{\text{GL}}$.

Given the smoothness bounds C, C_0 in Sect. 4.1 on the true covariance/precision matrices Zhou et al. demonstrate that the estimator is consistent, such that estimator risk converges in probability $\mathcal{R}(\hat{\boldsymbol{\Sigma}}(t)) - \mathcal{R}(\boldsymbol{\Sigma}^o(t)) \xrightarrow{P} 0$, even in the dynamic (non-identically distributed) case. The risk here is defined as:

$$\mathcal{R}(\boldsymbol{\Sigma}) = \mathrm{tr}(\boldsymbol{\Sigma}^{-1}\boldsymbol{\Sigma}_*) + \log \det(\boldsymbol{\Sigma}), \tag{15}$$

where $\boldsymbol{\Sigma}_*$ is the true covariance matrix such that $Y \sim \mathcal{N}(\mathbf{0}, \boldsymbol{\Sigma}_*)$. The convergence of covariance matrices $\hat{\boldsymbol{\Sigma}}$ and $\boldsymbol{\Sigma}^o$ refer respectively to the minimiser of the ML risk given by Eq. (3) (with $\hat{\boldsymbol{S}}$ replaced with $\hat{\boldsymbol{S}}(t)$), and the true risk[4] $\boldsymbol{\Sigma}^o = \arg\min_{\boldsymbol{\Sigma} \in S_t} \mathcal{R}(\boldsymbol{\Sigma})$, where the set of possible solutions is given as $S_t = \{\boldsymbol{\Sigma} | \boldsymbol{\Sigma} \succ \mathbf{0}, \|\boldsymbol{\Sigma}^{-1}\|_1 \leq L_t\}$. Zhou et al. also demonstrate consistency in the Frobenius norm, akin to Theorem 1 in the static case. For a sparsistency result with this estimator see the later work of Kolar et al. [22], however, this also requires an additional incoherence condition like Definition 1.

5.2   Regularised Temporal Variation

In Sect. 3 we introduced the M-estimation framework of Eq. (2). One can understand the inference of Zhou et al. [48] under this framework simply through the graphical lasso formulation (5) that we studied in the static case. In this section, we discuss how this framework can be harnessed to estimate structure corresponding to the two classes of edge and graph wise changepoints in the previous sections (Sects. 4.2 and 4.3).

The techniques presented here rely on adding a regularisation term to account for the kind of smoothness we wish to induce in the model. We previously discussed how the addition of an ℓ_1 penalty can induce sparsity in a set of parameters for precision matrix estimation. Work in univariate changepoint analysis, estimation of piecewise constant signals, and non-parametric smoothing, have also utilised this property of the ℓ_1 norm to induce sparsity in the difference between parameters. For example, imagine we have univariate data drawn $Y_t = u_t + \epsilon_t$ such that $\boldsymbol{y}^\top = (Y_1, \ldots, Y_T)$, Harchaoui et al. [19] propose an estimator to recover piecewise u_t of the form:

$$\hat{\boldsymbol{u}} := \arg\min_{\boldsymbol{u} \in \mathbb{R}^T} \frac{1}{T}\|\boldsymbol{y} - \boldsymbol{u}\|_2^2 + \lambda \sum_{i=1}^{T-1} |u_{i+1} - u_i|. \tag{16}$$

If we want to find changepoints in the signal u_t, we just needto find the points where $\hat{\boldsymbol{u}}$ changes. Such an estimator can be understood as a convex relaxation of the hard constraint that we set on the number of changepoints (for example in the edgewise case via Eq. 11). Harchaoui et al. demonstrate the relation between (16) and the relaxed formof Eq. (11) given as:

$$\arg\min_{\boldsymbol{u} \in \mathbb{R}^T} \frac{1}{T}\|\boldsymbol{y} - \boldsymbol{u}\|_2^2, \text{ subject to } \sum_{i=1}^{T-1} |u_{i+1} - u_i| \leq K^* J_{\max}^*, \tag{17}$$

---

[4] The matrix $\boldsymbol{\Sigma}^o$ is known as an *oracle* estimator, as it has access to the ground truth $\boldsymbol{\Sigma}_*$ through the risk function $\mathcal{R}(\cdot)$.

where $J_{\max} = \max_{1 \leq k \leq K^*} |u^*_{\tau_{k+1}} - u^*_{\tau_k}|$ and K^*, u^* respectively denote the true number of changepoints and function. Changepoints are obtained from the consideration of the active set (non-zero differences[5]), such that $\hat{\mathcal{A}} = \{t \in 1, T-1 \mid |\hat{u}_{t+1} - \hat{u}_t| \neq 0\}$. The changepoints themselves are then simply given by the entries in the active set: $\{\hat{\tau}_1, \ldots, \hat{\tau}_{\hat{K}}\} = \hat{\mathcal{A}}$, where $\hat{K} = |\hat{\mathcal{A}}|$ and such that $\hat{\tau}_1 < \ldots < \hat{\tau}_{\hat{K}}$.

Theorem 2. *Consistency of Changepoint Estimation* (Harchaoui 2010) [19].

Given some tail conditions on i.i.d ϵ_t, the distance between changepoints is not toosmall, and the regularisation λ is appropriately set, then the probability of recovering the true changepoints $\{\tau_1^*, \ldots \tau_{K^*}^*\}$ via (17) tends to one asympotically:

$$P(\max_{1 \leq k \leq K^*} |\hat{\tau}_k - \tau_k^*| \leq T\delta_T) \to 1 \quad \text{as } T \to \infty,$$

where δ_T is a non-increasing positive sequence in T.

Edge-Wise Smoothing. The above method for univariate changepoint detection motivates the application to the dynamic graphical modeling setting. In the edge-wise case a popular [1,10,18,32,44] form of smoothing for dynamic graphical models is given by the penalty:

$$R_{\text{IFGL}}(\boldsymbol{\Theta}) = \lambda_1 \sum_{t=1}^T \|\boldsymbol{\Theta}^t\|_1 + \lambda_2 \sum_{t=2}^T \|\boldsymbol{\Theta}^t - \boldsymbol{\Theta}^{t-1}\|_1. \tag{18}$$

We refer to the above as the *Independently Fused Graphical Lasso (IFGL)* penalty. Of particular note is the fact there are two regulariser terms, the second corresponding to λ_2 plays a similar smoothing role to (16), whilst the term associated with λ_1 enforces sparsity on the elements of the precision matrix themselves[6]. To construct an M-estimator, we also need to specify a loss function to go alongside our regulariser, the combination of different loss functions and regularisers can be seen to account for most of the methods currently available for dynamic graph estimation. The most popular choise is the log-det function associated with the Gaussian ML estimator (like in Eq. 3). However, in the dynamic setting, we need to allow for temporal flexibility in the estimation of $\{\boldsymbol{\Theta}^t\}_{t=1}^T$. Corresponding to (9) we construct the negative log-likelihood:

$$L(\boldsymbol{Y}, \{\boldsymbol{\Theta}^t\}_{t=1}^T) = \sum_{t=1}^T \left(-\log\det(\boldsymbol{\Theta}^t) + \text{trace}(\hat{\boldsymbol{S}}^t \boldsymbol{\Theta}^t) \right). \tag{19}$$

Minimising $L(\boldsymbol{Y}, \{\boldsymbol{\Theta}^t\}_{t=1}^T) + R_{\text{IFGL}}(\{\boldsymbol{\Theta}\}_{t=1}^T)$ we find the estimated graph to have properties consistent with an piecewise edge-smooth dynamic graphical model[7].

---

[5] We note that Harcharoui et al. perform their changepoint analysis in a reformulated lasso problem rather than considering directly jumps in $\hat{u}$ as presented here.

[6] In the univariate setting for functional approximation this is analogous to the fused lasso of Tibshirani et al. [40].

[7] If we choose $\hat{\boldsymbol{S}}^t$ to be estimated through a localised kernel as in (14) we obtain the SINGLE estimator of Monti et al. [32], if we use a Dirac delta kernel i.e. $\hat{\boldsymbol{S}}^t = \boldsymbol{y}^\top \boldsymbol{y}/2$

The edge-smooth behavior is borne out of the ℓ_1 smoothing penalty due to its linear separability with respect to the different elements $\theta_{i,j}$ for $i \neq j$. When solving the IFGL problem several works use this separability to enable more efficient optimisation by parralellising the constraint updating in an *Alternating Directed Method of Moments (ADMM)* [18, 32] or *block-coordinate descent* [44] scheme. For more on these optimisation methods in general please see [4, 5, 15, 46].

Graph-Wise Smoothing. Sometimes we have a-priori knowledge that particular variables may change in a grouped manner, that is changepoints across the edges may coincide. Such an assumption coincides with the graph-wise changepoint definition of (13), here we extend the fused estimation with the separable ℓ_1 norm to a non-separable ℓ_2 or Frobenius norm. Our recent work [18] extends the work of Bleakley et al. [4] in the multivariate smoothing setting, to graphical model estimation by introducing the Group-Fused Graphical Lasso penalty:

$$R_{\text{GFGL}}(\boldsymbol{\Theta}) = \lambda_1 \sum_{t=1}^{T} \|\boldsymbol{\Theta}^t\|_1 + \lambda_2 \sum_{t=2}^{T} \|\boldsymbol{\Theta}^t - \boldsymbol{\Theta}^{t-1}\|_F. \tag{20}$$

Such a penalty when associated with the loss in (19) is analysed in the paper [18], in that work the empirical properties of the estimator are compared to that of IFGL. It is demonstrated that both have similar recovery properties for graphical structure. However, when group changepoint structure exists GFGL seems to have an advantage at selecting changepoints. As expected, when using such a grouped penalty the graphs are allowed to change sparsity structure at many edges for each changepoint. A qualitative example of the kind of structure extracted by these two regularisation schemes is provided in the next section.

The study of changepoints effecting groups of edges is also related to the work of Kolar et al. [23] who consider a neighbourhood selection approach. Instead of a log-det problem, changepoint and graph selection is formulated according to a temporally sensitive neighbourhood selection problem, extending the static case given in Eq. 6. Combining a *temporal-difference lasso* regulariser:

$$R_{\text{td}}(\boldsymbol{\beta}) = 2\lambda_1 \sum_{t=1}^{T} \sum_{c \in \backslash a} |\beta_{c,t}| + 2\lambda_2 \sum_{t=1}^{T} \|\beta_{\cdot,t} - \beta_{\cdot,t-1}\|_2, \tag{21}$$

on the node-wise loss $L(\boldsymbol{\beta}) = \sum_{t \in [T]}(y_{t,a} - \sum_{c \in \backslash a} y_{t,c}\beta_{c,t})^2$, it is possible to recover a piecewise structure in $\beta_{c,\cdot}$ from which changepoints $\hat{\tau}_1, \ldots, \hat{\tau}_B$ can be obtained (akin to $\hat{u}$ in Eq. 17). The neighbourhood structure $\boldsymbol{\theta}_a^b$ for blocks $b = 1, \ldots, B = K + 1$ can then be obtained from the values of $\hat{\beta}_{\cdot,t}$ between changepoints. Formally, we construct $\boldsymbol{\theta}_a^b = \hat{\beta}_{\cdot,t}$ for all $t \in [\hat{\tau}_b : \hat{\tau}_{b+1}]$, the neighbourhood estimate for node a is then given by $\hat{E}_a^b := E(\hat{\boldsymbol{\theta}}_a^j) := \{c \in \backslash a | \hat{\theta}_{a,c}^b \neq 0\}$

---

then we recover the IFGL estimator of our previous work [18]. Note: the TESLA approach of Ahmed et al. [1] uses a regulariser term like R_{IFGL} but with a logistic loss function for binary variables.

Theorem 3. *Dynamic Graph Consistency* (Kolar et al. 2012) [23].

Subject to the eigenvalues of the true covariance matrices (between change-points), the ℓ_2 norm of the difference between blocks being bounded by a constant, and the precision coefficient sizes being bounded away from zero, then the block boundaries (or changepoints) are recoverable as in Theorem 2.

Additionally, given the incoherence condition in Definition 1 and all the blocks b are detected, then the neighbourhoods are recoverable:

$$P(E^b = E(\hat{\boldsymbol{\theta}}^b)) \stackrel{T\to\infty}{\to} 1, \quad \text{for all } b = 1,\ldots,K+1.$$

The proof of the above (see [23]) follows from analysis of the optimality conditions to the temporal difference regularised neighbourhood selection procedure, and extends the techniques of Harchaoui et al. [19].

6   Example Application

In this section we give a brief example of some dynamic graphical structure learning techniques applied to a financial time-series dataset. The dataset in question tracks the value-weighted monthly returns for seven industry classes over the period 1926–2015, aportion of this data-set[8] is also analysed in previous work [38]. Here we perform analysis on the log-returns of the portfolios centered by their empirical mean over the whole time-series (see Fig. 3). Analysis by Carvalho et al. suggested that sparse GGM's when used in portfolio construction can potentially lead to increased profit [8]. Methods that can shed insight on the dependency of such risks are obviously of great interest in the financial services sector. For the purposes of this paper, we limit our analysis to give a qualitative overview of the different methods performance. We do not consider setting hyper-parameters or tuning parameters in any kind of *optimal* sense. This could potentially be achieved through cross-validation or in-sample complexity measures such as BIC/AIC, we note Monti et al. and Kolar et al. [23,32] suggest a BIC approach, however, it is not well understood how to choose an appropriate number of *degrees of freedom* $\hat{s}$ to use in the dynamic equivalent of Eq. (4). Rather than specify an optimal value of (λ_1, λ_2), we examine how estimated changepoint and graphical structure emerges as a function of these tuning parameters. The smoothing parameter is of specific interest as it leads to the emergence of new changepoint positions (see Fig. 4). In this sense we are using our estimators like a structural sieve, a small λ_2 lets us keep small scale structure, a large λ_2 lets us only keep the larger scale structure.

In this example, we set $\lambda_1 = 0.2$ for both IFGL and GFGL and then examine the estimated structure across a range of λ_2. The results presented in Fig. 4 demonstrate some of the subtle differences between the edge-wise and graph-wise changepoint methods that motivate IFGL and GFGL. From the upper plots looking at the changepoint positions we notice that for a give λ_2 IFGL estimates

---

[8] The data can be obtained from Ken French's website http://mba.tuck.dartmouth.edu/pages/faculty/ken.french/data_library.html.

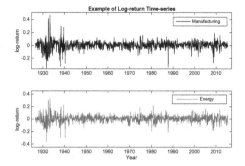

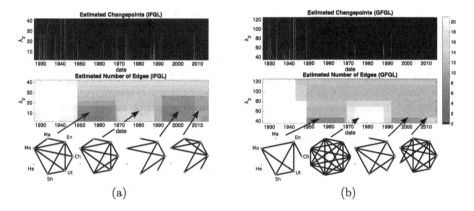

Fig. 3. Example of log-returns for manufacturing and energy asset classes. Right: Overview of economic classes for stocks under analysis.

Fig. 4. Overview of changepoints and edges estimated as a function of smoothness for (a) IFGL, and (b) GFGL.

a higher number of distinct changepoints (i.e. at different time-points) than GFGL. This is due to edges being able to vary independently, the smoothness measure can be decoupled across the graph (corresponding to the definition in Sect. 4.2) as the ℓ_1 penalty is separable. Where the GFGL estimator produces a sparsity pattern that adjusts from very dense to very sparse in adjacent blocks IFGL takes more changepoints and time to achieve such a graph wide change in structure.

It is interesting to note that there are also some strong similarities between the outputs. For example, both methods detect changepoints around 1970, and 1990, and around financial crises in 2008. In addition to this, the start of the second world war in 1940 appears to be detected, with another large change estimated in 1948. The period from 1926–1948 appears completely connected in the estimated models. This may be due to an estimated increase in volatility within this time-period, another study might consider penalising the partial correlation rather than partial covariance, this may help gauge out such sensitivity to marginal variation.

7   Conclusion

Dynamic graphical models are an emerging topic of study within the convergent disciplines of statistics, computer science, and signal processing. They have greater flexibility to model time-variation of dependencies than their static counterparts. The estimated structure of such models can help provide insight within complex dynamical systems.

There is a very wide class of time-varying component models [20] (of which dynamic GGM lie within) that aim to model not just contemporaneous relationships, but also the evolution of trends in a data-set [27,47], for example what happens when we let $\mu \neq 0$ and potentially depend on time. Merging these two classes of model to allow time-variation of trends and variation under a graphical model is a potential topic for future research. A further direction of interest, and one that is pervasive across high-dimensional modeling, is attempting to identify some level confidence to extracted structure, rather than simply report a point estimate. Although not covered here, Bayesian methods such as [27,38,42] can intuitively achieve this through analysis of posterior credibility intervals, however, efficient inference in such models remains a challenge. An alternative approach here is to test for changepoint structure within a graph, however, when one considers changes across the graph a multiple testing problem is formed, one must also consider the high-dimensional nature of such problems. Potentially some insight on such challenges can be gained from work in detecting changepoints in mean structure, for example the recent work of Enikeeva et al. [12].

In this paper we have presented a quick overview of some methods, results, and challenges involved in estimating dynamic graphical models and specifically a sub-class of dynamic Gaussian graphical models [2,10,18,22,23,32,37,48]. We propose that available methods in dynamic graphical modeling can be categorised by different assumptions on how the models change over time either producing continuously smooth, or piecewise constant models. Although several estimators have been proposed for these models, theoretical results considering the consistency of parameter estimation and the graph support are rare [22,23,37]. As in the static case, to obtain sparsistency results these estimators require rather strict incoherence assumptions (Definition 1) to be placed on the underlying graph. Whilst these may not be met in practice, it is of interest to be aware of these limitations. In a pragmatic setting the ability to interpret parameters (i.e. networks) inferred from dynamic GGM provide a powerful tool for exploratory data analysis of complex dynamic systems.

References

1. Ahmed, A., Xing, E.P.: Recovering time-varying networks of dependencies in social and biological studies. Proc. Natl. Acad. Sci. USA **106**, 11878–11883 (2009)
2. Angelosante, D., Giannakis, G.B.: Sparse graphical modeling of piecewise-stationary time series. In: International Conference on Acoustics, Speech and Signal Processing (ICASSP) (2011)

3. Banerjee, O., Ghaoui, L.E., D'Aspremont, A.: Model selection through sparse maximum likelihood estimation for multivariate Gaussian or binary data. J. Mach. Learn. **9**, 485–516 (2008)
4. Bleakley, K., Vert, J.P.: The group fused lasso for multiple change-point detection. Technical report HAL-00602121 (2011)
5. Boyd, S., Parikh, N., Chu, E.: Distributed optimization and statistical learning via the alternating direction method of multipliers. Found. Trends Mach. Learn. **3**, 1–122 (2011)
6. Boyd, S., Vandenberghe, L.: Convex Optimization. Cambridge University Press (2004)
7. Cai, T., Liu, W., Luo X.: A constrained L1 minimization approach to sparse precision matrix estimation. J. Am. Stat. Assoc. (2011)
8. Carvalho, C.M., West, M.: Dynamic matrix-variate graphical models matrix-variate dynamic linear models. Bayesian Anal. **2**, 69–97 (2007)
9. Cowell, R.G., Verrall, R.J., Yoon, Y.K.: Modelling operational risk with Bayesian networks. J. Risk Insur. **74**, 795–827 (2007)
10. Danaher, P., Wang, P., Witten, D.M.: The joint graphical lasso for inverse covariance estimation across multiple classes. J. R. Stat. Soc. Ser. B (Stat. Methodol.) **76**, 373–397 (2013)
11. Drton, M., Perlman, M.D.: Model selection for Gaussian concentration graphs. Biometrika **51**, 591–602 (2004)
12. Enikeeva, F., Harchaoui, Z.: High-dimensional change-point detection with sparse alternatives (2013). arXiv:1312.1900
13. Foygel, R., Drton, M.: Extended Bayesian information criteria for Gaussian graphical models. In: Advances in Neural Information Processing Systems, vol. 23 (2010)
14. Friedman, J., Hastie, T., Tibshirani, R.: Sparse inverse covariance estimation with the graphical lasso. Biostatistics **9**, 432–441 (2008)
15. Friedman, J., Hastie, T., Tibshirani, R.: Applications of the lasso and grouped lasso to the estimation of sparse graphical models (2010)
16. Gibberd, A.J., Nelson, J.D.B.: High dimensional changepoint detection with a dynamic graphical lasso. In: International Conference on Acoustics, Speech and Signal Processing (ICASSP) (2014)
17. Gibberd, A.J., Nelson, J.D.B.: Estimating multiresolution dependency graphs within the stationary wavelet framework. In: IEEE Global Conference on Signal and Information Processing (GlobalSIP) (2015)
18. Gibberd, A.J., Nelson, J.D.B.: Regularized estimation of piecewise constant Gaussian graphical models: the group-fused graphical lasso (2015). arXiv:1512.06171
19. Harchaoui, Z., Lévy-Leduc, C.: Multiple change-point estimation with a total variation penalty. J. Am. Stat. Assoc. **105**, 1480–1493 (2010)
20. Hastie, T., Tibshirani, R.: Varying-coefficient models. J. R. Stat. Soc. B **55**, 757–796 (1993)
21. Jordan, M.I.: Graphical models. Stat. Sci. **19**, 140–155 (2004)
22. Kolar, M., Xing, E.P: On time varying undirected graphs. In: Proceedings of the International Conference on Artificial Intelligence and Statistics (AISTATS) (2011)
23. Kolar, M., Xing, E.P.: Estimating networks with jumps. Electron. J. Stat. **6**, 2069–2106 (2012)
24. Lafferty, J., Liu, H., Wasserman, L.: Sparse nonparametric graphical models. Stat. Sci. **27**, 519–537 (2012)
25. Lam, C., Fan, J.: Sparsistency and rates of convergence in large covariance matrix estimation. Ann. Stat. **37**, 4254–4278 (2009)

26. Lauritzen, S.L.: Graphical Models. Oxford University Press, Oxford (1996)
27. Lèbre, S., Becq, J., Devaux, F., Stumpf, M.P.H., Lelandais, G.: Statistical inference of the time-varying structure of gene-regulation networks. BMC Syst. Biol. **4**, 130 (2010)
28. Lee, J.D., Hastie, T.J.: Learning the structure of mixed graphical models. J. Comput. Graph. Stat. **24**, 230–253 (2015)
29. Little, M.A., Jones, N.S.: Generalized methods and solvers for noise removal from piecewise constant signals. I. background theory. Proc. Math. Phys. Eng. Sci./R. Soc. 467, 3088–3114 (2011)
30. Loh, P., Wainwright, M.J.: Structure estimation for discrete graphical models: generalized covariance matrices and their inverses. In: Neural Information Processing Systems (NIPS) (2012)
31. Meinshausen, N., Bühlmann, P.: High-dimensional graphs and variable selection with the lasso. Ann. Stat. **34**, 1436–1462 (2006)
32. Monti, R.P., Hellyer, P., Sharp, D., Leech, R., Anagnostopoulos, C., Montana, G.: Estimating time-varying brain connectivity networks from functional MRI time series. NeuroImage **103**, 427–443 (2014)
33. Negahban, S.N., Ravikumar, P., Wainwright, M.J., Yu, B.: A unified framework for high-dimensional analysis of M-estimators with decomposable regularizers. Stat. Sci. **27**, 538–557 (2012)
34. Ravikumar, P., Wainwright, M.J., Lafferty, J.D.: High-dimensional Ising model selection using l_1-regularized logistic regression. Ann. Stat. **38**, 1287–1319 (2010)
35. Ravikumar, P., Wainwright, M.J., Raskutti, G., Yu, B.: High-dimensional covariance estimation by minimizing l_1-penalized log-determinant divergence. Electron. J. Stat. **5**, 935–980 (2011)
36. Rothman, A.J., Bickel, P.J., Levina, E., Zhu, J.: Sparse permutation invariant covariance estimation. Electron. J. Stat. **2**, 494–515 (2008)
37. Roy, S., Atchad, Y., Michailidis, G.: Change-point estimation in high-dimensional Markov random field models (2015). arXiv:1405.6176v2
38. Talih, M., Hengarter, N.: Structural learning with time-varying components: tracking the cross-section of financial time series. J. R. Stat. Soc. B **67**, 321–341 (2005)
39. Tibshirani, R.: Regression shrinkage and selection via the lasso. J. R. Stat. Soc. Ser. B (Stat. Methodol.) **73**, 273–282 (1996)
40. Tibshirani, R., Saunders, M., Rosset, S., Zhu, J., Knight, K.: Sparsity, smoothness via the fused lasso. J. R. Stat. Soc. Ser. B (Stat. Methodol.) **67**, 91–108 (2005)
41. Wang, H.: Bayesian graphical lasso models and efficient posterior computation. Bayesian Anal. **7**, 867–886 (2012)
42. Xuan, X., Murphy, K.: Modeling changing dependency structure in multivariate time series. In: International Conference on Machine Learning (2007)
43. Yang, E., Ravikumar, P.K., Allen, G.I., Liu, Z.: On Poisson graphical models. In: Advances in Neural Information Processing Systems (NIPS) (2013)
44. Yang, S., Pan, Z., Shen, X., Wonka, P., Ye, J.: Fused multiple graphical lasso (2012)
45. Yi-Ching, Y., Au, S.T.: Least-squares estimation of a step function. Indian J. Stat. Ser. A **51**, 370–381 (1989)
46. Yuan, X.: Alternating direction method for covariance selection models. J. Sci. Comput. **51**, 261–273 (2011)
47. Zhang, B., Geng, J., Lai, L.: Multiple change-points estimation in linear regression models via sparse group lasso. IEEE Trans. Signal Process. **63**, 2209–2224 (2014)
48. Zhou, S., Lafferty, J., Wasserman, L.: Time varying undirected graphs. Mach. Learn. **80**, 295–319 (2010)

Metric Learning for Time Series Comparison

A Multi-modal Metric Learning Framework for Time Series kNN Classification

Cao-Tri Do[1,2,3], Ahlame Douzal-Chouakria[2(✉)], Sylvain Marié[1], and Michèle Rombaut[3]

[1] Schneider Electric, Paris, France
[2] LIG, University of Grenoble Alpes, Grenoble, France
ahlame.douzal@imag.fr
[3] GIPSA-Lab, University of Grenoble Alpes, Grenoble, France

Abstract. This work proposes a temporal and frequential metric learning framework for a time series nearest neighbor classification. For that, time series are embedded into a pairwise space where a combination function is learned based on a maximum margin optimization process. A wide range of experiments are conducted to evaluate the ability of the learned metric on time series kNN classification.

Keywords: Metric learning · Time series · kNN · Classification · Spectral metrics

1 Introduction

Nowadays, time series are present in various fields, particularly in emerging applications such as sensor networks, smart buildings, social media networks or Internet of Things [1–4]. Due to their temporal and frequential nature, time series constitute complex data to analyze by standard machine learning approaches [5].

In order to classify such challenging data, distance features must be used to bring closer time series of identical classes and separate those of different classes. Temporal data may be compared on their values. The most frequently used value-based metrics are the Euclidean distance and the Dynamic Time Warping DTW to cope with delays [6,7]. They can also be compared on their dynamics and frequential characteristics [8,9]. Promising approaches aims to learn the Mahalanobis distance or kernel function for a specific classifier [10,11]. Other work investigate the representation paradigm by representating objects in a dissimilarity space where dissimilarity combinations and metric learning are investigated [12,13]. The idea in this paper is to combine several basic metrics into a single discriminative metric for a kNN classifier. Our work follows a general metric learning approach driven by nearest neighbors (Weinberger and Saul [10]), in particular we extend the work of Do et al. in [14] to temporal and frequential characteristics. The main idea is to embed pairs of time series in a space whose dimensions are basic temporal and frequential metrics, where a combination function is learned based on a large margin optimization process.

© Springer International Publishing Switzerland 2016
A. Douzal-Chouakria et al. (Eds.): AALTD 2015, LNAI 9785, pp. 131–143, 2016.
DOI: 10.1007/978-3-319-44412-3_9

The rest of the paper is organized as follows. Section 2 recalls briefly the major metrics for time series. In Sect. 3, we present the proposed metric learning approach. Finally, Sect. 4 presents the experiments conducted and discusses the results obtained.

The main contributions of the paper are:

- Propose a new temporal and frequential metric learning framework for time series nearest neighbors classification,
- Learn a combination metric involving amplitude, behavior and frequential characteristics,
- Conduct large experimentations to study the ability of learned metric.

2   Time Series Metrics

Let $\mathbf{x}_i = (x_{i1}, ..., x_{iT})$ and $\mathbf{x}_j = (x_{j1}, ..., x_{jT})$ be two time series of time length T. Time series metrics fall at least within three main categories. The first one concerns value-based metrics, where time series are compared according to their values regardless of their behaviors. Among these metrics are the Euclidean distance, the Minkowski distance and the Mahalanobis distance [7]. In our work, we consider the Euclidean distance as our value-based metric d_V:

$$d_V(\mathbf{x}_i, \mathbf{x}_j) = \sqrt{\sum_{t=1}^{T}(x_{it} - x_{jt})^2} \tag{1}$$

The second category, commonly used in signal processing, relies on comparing time series based on their frequential properties (e.g. Fourier Transform, Wavelet, Mel-Frequency Cepstral Coefficients [15–17]). In our work, we limit the frequential comparison to Discrete Fourier Transform [18], but other frequential properties can be used as well. Thus, for time series comparison, first the time series $\mathbf{x}_i$ are transformed into their Fourier representation $\tilde{\mathbf{x}}_i = [\tilde{x}_{i1}, ..., \tilde{x}_{iF}]$, with $\tilde{x}_{if}$ the complex component at frequential index f. The Euclidean distance is then used between their respective complex number modules $\tilde{x}_{if}$, noted $|\tilde{x}_{if}|$:

$$d_F(\mathbf{x}_i, \mathbf{x}_j) = \sqrt{\sum_{f=1}^{F}(|\tilde{x}_{if}| - |\tilde{x}_{jf}|)^2} \tag{2}$$

Note that times series of similar frequential characteristics may have distinctive global behavior.

A third category of metrics aims to compare time series based on their shape or behavior despite the range of their amplitudes. By time series of similar behavior, it is generally intended that for all temporal window $[t, t']$, they increase or decrease simultaneously with the same growth rate. On the contrary, they are said of opposite behavior if for all $[t, t']$, if one time series increases, the other one decreases and (vise-versa) with the same growth rate in absolute value.

Finally, time series are considered of different behaviors if they are not similar, nor opposite. Many applications refer to the Pearson correlation [19,20] for behavior comparison. A generalization of the Pearson correlation is introduced in [8]:

$$cort_r(\mathbf{x}_i, \mathbf{x}_j) = \frac{\sum\limits_{t,t'} (x_{it} - x_{it'})(x_{jt} - x_{jt'})}{\sqrt{\sum\limits_{t,t'} (x_{it} - x_{it'})^2} \sqrt{\sum\limits_{t,t'} (x_{jt} - x_{jt'})^2}} \tag{3}$$

where $|t - t'| \leq r, r \in [1, ..., T-1]$ being a parameter that can be learned or fixed a priori. The optimal value of r is noise dependent. For $r = T - 1$, Eq. 3 leads to the Pearson correlation. As $cort_r$ is a similarity measure, it is transformed into a dissimilarity measure:

$$d_B(\mathbf{x}_i, \mathbf{x}_j) = \frac{1 - cort_r(\mathbf{x}_i, \mathbf{x}_j)}{2} \tag{4}$$

In most classification problems, it is not known a priori if time series of a same class exhibit same characteristics based on their amplitude, behavior or frequential components alone. In some cases, several components (value, behavior and/or frequential) may be implied. Some propositions show the benefit of involving them through a combination function. They mainly combine value-(d_V) and behavior-based (d_B) metrics together to obtain a single metric used after that in a classifier. The most classical combination functions combine through linear and geometric functions:

$$D_{Lin}(\mathbf{x}_i, \mathbf{x}_j) = \alpha d_B(\mathbf{x}_i, \mathbf{x}_j) + (1 - \alpha)d_V(\mathbf{x}_i, \mathbf{x}_j) \tag{5}$$

$$D_{Geom}(\mathbf{x}_i, \mathbf{x}_j) = (d_B(\mathbf{x}_i, \mathbf{x}_j))^{\alpha}(d_V(\mathbf{x}_i, \mathbf{x}_j))^{1-\alpha} \tag{6}$$

where $\alpha \in [0; 1]$ defines the trade-off between the value d_V and the behavior d_B components, and is thus application dependent. In general, it is learned through a grid search procedure. Without being restrictive, these combinations can be extended to take into account more basic metrics.

More specific work on d_V and $cort$ propose to combine the two components through a sigmoid combination function [8]:

$$D_{Sig}(\mathbf{x}_i, \mathbf{x}_j) = \frac{2d_V(\mathbf{x}_i, \mathbf{x}_j)}{1 + \exp(\alpha cort_r(\mathbf{x}_i, \mathbf{x}_j))} \tag{7}$$

where α is a parameter that defines the compromise between behavior and amplitude components. When α is fixed to 0, the metric only includes the value proximity component. For $\alpha \geq 6$, the metric completely includes the behavior proximity component as a penalizer of the value component.

Figures 1 and 2 illustrate the value of the resulting combined metrics (D_{Lin}, D_{Geom} and D_{Sig}) in 2-dimensional space using contour plots for different values of the trade-off α. For small value of α ($\alpha = 0$), the three metrics only includes d_V. For high value of α ($\alpha = 1$), D_{Lin} and D_{Geom} only includes d_B. For $\alpha = 6$,

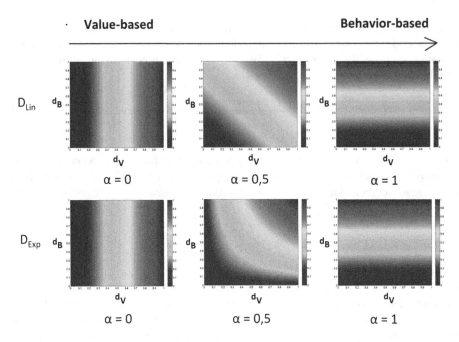

Fig. 1. Contour plot of the resulting combined metrics: D_{Lin} (1st line) and D_{Geom} (2nd line) for different values of α ($\alpha = 0; 0.5; 1$). The first and second dimensions are respectively the amplitude-based metric d_V and the behavior-based metric d_B.

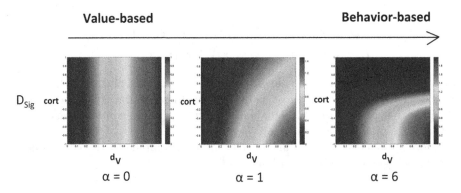

Fig. 2. Contour plot of the resulting combined metrics D_{Sig} for different values of α ($\alpha = 0; 1; 6$). The first and second dimensions are respectively the amplitude-based metric d_V and the temporal correlation $cort_r$.

D_{Sig} doesn't include completely $cort$. Note that for these combinations, to ensure comparable range between the two components (value d_V and behavior d_B), a Z-normalization of their log distributions is used.

Standard propositions for D_{Lin}, D_{Geom} and D_{Sig} combine both d_V and d_B components [8]. The functions D_{Lin} and D_{Geom} could be easily extended to more metrics (*e.g.*, frequential-based metrics d_F) but this requires additional parameters to optimize. In [8], the function D_{Sig} is restricted to two components and has been studied for a combination of d_V and d_B. In the following, for simplification purpose, we restrict D_{Lin}, D_{Geom} and D_{Sig} to a combination of d_V and d_B components.

It can be observed that these combinations are fixed and defined independently from the analysis task at hand. Moreover, in the case of D_{Sig}, only two variables are taking into account in these combined metrics and the component $cort_r$ can be seen as a penalizing factor of d_V. It doesn't represent a real compromise between value and behavior components. Finally, by adding metrics, the grid search to find the best parameters can become time consuming.

Our aim in this paper is to propose a new framework to learn a combined temporal metric D that combines several (more than 2) basic metrics for a robust kNN. In the next section, we first recall the metric learning framework proposed by Weinberger and Saul [10]. Then, we detail how this work is extended to learn a metric from multiple basic metrics.

3   Temporal and Frequential Metric Learning for a Large Margin kNN

Let $\mathbf{X} = \{\mathbf{x}_i, y_i\}_{i=1}^N$ be a set of N static vector samples, $\mathbf{x}_i \in \mathbb{R}^p$, p being the number of descriptive features and y_i the class labels. Weinberger and Saul proposed in [10] an approach to learn a dissimilarity metric D for a large margin kNN. It is based on two intuitions: first, each training sample $\mathbf{x}_i$ should have the same label y_i as its k nearest neighbors; second, training samples with different labels should be widely separated. For this, they introduced the concept of target for each training sample $\mathbf{x}_i$. Target neighbors of $\mathbf{x}_i$, noted $j \rightsquigarrow i$, are the k closest $\mathbf{x}_j$ of the same class ($y_j = y_i$). The target neighborhood is defined with respect to an initial metric D_{ini}. The aim is to learn a metric D that pulls the targets and pushes away the ones of different class as illustrated in Fig. 3. Note that as opposed to the initial approach [10], we propose to push away all samples of different class - not only those (initially called "impostors") invading the target space. We note these samples "undesired" samples.

Let $d_1, ..., d_h..., d_p$ be p given dissimilarity metrics that allow to compare samples. The computation of a metric always takes into account a pair of samples. Therefore, we use the pairwise representation introduced in Do et al. [14]. In this space illustrated in Fig. 4, a vector $\mathbf{x}_{ij}$ represents a pair of samples $(\mathbf{x}_i, \mathbf{x}_j)$ described by the p basics metrics d_h: $\mathbf{x}_{ij} = [d_1(\mathbf{x}_i, \mathbf{x}_j), ..., d_p(\mathbf{x}_i, \mathbf{x}_j)]^T$. If $\mathbf{x}_{ij} = \mathbf{0}$ then $\mathbf{x}_j$ is identical to $\mathbf{x}_i$ according to all metrics d_h.

A combination function D of the metrics d_h can be seen as a function in this space. We propose in the following to use a linear combination of d_h: $D_{\mathbf{w}}(\mathbf{x}_i, \mathbf{x}_j) = \sum_h w_h d_h(\mathbf{x}_i, \mathbf{x}_j)$. Its pairwise notation is :

$$D_{\mathbf{w}}(\mathbf{x}_{ij}) = \mathbf{w}^T \mathbf{x}_{ij} \tag{8}$$

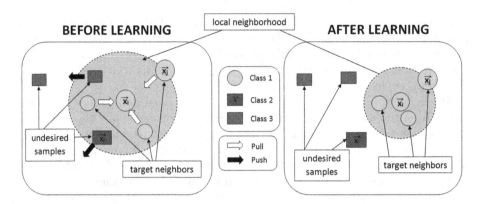

Fig. 3. Pushed and pulled samples in the $k = 3$ target neighborhood of $\mathbf{x}_i$ before (left) and after (right) learning. The pushed (vs. pulled) samples are indicated by a white (vs. black) arrows (Weinberger and Saul [10]).

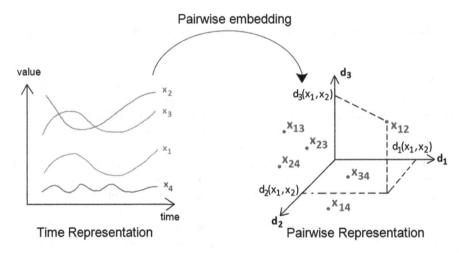

Fig. 4. Example of embedding of 4 time series $\mathbf{x}_1, \ldots, \mathbf{x}_4$ from the temporal space (left) into the pairwise space (right). In this example, a pair of time series $(\mathbf{x}_1, \mathbf{x}_2)$ is projected into the pairwise space as a vector $\mathbf{x}_{12}$ described by $p = 3$ basic metrics: $\mathbf{x}_{12} = [d_1(\mathbf{x}_1, \mathbf{x}_2), d_2(\mathbf{x}_1, \mathbf{x}_2), d_3(\mathbf{x}_1, \mathbf{x}_2)]^T$.

The main steps of the proposed approach to learn the metric, detailed hereafter, can be summarized as follows:

1. Embed each pair $(\mathbf{x}_i, \mathbf{x}_j)$ into the pairwise space $\mathbb{R}^p$.
2. Scale the data within the pairwise space.
3. Define for each $\mathbf{x}_i$ its targets.
4. Scale the neighborhood of each $\mathbf{x}_i$.
5. Learn the combined metric $D_{\mathbf{w}}$.

Data Scaling. The scale between the p basic metrics d_h can be different. Thus, a normalization is performed to scale the data within the pairwise space and ensure comparable ranges for the p basic metrics d_h. In our experiment, we use dissimilarity measures with values in $[0; +\infty[$. Therefore, we propose to Z-normalize their log distributions.

Target Set. For each $\mathbf{x}_i$, we define its target neighbors as the k nearest neighbors $\mathbf{x}_j$ ($j \leadsto i$) of the same class according to an initial metric D_{ini}. In this paper, we choose a L_2-norm of the pairwise space as the initial metric ($D_{ini} = \sqrt{\sum_h d_h^2}$). Other metrics could be chosen. We emphasize that target neighbors are fixed *a priori* (at the first step) and do not change during the learning process.

Neighborhood Scaling. In real datasets, local neighborhoods can have very different scales. To make the target neighborhood spreads comparable, we propose for each $\mathbf{x}_i$ to scale its neighborhood vectors $\mathbf{x}_{ij}$ such that the norm of the farthest target according to the initial metric D_{ini} is 1 (in our case, the L_2-norm). (Fig. 5). Before scaling, local margins between target samples and undesired samples have very different scales. The smallest neighborhood has the smallest margin, and therefore would have a greater influence on a margin-based optimisation solver. After scaling, both margins are comparable, which would ensure equal impact on the solver.

Learning the Combined Metric $D_\mathbf{w}$. Let $\{\mathbf{x}_{ij}, y_{ij}\}_{i,j=1}^N$ be the training set with $y_{ij} = -1$ if $y_j = y_i$ and $+1$ otherwise. Our objective is to define a metric $D_\mathbf{w}$ as a linear combination of the p basic metrics (Eq. 8). In the pairwise space, the metric $D_\mathbf{w}$ should:

- **pull** all pairs $\mathbf{x}_{ij}$ of same labels ($y_{ij} = -1$) representing a k nearest neighbor pair ($j \leadsto i$) - noted "target pairs".
- **push** away from the origin all pairs $\mathbf{x}_{il}$ of different classes ($y_{il} = +1$) - noted "undesired pairs".

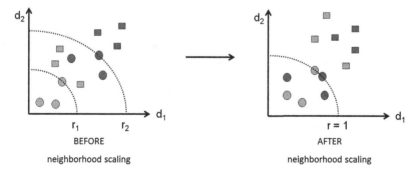

Fig. 5. Effect of neighborhood scaling before (left) and after (right) on the neighborhood of two time series $\mathbf{x}_1$ (green) and $\mathbf{x}_2$ (red). Circle represent target pairs $\mathbf{x}_{ij}$ with $y_j = y_i$ and square represents pairs of time series $\mathbf{x}_{il}$ of different labels $y_l \neq y_i$ for $k = 3$ neighbors. (Color figure online)

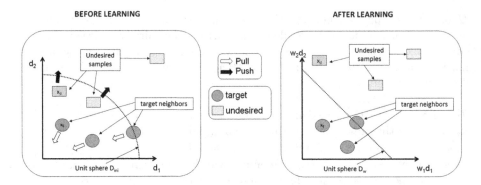

Fig. 6. Geometric representation of the adaptation of metric learning problem in the pairwise space for a $k = 3$ target neighborhood of $\mathbf{x}_i$ with initial metric D_{ini} as a L_2-norm. Before learning (left), undesired samples $\mathbf{x}_l$ invade the unitary sphere, that is the targets $\mathbf{x}_j$ perimeter (after radius normalization). The aim of metric learning is to push $\mathbf{x}_{il}$ away (black arrows), and pull $\mathbf{x}_{ij}$ towards the origin (white arrows).

Figure 6 illustrates our idea. For each time series $\mathbf{x}_i$, we build the set of target pairs $\mathbf{x}_{ij}$ ($j \rightsquigarrow i$) and the set of undesired pairs $\mathbf{x}_{il}$ ($y_{il} = +1$). Then, we optimise the weight vector $\mathbf{w}$ so that the pairs $\mathbf{x}_{ij}$ are pulled to the origin and the pairs $\mathbf{x}_{il}$ are pushed from the origin. Learning $D_{\mathbf{w}}$ for a large margin kNN classifier can be formalized as the following optimization problem:

$$\min_{\mathbf{w},\xi} \underbrace{\sum_{i,j\rightsquigarrow i} D_{\mathbf{w}}(\mathbf{x}_{ij})}_{pull} + C \underbrace{\sum_{i,j\rightsquigarrow i,l} \frac{1+y_{il}}{2}\xi_{ijl}}_{push}$$

$$\text{s.t. } \forall j \rightsquigarrow i, y_l \neq y_i,$$
$$D_{\mathbf{w}}(\mathbf{x}_{il}) - D_{\mathbf{w}}(\mathbf{x}_{ij}) \geq 1 - \xi_{ijl} \qquad (9)$$
$$\xi_{ijl} \geq 0$$
$$w_h > 0 \ \forall h = 1...p$$

where ξ_{ijl} are slack variables and C is a trade-off between the push and pull term. The parameter C can be learned through a cross-validation and grid search procedure.

To ensure that $D_{\mathbf{w}}$ is a valid metric, we set $w_h \geq 0$ for all $h = 1...p$. The "pull" term can be written:

$$\sum_{i,j\rightsquigarrow i} D_{\mathbf{w}}(\mathbf{x}_{ij}) = \sum_{i,j\rightsquigarrow i} \mathbf{w}^T \mathbf{x}_{ij}$$
$$= \mathbf{w}^T \left(\sum_{i,j\rightsquigarrow i} \mathbf{x}_{ij} \right)$$
$$= (N.k).\mathbf{w}^T \bar{\mathbf{x}}_{ij}$$

where N is the number of time series. Note that the pull term is a L_1-Mahalanobis norm weighted by the average target sample $\bar{\mathbf{x}}_{ij} = \sum\limits_{i,j \rightsquigarrow i} \mathbf{x}_{ij}/(N.k)$.
Therefore, it behaves like a L_1-norm in the optimization problem.

Testing Phase. Let $\mathbf{x}_{test}$ be a new sample to classify and $\mathbf{x}_{test,i}$ $(i = 1, ..., N)$ the corresponding vectors into the pairwise embedding space. We first normalize all pairs $\mathbf{x}_{test,i}$ according to the *Data Scaling* step. Then $\mathbf{x}_{test}$ is classified based on a standard kNN and $D_{\mathbf{w}}$.

4 Experiments

In this section, we compare kNN classifier performances for several metrics on reference time series datasets [21–24] described in Table 1. The proposed algorithm has been designed for a general kNN classifier. In this work, to compare with the reference results in [7,21], the experiments are conducted with the same protocols as in Do et al. [14]: k is set to 1; train and test set are given a priori. For computation time reasons, small datasets with short time series are retained. As the test sets are given, each experiment is only run once.

In this experimentation, we consider basic metrics d_V, d_F and d_B. Then, we learn a combined metric $D_{\mathbf{w}}$ according to the procedure described in Sect. 3.

Table 1. Dataset description giving the number of classes (Nb. Class), the number of time series for the training (Nb. Train) and the testing (Nb. Test) sets, and the length of each time series (TS length).

Dataset	Nb. Class	Nb. Train	Nb. Test	TS length
SonyAIBO	2	20	601	70
MoteStrain	2	20	1252	84
GunPoint	2	50	150	150
PowerCons	2	73	292	144
ECG5Days	2	23	861	136
SonyAIBOII	2	27	953	65
Coffee	2	28	28	286
BME	3	48	102	128
UMD	3	46	92	150
ECG200	2	100	100	96
Beef	5	30	30	470
DiatomSizeReduction	4	16	306	345
FaceFour	4	24	88	350
Lighting-2	2	60	61	637
Lighting-7	7	70	73	319
OliveOil	4	30	30	570

Table 2. Parameter ranges

Method	Parameter	Parameter range
d_{B_r}	r	$[1, 2, 3, , ..., T]$
D_{Lin}, D_{Geom}	α	$[0, 0.1, 0.2, ..., 1]$
D_{Sig}	α	$[0, 1, 2, ..., 6]$
D_2, D_3	C	$[10^{-4}, 10^{-3}, ..., 10^8]$

First, two basic temporal metrics are considered (d_V and d_B), the resulting learned metric $D_{\mathbf{w}}$ is noted D_2 (as in Do et al. [14]). Second, we consider a combination between temporal and frequential metrics in D_3 (d_V, d_B and d_F). Cplex library [25] has been used to solve the optimization problem in Eq. 9. We learn the optimal parameter values of these metrics by minimizing a leave-one out cross-validation criterion. Thirdly, to benchmark the learned metric D_2 and D_3, three a priori combinations of d_V and d_B are also evaluated : D_{Lin}, D_{Geom} and D_{Sig}. In order for these combinations to perform well, data is first scaled according to the procedure described in Sect. 3.

As the training dataset sizes are small, we propose a hierarchical error criterion:

1. Minimize the kNN error rate
2. Minimize $\frac{d_{intra}}{d_{inter}}$ if several parameter values obtain the minimum kNN error.

where d_{intra} and d_{inter} stand respectively for the mean of all intraclass and interclass distances according to the metric at hand. Table 2 gives the range of the grid search considered for the parameters. In the following, we consider only the raw series and don't align them using a Dynamic Time Warping DTW algorithm for example. For all reported results (Table 3), the best one is indexed with a star and the ones significantly similar from the best one (Z-test at 10 % risk) are in bold [26].

From Table 3, if we compare only value- and/or behavior-based metrics (d_V, d_B, the 3 a priori combined metrics and D_2), many observations arises. First, D_{Geom} is the best overall combined metric, but it rarely had better results than the best of basic metrics except for Beef where the improvement is non-significant. Second, D_{Sig} is almost as good as D_{Geom} on average, but it performs better than the best of basic metrics on a couple databases (SonyAIBO where the result is significative; DiatomSizeReduction where the result is non-significative). Thirdly, learning a combination of d_V and d_B with our proposed method D_2 reaches similar performance than a priori combinations on most datasets or achieves better results (PowerCons). However, it never outperforms basic metrics. According to the Z-test, note that D_2 always achieves statistically equivalent or better results compared to D_{Lin}.

Adding metrics in $D_{\mathbf{w}}$, here frequency-based metric d_F, improves its performance on some datasets (FaceFour - non significative, Lighting-2 - non significative, Lighting 7 - non significative). For the learned metric D_2 and D_3,

Table 3. Error rate of 1NN classifier for different metrics without DTW. D_2 is computed using d_V and d_B; D_3 uses the 3 basic metrics (d_V, d_B, d_F). The metric with the best performance for each dataset is indicated by a star (*) and the ones with equivalent performances are in bold.

Dataset	Metrics							
	Basic			A priori combined			Learned combined	
	d_V	d_B	d_F	D_{Lin}	D_{Geom}	D_{Sig}	D_2	D_3
SonyAIBO	0.305	0.308	**0.258***	0.308	0.308	0.293	0.308	**0.259**
MoteStrain	**0.121***	0.264	0.278	0.217	0.197	0.231	0.210	0.277
GunPoint	0.087	0.113	**0.027***	0.113	0.113	0.093	0.113	0.073
PowerCons	**0.370**	0.445	**0.315***	0.445	0.431	0.421	0.384	0.410
ECG5Days	0.203	0.153	**0.006***	0.153	0.153	0.184	0.153	0.156
SonyAIBOII	0.141	0.142	**0.128***	0.142	0.142	0.144	0.142	0.142
Coffee	0.250	**0***	0.357	**0***	**0***	0.071	**0***	**0***
BME	0.128	**0.059***	0.412	**0.059***	**0.059***	**0.059***	**0.059***	0.078
UMD	**0.185***	0.207	0.315	0.207	0.207	0.207	0.207	**0.185***
ECG200	0.120	**0.070***	0.166	**0.070***	**0.070***	**0.070***	**0.070***	**0.070***
Beef	**0.467**	**0.300**	0.500	0.367	**0.267***	0.467	**0.300**	0.367
DiatomSizeReduction	0.065	0.075	0.069	0.065	0.065	**0.062***	0.075	0.075
FaceFour	0.216	0.216	0.239	0.216	0.216	0.216	0.216	**0.205***
Lighting-2	0.246	0.246	**0.148***	0.246	0.246	0.246	0.246	0.213
Lighting-7	0.425	0.411	0.315	0.425	0.411	0.424	0.411	**0.288***
OliveOil	**0.133***	**0.133***	0.200	**0.133***	**0.133***	**0.133***	**0.133***	**0.133***

the L_1 regularization allows to reveal the most discriminative metrics implied in the combination. For example, for some datasets (*e.g.*, Coffee, BME, Beef), the learned metric D_2 or D_3 achieve similar results compared to the basic metrics. Compared to the a priori combinations, the proposed framework allows to add more metrics without adding new parameters to optimize. In this work, the proposition is restricted to a linear combination of the metric $D_{\mathbf{w}}$. For a non-linear combination, the considered optimization problem is similar to an SVM problem. For that, the optimization problem is transformed into a dual form involving only dot products that allows the use of kernel trick.

Compared to the basic metrics, the proposed framework allows to test many basic metrics without testing them one by one. It brings a new framework to learn combined metrics in general and for time series in particular. However, as the results are not always improved by adding new metrics (*e.g.*, MoteStrain, PowerCons, ECG5Days), we believe that some improvements can be made. Firstly, like the framework of Weinberger and Saul [10], the proposed method is sensitive to the choice of the initial metric (L_2-norm). Secondly, in this work, we choose to consider for the "undesired pairs" all the pairs $\mathbf{x}_{il}$ of different classes. As the objective is to learn a metric for a kNN classifier, this may imply more constraints in the optimization problem than what is needed. Thirdly, to ensure the positivity of the metric, additional constraints of the $\mathbf{w}$ is added but with the risk to exclude optimal solutions for D.

5 Conclusion

For nearest neighbor time series classification, we propose to learn a metric as a combination of temporal and frequential metrics based on a large margin optimization process. The new approach allows us to extend combination functions to many metrics without having to cope with additional parameters in grid search and without testing every basic metric independently to retain the best one.

For future work, we are looking for some improvements. **First**, the choice of the initial metric is crucial. It has been set here as the L_2-norm of the pairwise space but a different metric could provide better *target* sets. Otherwise, using an iterative procedure (reusing $D_{\mathbf{w}}$ to generate new *target* sets and learn $D_{\mathbf{w}}$ again) could be another solution. **Second**, we note that the L_1-norm on the "pull" term leads to sparcity. Changing it into a L_2-norm could allow for non-sparse solutions and also extend the approach to non-linear metric combination functions thanks to the Kernel trick. **Finally**, we could extend this framework to multivariate, regression or clustering problems.

References

1. Najmeddine, H., Jay, A., Marechal, P., Marié, S.: Mesures de similarité pour l'aide à l'analyse des données énergétiques de bâtiments. In: RFIA (2012)
2. Yin, J., Gaber, M.: Clustering distributed time series in sensor networks. In: ICDM (2008)
3. Nguyen, L., Wu, P., Chan, W., Peng, W., Zhang, Y.: Predicting collective sentiment dynamics from time-series social media. In: WISDOM (2012)
4. Díaz, M., Juan, G., Lucas, O., Ryuga, A.: Big data on the internet of things: an example for the E-health. In: IMIS (2012)
5. Fu, T.C.: A review on time series data mining. Eng. Appl. Artif. Intell. **24**, 164–181 (2011)
6. Sakoe, H., Chiba, S.: Dynamic programming algorithm optimization for spoken word recognition. IEEE Trans. Acoust. Speech Signal Process. **26**, 43–49 (1978)
7. Ding, H., Trajcevski, G., Scheuermann, P.: Querying, mining of time series data: experimental comparison of representations and distance measures. In: VLDB (2008)
8. Douzal-Chouakria, A., Amblard, C.: Classification trees for time series. Pattern Recogn. J. **45**, 1076–1091 (2011)
9. Lhermitte, S., Verbesselt, J., Verstraeten, W.W., Coppin, P.: A comparison of time series similarity measures for classification and change detection of ecosystem dynamics. Remote Sens. Environ. **115**, 3129–3152 (2011)
10. Weinberger, K., Saul, L.: Distance metric learning for large margin nearest neighbor classification. J. Mach. Learn. Res. **10**, 207–244 (2009)
11. Gönen, M., Alpaydin, E.: Multiple kernel learning algorithms. J. Mach. Learn. Res. **12**, 2211–2268 (2011)
12. Duin, R.P.W., Bicego, M., Orozco-Alzate, M., Kim, S.-W., Loog, M.: Metric learning in dissimilarity space for improved nearest neighbor performance. In: Fränti, P., Brown, G., Loog, M., Escolano, F., Pelillo, M. (eds.) S+SSPR 2014. LNCS, vol. 8621, pp. 183–192. Springer, Heidelberg (2014)

13. Ibba, A., Duin, R., Lee, W.: A study on combining sets of differently measured dissimilarities. In: Proceedings International Conference on Pattern Recognition, pp. 3360–3363 (2010)
14. Do, C., Douzal-Chouakria, A., Marié, S., Rombaut, M.: Multiple metric learning for large margin kNN classification of time series. In: Proceedings of the 23rd European Signal Processing Conference (EUSIPCO), Nice, France, pp. 2391–2395 (2015)
15. Sahidullah, M., Saha, G.: Design, analysis and experimental evaluation of block based transformation in MFCC computation for speaker recognition. Speech Commun. **54**(4), 543–565 (2012)
16. Torrence, C., Compo, G.P.: A practical guide to wavelet analysis. Bull. Am. Meteorol. Soc. **79**(1), 61–78 (1998)
17. Brigham, E.O., Morrow, R.E.: The fast fourier transform. Spectr. IEEE **4**(12), 63–70 (1967)
18. Lhermitte, S., Verbesselt, J., Verstraeten, W.W., Coppin, P.: A comparison of time series similarity measures for classification and change detection of ecosystem dynamics. Remote Sens. Environ. **115**(12), 3129–3152 (2011)
19. Abraham, Z., Tan, P.N.: An integrated framework for simultaneous classification and regression of time-series data. In: ACM SIGKDD (2010)
20. Benesty, J., Chen, J., Huang, Y., Cohen, I.: Pearson correlation coefficient. In: Cohen, I., Huang, Y., Chen, J., Benesty, J. (eds.) Noise Reduction in Speech Processing. Springer Topics in Signal Processing, vol. 2, pp. 1–4. Springer, Heidelberg (2009)
21. Keogh, E., Zhu, Q., Hu, B., Hao, Y., Xi, X., Wei, L., Ratanamahatana, C.A.: The UCR time series classification/clustering homepage (2011)
22. Bache, K., Lichman, M.: UCI Machine Learning Repository (2013). http://archive.ics.uci.edu/ml
23. LIG-AMA Machine Learning Datasets Repository (2014)
24. Frambourg, C., Douzal-Chouakria, A., Gaussier, E.: Learning multiple temporal matching for time series classification. In: Tucker, A., Höppner, F., Siebes, A., Swift, S. (eds.) IDA 2013. LNCS, vol. 8207, pp. 198–209. Springer, Heidelberg (2013)
25. IBM Cplex. http://www-01.ibm.com/software/commerce/optimization/cplex-optimizer/
26. Dietterich, T.: Approximate statistical tests for comparing supervised classification learning algorithms. Neural Comput. **10**, 1895–1923 (1997)

A Comparison of Progressive and Iterative Centroid Estimation Approaches Under Time Warp

Saeid Soheily-Khah[✉], Ahlame Douzal-Chouakria, and Eric Gaussier

Université Grenoble Alpes, CNRS - LIG/AMA, Grenoble, France
{Saeid.Soheily,Ahlame.Douzal,Eric.Gaussier}@image.fr

Abstract. Estimating the centroid of a set of time series under time warp is a major topic for many temporal data mining applications, as summarization a set of time series, prototype extraction or clustering. The task is challenging as the estimation of centroid of time series faces the problem of multiple temporal alignments. This work compares the major progressive and iterative centroid estimation methods, under the dynamic time warping, which currently is the most relevant similarity measure in this context.

Keywords: Centroid estimation · Multiple temporal alignment · Dynamic time warping · Time series

1 Introduction

Time series centroid estimation is a major issue for many temporal data analysis and mining applications. Estimating the centroid of a set of time series under time warp however faces the tricky multiple temporal alignment problem [1–4]. Temporal warping alignment of time series has been an active research topic in many scientific disciplines. To estimate the centroid of two time series under temporal metrics, as the dynamic time warping [5–7], one standard way is to embed the time series into a new Euclidean space defined by their temporal warping alignment. In this space, the centroid can be estimated as the average of the linked elements. The problem becomes more complex where the number of time series is more than two, as one needs to determine a multiple alignment that links simultaneously all the time series on their commonly shared elements.

A first manner to determine a multiple alignment is to search, by dynamic programming, the optimal path within an N-dimensional grid that crosses the N time series. The complexity of this approach nevertheless prevents its use, as it constitutes an NP-complete problem with a complexity of $O(T^N)$ that increases exponentially with the number of time series N and the time series length T. A second way, that characterizes progressive approaches, is based on combining progressively pairs of time series centroids to estimate the global centroid. Such progressive approaches may suffer from the error propagation problem through the set of pairwise centroid combinations. The third approach

© Springer International Publishing Switzerland 2016
A. Douzal-Chouakria et al. (Eds.): AALTD 2015, LNAI 9785, pp. 144–156, 2016.
DOI: 10.1007/978-3-319-44412-3_10

is iterative. It works similarly to the progressive approach but reduces the error propagation by repeatedly refining the centroid and realigning it to the initial time series.

The main contribution of this work is to present some major progressive and iterative approaches for time series centroid estimation, prior to present their characteristics. It also reviews an extensive comparison between the approaches through public real and synthetic datasets. To the best of our knowledge, such a comparison has never been conducted before.

The remainder of the paper is organized as follows: In the next section, different related progressive and iterative approaches are presented. Section 3 presents the experiments conducted for comparison purposes and discuss the results obtained. Lastly, Sect. 4 concludes the paper.

2 Progressive and Iterative Approaches

The progressive and iterative approaches for time series centroid estimation are mainly derived from the multiple sequence alignment methods to address the challenging problem of aligning more than two time series [8–11]. To estimate the centroid of more than two time series, several heuristic approaches have been proposed. Here, we review some major progressive and iterative approaches for time series averaging under the dynamic time warping.

2.1 Progressive Approaches

NonLinear Alignment and Averaging Filters (NLAAF). In the past decades, many averaging methods have been introduced, but only a few of them have been adapted to time series averaging, clustering and mining. For instance, Gupta et al. [12], proposed a time series averaging method based on a tournament scheme, called *"NonLinear Alignment and Averaging Filters* (NLAAF)*"*. First, pairs of time series are selected randomly, and then aligned according to the dynamic time warping. That way, $(N/2)$ averaged sequences are created. The same process is iterated on the centroids estimated, until one sequence is obtained as a global centroid. In this approach, the averaging method between two time series is applied $(N-1)$ times, as illustrated in Fig. 1, where $\mathbf{c}(\mathbf{x}_i, \mathbf{x}_j)$ refers to the estimated centroid of time series $\mathbf{x}_i$ and $\mathbf{x}_j$.

In NLAAF, each element of a centroid is computed as the mean of each linked elements in the DTW alignment. The main drawback of NLAAF approach lies in the growth of its resulting length, because each use of averaging method can almost double the length of the average sequence. As classical datasets comprise hundreds of time series, with each one including hundreds of data points, simply storing the resulting average may be impossible. This length problem is moreover worsened by the complexity of DTW, that grows bi-linearly with the lengths of the sequences. That is why NLAAF is generally used in conjunction with a process reducing the length of the average, unfortunately leading to information loss and unsatisfactory approximation. Additionally, the average strongly depends on the random selection of sequences and different choices lead to different results.

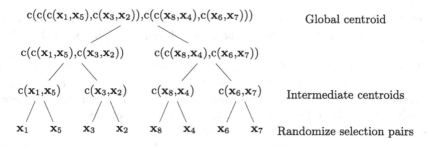

$c(c(c(\mathbf{x}_1,\mathbf{x}_5),c(\mathbf{x}_3,\mathbf{x}_2)),c(c(\mathbf{x}_8,\mathbf{x}_4),c(\mathbf{x}_6,\mathbf{x}_7)))$ Global centroid

$c(c(\mathbf{x}_1,\mathbf{x}_5),c(\mathbf{x}_3,\mathbf{x}_2))$ $c(c(\mathbf{x}_8,\mathbf{x}_4),c(\mathbf{x}_6,\mathbf{x}_7))$

$c(\mathbf{x}_1,\mathbf{x}_5)$ $c(\mathbf{x}_3,\mathbf{x}_2)$ $c(\mathbf{x}_8,\mathbf{x}_4)$ $c(\mathbf{x}_6,\mathbf{x}_7)$ Intermediate centroids

$\mathbf{x}_1$ $\mathbf{x}_5$ $\mathbf{x}_3$ $\mathbf{x}_2$ $\mathbf{x}_8$ $\mathbf{x}_4$ $\mathbf{x}_6$ $\mathbf{x}_7$ Randomize selection pairs

Fig. 1. Centroid estimation by random pairwise centroid combination.

Prioritized Shape Averaging (PSA). To avoid the bias induced by random selection, Niennattrakul et al. among others [8,16,17] proposed a framework of shape averaging called *"Prioritized Shape Averaging* (PSA)*"* based on hierarchical clustering. The pairwise time series centering is guided by the dendrogram obtained through hierarchical clustering strategy.

The PSA uses hierarchical clustering as a way to identify priorities between time series. In particular, to estimate a global centroid, the set is first clustered using the agglomerative clustering to get a hierarchical relationship among the whole time series. The simple or complete linkage is considered in general to fasten the dendrogram build, where almost the average linkage or centroids are the best-performed methods. Subsequently, the pairwise time series centroids are combined respectively to their clustering order in the dendrogram. Each parent node is averaged in a bottom-up manner using a weighted DTW averaging. Therefore, the most similar time series are averaged first. Note that the weight of an averaged sequence is calculated from the number of time series upon which the averaged sequence is formed. Initially, all time series have the same weight of one.

Figure 2 describes an example of averaging six sample time series using PSA. According to the dendrogram, first the time series $\mathbf{x}_2$ and $\mathbf{x}_3$ are averaged.

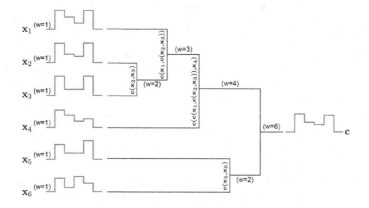

Fig. 2. Example of six time series sequence averaging using PSA

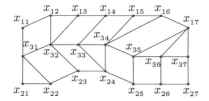

	1	2	...	7
$\mathbf{x_1}$	x_{11}	x_{12}, x_{13}	...	x_{17}
$\mathbf{x_2}$	x_{21}, x_{22}	x_{23}	...	x_{27}
$\mathbf{x_3}$	x_{31}	x_{32}	...	x_{37}
$\mathbf{c}$	$\mathrm{avg}(x_{11}, x_{21}, x_{22}, x_{31})$	$\mathrm{avg}(x_{12}, x_{13}, x_{23}, x_{32})$	...	$\mathrm{avg}(x_{17}, x_{27}, x_{37})$

Fig. 3. Centroid estimation based on a reference time series. The DTW is performed between $\mathbf{x_1}$, $\mathbf{x_2}$ and the reference time series $\mathbf{x_3}$ (left). $\mathbf{x_1}$ and $\mathbf{x_2}$ are embedded in the space defined by $\mathbf{x_3}$ (right) where the centroid is estimated, and 'avg' is the standard mean function.

The average sequence denoted by $\mathbf{c}(\mathbf{x_2}, \mathbf{x_3})$, has the weight of two. The intermediate centroid $\mathbf{c}(\mathbf{x_1}, \mathbf{c}(\mathbf{x_2}, \mathbf{x_3}))$ is then computed by averaging the time series $\mathbf{x_1}$ and the average sequence $\mathbf{c}(\mathbf{x_2}, \mathbf{x_3})$. The intermediate centroid $\mathbf{c}(\mathbf{x_1}, \mathbf{c}(\mathbf{x_2}, \mathbf{x_3}))$ will have the weight of three, since the time series sequences $\mathbf{x_1}$ and $\mathbf{c}(\mathbf{x_2}, \mathbf{x_3})$ have weight of one and two, respectively. The process goes on till one obtains a global centroid.

Although this hierarchical averaging method aims to remove the bias induced by random selection, growth length of the average sequence remains a problem. Furthermore, local averaging strategies like NLAAF or PSA may let an initial approximation error propagate throughout the averaging process. If averaging process has to be repeated (e.g., during k-means iterations), the effects may dramatically alter the quality of the result. This is why a global approach is desirable, where time series would be averaged all together, with no sensitivity to their order of consideration.

Cross-Word Reference Template (CWRT). A direct manner to estimate the centroid is proposed in Abdulla et al. [1], where a dynamic time warping between each time series and a reference one, generally the time series medoid, is first performed. Each time series is then described in the representation space defined by the reference medoid by resampling, stretching and shortening operations, as in Fig. 3. Finally the global centroid is computed by averaging the time-aligned time series across each point. The method is called "*Cross-Words Reference Template* (CWRT)".

The global estimated centroid has the same length as the medoid, and the result does not depend on the order in which time series are processed.

2.2   Iterative Approaches

Dtw Barycenter Averaging (DBA). Petitjean et al. [3] proposed a global averaging method, called "*Dtw Barycenter Averaging* (DBA)". The method consists in iteratively refining an initially average sequence, in order to minimize its distance to the set of time series. The aim is to minimize the sum of squared DTW distances from the average sequence to the set of time series. Technically,

DBA works in two steps for each refinement. First, computing DTW between each time series and the temporary average sequence, and secondly, updating each element of the average sequence with the barycenter of the elements aligned to it during the first step. In a nutshell, the DBA under temporal warping is a global approach that can average a set of time series all together. The global estimated centroid has the same length as the initial average sequence, and like CWRT, the result is not depending on the order in which time series are processed. However the time complexity of DBA is smaller than NLAAF and PSA [3], but the time complexity problem remains.

Weighted DTW Averaging (WDTW). To circumvent the tricky multiple temporal alignments and the above mentioned limitations, we proposed a tractable and fast centroid estimation that captures both global and local temporal features under weighted time warp measures [20]. It formalizes the multiple time series averaging problem as an optimization problem and propose a solution yielding a local optimum.

For that, we propose to estimate both the time series centroid $\mathbf{c}$ and the weight vector $\mathbf{w}$ that measures the representativeness of the centroid's regions. In addition, we introduce a weighted warping function $f(w_t)$ that guides the learned alignments according to the importance of the centroid elements to capture the shared global and local temporal features.

Let $\mathbf{X} = \{\mathbf{x}_1, \mathbf{x}_2, \ldots, \mathbf{x}_N\}$ be a set of time series, and WDTW the weighted dissimilarity between $\mathbf{x}_i$ and the weighted centroid $(\mathbf{c}, \mathbf{w})$. The averaging problem, as formalized in [20], is defined as:

$$\underset{\mathbf{c}, \, \mathbf{w}}{\operatorname{argmin}} \sum_{i=1}^{N} \mathrm{WDTW}(\mathbf{x}_i, (\mathbf{c}, \mathbf{w}))$$

with

$$\mathrm{WDTW}(\mathbf{x}, (\mathbf{c}, \mathbf{w})) = \min_{\pi \in \mathcal{A}} \underbrace{\frac{1}{|\pi|} \sum_{(t', t) \in \pi} f(w_t) \, \varphi(x_{t'}, c_t)}_{C(\pi)}$$

where $f : (0, 1] \to \mathbb{R}^+$ is a non-increasing function (e.g. $f(w_t) = w_t^{-\alpha}$) and $\varphi : \mathbb{R} \times \mathbb{R} \to \mathbb{R}^+$ is a positive, real-valued, dissimilarity function. The cost function C computes the sum of the weighted dissimilarities φ between $\mathbf{x}$ and $(\mathbf{c}, \mathbf{w})$ through the alignment π. When the weights are uniform (or f is a constant function) and when φ is the Euclidean distance, corresponds to the well known Dynamic Time Warping (DTW) [5, 7].

The problem given above, can be solved by computing the partial derivatives of Lagrangian with respect to $\mathbf{c}$ to 0 and solving for $\mathbf{c}$, and with respect to $\mathbf{w}$ to 0 and solving for $\mathbf{w}$, described more in details in [20].

Let us summarize the main characteristics of the above approaches. In both NLAAF and PSA, the length of the global centroid increases with the number of time series to average, inducing an increase of the space and time complexity that is particularly critical under the DTW. The length of the centroids estimated by CWRT, DBA and WDTW averaging is however the same as the reference time series length. Furthermore, all the progressive approaches as well as DBA method are heuristic, with no guarantee of optimality. Even, if the provided approximations are accurate for globally similar time series, they are in general poor for time series that share local characteristics with distinctive global behaviors. In this view, WDTW is a tractable fast and accurate averaging method that captures both global and local temporal features, as shown in [20].

3   Experimental Study

The experiments are conducted to compare the above approaches on classes of time series composing various datasets. The datasets can be divided into two categories. The first one is composed of time series that have similar global behavior within the classes, where the time series of the second category may have distinct global behavior, while sharing local characteristics [19]. For the comparison, the induced inertia reduction rate and the required run time are evaluated as well as the qualitative comparison of the centroids obtained by a visualization. In the following, we first describe the datasets used, then specify the validation process and discuss the obtained results.

3.1   Data Description

The experiments are first carried out on four well known public datasets CBF, CC, DIGITS and CHARACTER TRAJ. [14,15]. These data define a favorable case for the averaging task as time series behave similarly within the classes, as illustrated in Fig. 4.

We then consider more complex datasets: BME[1], UMD (see Footnote 1) [19], SPIRAL [4], NOISED SPIRAL (see Footnote 1) and CONSSEASON [14]. They are composed of time series that behave differently within the same classes while sharing several local characteristics.

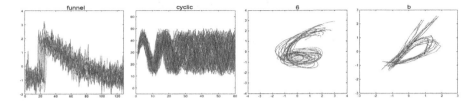

Fig. 4. The time series behaviors with the classes "Funnel", "Cyclic", "6" and "b" of the datasets CBF, CC, DIGITS and CHARACTER TRAJ., respectively

---

[1] http://ama.liglab.fr/douzal/data.

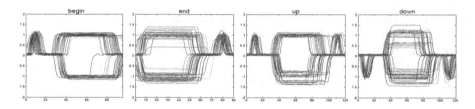

Fig. 5. The time series behaviors with the classes "Begin" and "End" of the dataset BME (left), "Up" and "Down" of the dataset UMD (right)

BME includes two challenging classes BEGIN and END (Fig. 5-left), which characterized by a small bell arising at the initial and final period respectively. The overall behavior may be different depending on whether the large bell is pointing upward or downward. UMD introduces more complexity with the classes UP and DOWN (Fig. 5-right) characterized by a small bell that may occur at different time stamps.

The SPIRAL data, proposed in [18], consists of 3-D spatio-temporal time series (2-D spatial and 1-D temporal) generated from latent time series:

$$\mathbf{X}_i = \begin{bmatrix} \mathbf{U}_i^T(\mathbf{Z} + \mathbf{b}_i \mathbf{1}_l^T)\mathbf{M}_i \\ \mathbf{e}_i^T \end{bmatrix} \in \mathbb{R}^{3*n_i}$$

where the canonical time series $\mathbf{Z} \in \mathbb{R}^{2*l}$ is a curve in two dimensions (x, y). $\mathbf{U}_i \in \mathbb{R}^{2*2}$ and $\mathbf{b}_i \in \mathbb{R}^2$ are randomly generated projection matrix and translation vector respectively. The binary matrix $\mathbf{M}_i \in \{0,1\}^{l*n_i}$ is generated by randomly choosing $n_i \leq l$ columns from $\mathbf{I}_l$ for temporal distortion. The spatial dimension $\mathbf{e}_i \in \mathbb{R}^{n_i}$ is generated with zero-mean Gaussian noise. The latent time series $\mathbf{Z}$ and three generated time series are visualized in Fig. 6.

SPIRAL2 extends SPIRAL data to more challenging time series that are highly noisy and globally behave differently while sharing a three dimensional latent time series that may appear randomly at different time stamps. The latent time series $\mathbf{Z}$ and three generated time series are visualized in Fig. 7.

Finally, CONSSEASON data provides the electric power consumption recorded in a personal home over almost one year. CONSSEASON is composed of time series distributed in two season classes (*Warm* and *Cold*) depending on whether the

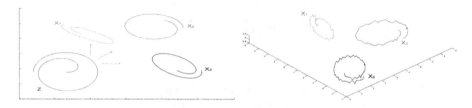

Fig. 6. Latent curve Z and three induced instances X_1, X_2, X_3 without noise (left), and with noise e_i (right) - SPIRAL dataset

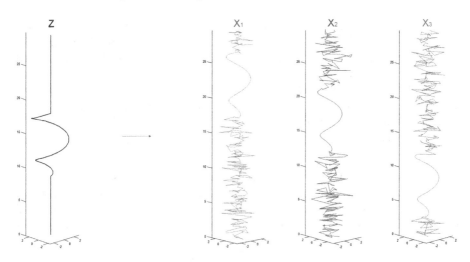

Fig. 7. Latent curve Z and 3 induced instances X_1, X_2, X_3 sharing local characteristics for the SPIRAL2 dataset

Table 1. Data description

DATASET	NB. CLASS	NB. TS.	NB. ATT.	TS. LENGTH	TYPE
CBF	3	930	1	128	GLOBAL
CC	6	600	1	60	
DIGITS	10	220	2	85	
CHARACTER TRAJ.	20	200	3	20	
BME	3	150	1	90	LOCAL
UMD	3	150	1	121	
SPIRAL	1	50	3	95	
NOISED SPIRAL	1	50	3	300	
CONSSEASON	2	365	1	144	

power consumption is recorded during the warm (from April to September) or cold (from October to March) season. Note that the electric power consumption profiles differ markedly within classes.

Table 1 indicates for each data set: the number of classes it includes (NB. CLASS), the number of instances (NB. TS.), the number of attributes (NB. ATT.), the time series length (TS. LENGTH) and the global or local nature of similarity within the classes (TYPE).

3.2 Validation Process

The five mentioned methods NLAAF, PSA, CWRT, DBA and WDTW described in Sect. 2 are compared together. The performances of these approaches are evaluated through the centroid estimation of each class of the above described datasets. Particularly, the efficiency of each approach is measured through: (a) the reduction rate of the inertia criterion; the initial inertia being evaluated around the time series medoid that minimizes the distances to the rest of time series and (b) the space and time complexity. The results reported hereafter are averages of 10 repetitions of the corresponding algorithms. Finally for all reported results, the one which is significantly different from the rest (two-sided t-test at 5 % risk) is indicated in bold.

Inertia Reduction Rate. Time series averaging approaches are used to estimate centroid of the time series classes described above, then the inertia w.r.t. the centroids is measured. Lower is the inertia higher representative is the extracted centroid. Table 2, gives the obtained inertia reduction rates (IRR), averaged per dataset, as:

$$IRR = 1 - \frac{\sum_{i=1}^{N} D(\mathbf{x}_i, \mathbf{c})}{\sum_{i=1}^{N} D(\mathbf{x}_i, \mathbf{m})}$$

where $\mathbf{x}_1, ..., \mathbf{x}_N$ are the set of time series, D is the distance metric, $\mathbf{c}$ is the determined centroid and $\mathbf{m}$ the initial medoid. The alternative of a centroid is a medoid. Medoid is a time series in a set that minimizes sum of the distances to all other time series within the same set. Note that, we use the medoid in the criteria defined above to make the results comparable. In the case, we compare the obtained centroid of each method with a specific time series in the set (i.e. medoid) as its alternative one. Table 2 shows that the WDTW provides the highest IRR for the most datasets, followed by DBA and PSA. Notice that, the results presented by PSA is obtained through the centroid linkage, which outperformed the other linkage (e.g. simple linkage, complete linkage), mostly. Some negative rates observed indicate an inertia increase.

Table 2. The mean of inertia reduction rate (in %) and standard deviations ($\pm\sigma$)

DATASET	NLAAF	PSA	CWRT	DBA	WDTW
CBF	$8.3^{\pm4.0}$	12.3	$-61.3^{\pm9.1}$	$32.1^{\pm1.4}$	$\mathbf{82.6^{\pm1.8}}$
CC	$9.8^{\pm6.6}$	28.6	$6.8^{\pm5.0}$	$34.2^{\pm0.9}$	$\mathbf{70.5^{\pm0.7}}$
DIGITS	$26.1^{\pm7.2}$	$\mathbf{79.5}$	$\mathbf{77.6^{\pm2.4}}$	$\mathbf{82.2^{\pm1.7}}$	$\mathbf{87.6^{\pm1.3}}$
CHARACTER TRAJ.	$67.1^{\pm8.6}$	$\mathbf{87.7}$	$\mathbf{85.2^{\pm5.1}}$	$\mathbf{90.6^{\pm2.3}}$	$\mathbf{93.1^{\pm2.0}}$
BME	$34.9^{\pm5.4}$	43.1	$-11.8^{\pm9.2}$	$59.4^{\pm2.7}$	$\mathbf{91.2^{\pm3.1}}$
UMD	$25.6^{\pm9.7}$	51.1	$-56.2^{\pm9.4}$	$48.8^{\pm1.9}$	$\mathbf{78.5^{\pm1.5}}$
SPIRAL	$\mathbf{59.8^{\pm2.5}}$	$\mathbf{64.4}$	$64.2^{\pm1.1}$	$65.8^{\pm1.1}$	$\mathbf{72.8^{\pm0.9}}$
NOISED SPIRAL	$61.4^{\pm4.2}$	66.3	$9.3^{\pm14.7}$	$9.8^{\pm3.2}$	$\mathbf{98.9^{\pm0.4}}$
CONSSEASON	$\mathbf{84.1^{\pm3.2}}$	70.5	$4.6^{\pm12.7}$	$21.4^{\pm1.6}$	$\mathbf{95.5^{\pm1.7}}$

Table 3. Comparison of Time/Space complexity

DATASET	NLAAF		PSA		DBA		WDTW	
	LENGTH	TIME	LENGTH	TIME	LENGTH	TIME(NB-IT.)	LENGTH	TIME(NB-IT.)
CBF	8283	392.32	35042	9999.89	128	42.91(30)	128	**33.42**(25)
CC	992	**4.15**	1677	12.75	60	6.46(40)	60	**3.91**(20)
DIGITS	313	**0.52**	530	1.09	85	**0.51**(15)	85	**0.47**(10)
CHAR. TRAJ.	33	0.06	29	0.06	20	**0.03**(10)	20	**0.02**(05)
BME	2027	5.46	2781	11.92	90	3.93(30)	90	**3.04**(15)
UMD	2729	10.32	4280	28.87	121	4.75(30)	121	**3.43**(15)
SPIRAL	660	1.62	1122	3.33	95	1.19(10)	95	**0.83**(05)
NOISED SPIRAL	1699	**16.13**	9030	269.93	300	34.84(25)	300	**15.74**(10)
CONSSEASON	5741	77.10	32706	3680.81	144	29.79(35)	144	**21.85**(20)

Time and Space Complexity. In Table 3 the studied approaches are compared w.r.t their space and time complexity. Are reported the length of the extracted centroid (LENGTH), the time consumption in seconds (TIME) and for the iterative methods the request number of iterations (ITER NB.). The results, averaged per dataset, reveal almost WDTW the faster method, followd by DBA, and PSA the slowest one. The CWRT approach is not comparable to the rest of the methods as it performs directly an euclidean distance on the time series once the initial DTW matrix evaluated. Remark that for NLAAF and PSA the centroid lengths are very large making these approaches unusable for large time series, while the centroid lengths for the remaining methods are equal to the length of the initial medoid. The higher time consumptions observed for NLAAF and PSA are mainly explained by the progressive increase of the centroid length during the pairwise combination process.

3.3   Discussion

From Table 2, we can see that WDTW lead to the highest inertia reduction rates for almost all datasets, where the best scores (significantly different) indicated in bold. As expected, the DBA method that iteratively optimizes an inertia criterion, in general, reaches higher values than the non-iterative methods (NLAAF, PSA and CWRT). Finally, CWRT has the lowest inertia reduction rates. The negative rates observed for CWRT indicate an inertia increase.

From Table 3, the results reveal WDTW the fastest method and the PSA the slowest one. For NLAAF and PSA the estimated centroids have a drastically large dimension (i.e. a length around 10^4) making these approaches unusable for large time series datasets. The NLAAF and PSA methods are highly time consuming, largely because of the progressive increase of the centroid length during the pairwise combination process. The centroid lengths for the remaining methods are equal to the length of the initial medoid (Table 3). Finally, PSA appears

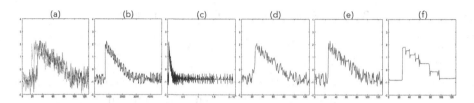

Fig. 8. CBF-"funnel" centroids: (a) ground through, (b) NLAAF, (c) PSA, (d) CWRT, (e) DBA, (f) WDTW

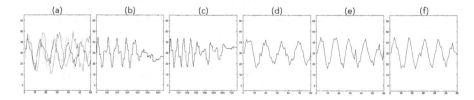

Fig. 9. CC-"cyclic" centroids: (a) ground through, (b) NLAAF, (c) PSA, (d) CWRT, (e) DBA, (f) WDTW

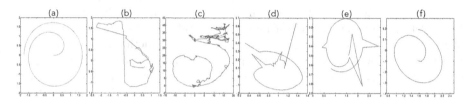

Fig. 10. SPIRAL-1 centroids: (a) ground through, (b) NLAAF, (c) PSA, (d) CWRT, (e) DBA, (f) WDTW

greatly slower than NLAAF; this is due to the hierarchical clustering on the whole time series.

We finally visualize here some of the centroids obtained by the different methods to compare their shape to the one of the time series they represent. Figures 8, 9, 10, 11 and 12 display the centroids obtained by the mentioned methods for the class "*funnel*" of CBF, "*cyclic*" of data set CC, the SPIRAL1, "*begin*" of BME and "*down*" of data set UMD, respectively. As one can note, for global datasets, almost all approaches succeed in obtaining centroids more or less similar to the initial time series. However, we observe generally less representative centroids for NLAAF and PSA, with a drastically large centroid's length of about 10^4 elements vs. 10^2 for the other methods. For the more complex (e.g. SPIRAL), Fig. 10 shows the ability of the DBA method, in obtaining centroids more or less similar to the initial time series, but one should circumvent the noise problem. Finally, as shown in the figures, the WDTW provide the most representative centroid for all datasets. For complex dataset, one can see the ability of the WDTW to circumvent the noise problem and to reveal the locally shared signature.

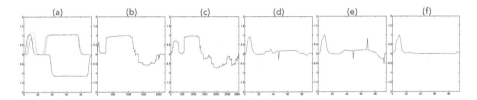

Fig. 11. BME-"begin" centroids: (a) ground through, (b) NLAAF, (c) PSA, (d) CWRT, (e) DBA, (f) WDTW

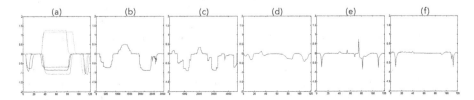

Fig. 12. UMD-"down" centroids: (a) ground through, (b) NLAAF, (c) PSA, (d) CWRT, (e) DBA, (f) WDTW

4   Conclusion

The DTW is among the most frequently used metrics for time series in several domains as signal processing, temporal data analysis and mining or machine learning. However, for time series clustering, approaches are generally limited to k-medoid to circumvent time series averaging under dynamic time warping and tricky multiple temporal alignments. The present study compares the major progressive and iterative time series averaging methods under the dynamic time warping. The experimental validation is based on standard datasets in which time series share similar behaviors within classes, as well as on more complex datasets. They are multidimensional, noisy and share only local characteristics. Both the quantitative evaluation, based on an inertia criterion (i.e. IRR), time and space complexity, and the qualitative one (consisting in the visualization of the centroids obtained by different methods) show the effectiveness of WDTW method to provide fastly accurate time series averaging for standard and complex datasets. The centroids obtained through WDTW are more representative of the set than the centroids obtained by the other methods, and the time requirements are lower than the rest. Following WDTW approach, the DBA, the second best method that iteratively optimizes an inertia criterion, reaches higher values than the non iterative methods (NLAAF, PSA and CWRT).

References

1. Abdulla, W.H., Chow, D., Sin, G.: Cross-words reference template for DTW-based speech recognition systems. In: Proceedings of TENCON, vol. 2, pp. 1576–1579 (2003)

2. Hautamaki, V., Nykanen, P., Franti, P.: Time-series clustering by approximate prototypes. In: 19th International Conference on Pattern Recognition (2008)
3. Petitjean, F., Ketterlin, A., Gançarski, P.: A global averaging method for dynamic time warping, with applications to clustering. Pattern Recogn. **44**, 678–693 (2011)
4. Zhou, F., De la Torre, F.: Generalized time warping for multi-modal alignment of human motion. In: Computer Vision and Pattern Recognition (CVPR), pp. 1282–1289. IEEE (2012)
5. Kruskall, J.B., Liberman, M.: The symmetric time warping algorithm: from continuous to discrete. Time Warps Journal. Addison-Wesley (1983)
6. Sakoe, H., Chiba, S.: Dynamic programming algorithm optimization for spoken word recognition. IEEE Trans. Acoust. Speech, Signal Process. **26**, 43–49 (1978)
7. Sankoff, D., Kruskal, J.B.: Time Warps, String Edits, and Macromolecules: The Theory and Practice of Sequence Comparison. Cambridge University Press, Addison-Wesley, Reading (1983)
8. Thompson, J.D., Higgins, D.G., Gibson, T.J.: CLUSTAL W: improving the sensitivity of progressive multiple sequence alignment through sequence weighting, position-specific gap penalties and weight matrix choice. J. Comput. Biol. **22**(22), 4673–4680 (1994)
9. Notredame, C., Higgins, D.-G., Heringa, J.: T-Coffee: a novel method for fast and accurate multiple sequence alignment. J. Mol. Biol. - J MOL BIOL **302**(1), 205–217 (2000)
10. Sze, S.-H., Lu, Y., Yang, Q.: A polynomial time solvable formulation of multiple sequence alignment. J. Comput. Biol. **13**(2), 309–319 (2006)
11. Carrillo, H., Lipman, D.: The multiple sequence alignment problem in biology. SIAM J. Appl. Math. **48**, 1073–1082 (1988). Society for Industrial and Applied Mathematics, Philadelphia, PA, USA
12. Gupta, L., Molfese, D., Tammana, R., Simos, P.: Nonlinear alignment and averaging for estimating the evoked potential. IEEE Trans. Biomed. Eng. **43**(4), 348–356 (1996)
13. Soheily-Khah, S., Douzal-Chouakria, A., Gaussier, E.: Progressive and iterative approaches for time series averaging. In: ECML-PKDD (Advanced Analytics and Learning on Temporal Data) (2015)
14. UCI Machine Learning Repository. http://archive.ics.uci.edu/ml/
15. UCR Time Series Classification Archive. http://www.cs.ucr.edu/~eamonn/
16. Niennattrakul, N., Ratanamahatana, C.: On clustering multimedia time series data using K-means and dynamic time warping. In: International onference on IEEE Multimedia and Ubiquitous Engineering, MUE 2007, pp. 733–738 (2007)
17. Niennattrakul, N., Ratanamahatana, C.: Shape averaging under time warping. In: ECTI-CON 6th International Conference on Electrical Engineering/Electronics, Computer, Telecommunications and Information Technology. IEEE, vol. 2, pp. 626–629, May 2009
18. Zhou, F., De la Torre, F.: Canonical time warping for alignment of human behavior. Adv. Neural Inf. Process. Syst. **22**, 2286–2294 (2009)
19. Frambourg, C., Douzal-Chouakria, A., Gaussier, E.: Learning multiple temporal matching for time series classification. In: Tucker, A., Höppner, F., Siebes, A., Swift, S. (eds.) IDA 2013. LNCS, vol. 8207, pp. 198–209. Springer, Heidelberg (2013)
20. Soheily-Khah, S., Douzal-Chouakria, A., Gaussier, E.: Generalized k-means-based clustering for temporal data under weighted and kernel time warp. J. Pattern Recogn. Lett. **75**, 63–69 (2016). doi:10.1016/j.patrec.2016.03.007

Coarse-DTW for Sparse Time Series Alignment

Marc Dupont[1,2][✉] and Pierre-François Marteau[1]

[1] IRISA, Université de Bretagne Sud, Campus de Tohannic, Vannes, France
marc.dupont@univ-ubs.fr
[2] Thales Optronique, 2 Avenue Gay Lussac, Elancourt, France

Abstract. Dynamic Time Warping (DTW) is considered as a robust measure to compare numerical time series when some *time elasticity* is required. However, speed is a known major drawback of DTW due to its quadratic complexity. Previous work has mainly considered designing speed optimization based on early-abandoning strategies applied to nearest-neighbor classification, although some of these optimizations are restricted to uni-dimensional time series. In this paper, we introduce Coarse-DTW, a reinterpretation of DTW for sparse time series, which exploits adaptive downsampling to achieve speed enhancement, even when faced with multidimensional time series. We show that Coarse-DTW achieves nontrivial speedups in nearest-neighbor classification and even admits a positive-definite kernelization suitable for SVM classification, hence offering a good tradeoff between speed and accuracy.

1 Introduction

Since the Frechet's distance [8] proposed at the dawn of the previous century, *time-elastic* matching of time series or symbolic sequences has attracted much attention of the scientific community in domains such as information indexing and retrieval, pattern analysis extraction and recognition, data mining, etc., with a very large spectrum of applications spreading in almost all the socioeconomic areas (environment, industry, health, energy, defense and so on).

Among other measures, Dynamic Time Warping (DTW) has been widely popularized during the seventies with the advent of speech recognition systems [21,25]. However, one of the main drawbacks of such a *time-elastic* measure is its quadratic computational complexity ($O(N^2)$) which, as is, prevents processing a very large amount of lengthy temporal data. Recent research has thus mainly focused on circumventing this complexity barrier. The original approach proposed in this paper is to cope directly and explicitly with the potential sparsity of the time series during their *time-elastic* alignment.

Our main contribution is three-fold: (i) an on-line downsampling algorithm whose aim is to provide a sparse representation of time series in $O(N)$; (ii) Coarse-DTW, a DTW variant that copes efficiently with the sparsity of time series; (iii) a kernelization of Coarse-DTW that allows for the design of accurate time-elastic SVM. Furthermore, an experimentation section is provided that highlights the tradeoff between speedup and accuracy on a large number of time series datasets (mainly unidimensional with a few multidimensional).

© Springer International Publishing Switzerland 2016
A. Douzal-Chouakria et al. (Eds.): AALTD 2015, LNAI 9785, pp. 157–172, 2016.
DOI: 10.1007/978-3-319-44412-3_11

2   Previous Work

DTW speed-up approaches mostly fall into one or several of the following categories:

1. **Reducing the search space**, when looking for the optimal alignment path. In [10,21] the search space is reduced by using a fixed corridor with a band (resp. parallelogram) shape displayed around the main alignment diagonal. For these corridor approaches, finding the optimal alignment path is obviously not guaranteed. Recently, [1] proposed the SparseDTW algorithm that exploits the concept of sparse alignment matrix to dynamically reduce the search space without optimality loss. SparseDTW provides thus an exact DTW computation with efficiency improvement in average.
2. **Reducing the dimensionality** of the data, along the spatial or temporal axis. Reducing the time series along the temporal axis leads to a straightforward speed-up (reducing by 2 the number of samples provides a by 4 speedup). [12,27] have proposed a piecewise aggregate approximation (PAA) of time series using segments of constant size. In [14] a modification of DTW, called PDTW, has been proposed to cope explicitly with PAA. Adaptive Piecewise Constant Approximation (APCA) has also been used [4] to comprees furthermore the representation of time series. Symbolic representation of time series such as SAX [20] or its variants falls also in this category. Recently, in [19] authors have shown that in the context of isolated gesture recognition sampled using depth-camera or motion capture systems, drastic down-sampling along the time axis in general enhances the accuracy.
3. **Approaching DTW by a low complexity lower bounding function** in an early abandoning strategy to reduce (drastically) the number of DTW calculations. This idea has been first proposed by [26] then progressively improved by [13,15] that have successively introduced tighter lower bounding functions.

   Some mixed approaches have been also proposed such as in ID-DTW (Iterative Deepening DTW) [6] which uses multi-resolution approximations with an early abandoning strategy or Fast-DTW [23] which also exploits multi-resolution approximations on a divide-and-conquer principle. [22,24] have also proposed approaches mixing APCA with a lower bounding strategy.

   Speeding up DTW algorithm is thus addressed either with or without accuracy loss. However, in the context of time series similarity, this simple choice may have a non trivial answer, depending on what meaning we give to accuracy. Are we interested in computing with accuracy the exact DTW measure? Or are we trying to maximize the accuracy of some task (regression, categorization, clustering or search for nearest neighbors) according to a given ground truth? Some elastic distance variants have been proposed, such as ERP [5] or TWED [17] with some gain in classification accuracy, but with no speed-up strategy designed so far.

   Attempts to improve a 1-NN DTW classification accuracy using more sophisticated approaches such as Support Vector Machine (SVM) with a direct DTW distance substituting Gaussian kernel has also been investigated, but has led to relatively poor results comparatively to 1-NN classification [9]. Observing that this kind of kernel is not definite, and as such could lead to some discrepancies when used in a kernel machine, recent works [7,18] have proposed new kernel regularization techniques for time-elastic kernels which lead, in general, to very significant classification accuracy improvements. These approaches can even be used in conjunction with a symmetric corridor that allows for a speedup based on the reduction of the search space, at the price of a lower accuracy in general.

Obviously, optimizing the accuracy/speedup tradeoff is thus a natural concern, and within this line of research, mixing speedup strategies with a dedicated DTW variant and a *time-elastic* kernel seems quite promising. This paper specifically contributes to this focus.

3   Presentation of Coarse-DTW

3.1   Classical DTW

Let us first review the classical formulation of DTW. If d is a fixed positive integer, we define a *dense time series* of length n as a multidimensional sequence (v_i), i.e. :

$$v : \{1, \dots, n\} \to \mathbb{R}^d.$$

Let (u_i) and (v_j) be two dense time series with respective lengths n and m. A *warping path* $\gamma = (\gamma_k)$ of length p is a sequence

$$\gamma : \{1, \dots, p\} \to \{1, \dots, n\} \times \{1, \dots, m\}$$

such that $\gamma_1 = (1, 1)$, $\gamma_p = (n, m)$, and (using the notation $\gamma_k = (i_k, j_k)$), for all k in $\{1, \dots, p-1\}$, $\gamma_{k+1} = (i_{k+1}, j_{k+1}) \in \{(i_k+1, j_k), (i_k, j_k+1), (i_k+1, j_k+1)\}$.

In other words, a warping path is required to travel along both time series from their beginnings to their ends; it cannot skip a point, but it can advance one timestep on one series without advancing the other, effectively amounting to "time-warping".

Now let δ be a distance on $\mathbb{R}^d$; let us define the *cost* of a warping path γ as the sum of distances between pairwise elements of the time series along γ, i.e.:

$$\text{cost}(\gamma) = \sum_{(i_k, j_k) \in \gamma} \delta(v_{i_k}, w_{j_k})$$

A common choice of distance on $\mathbb{R}^d$ is the one induced by the L^2 norm:

$$\delta(x, y) = \|x - y\|_2 = \sqrt{\sum_{s=1}^d (x_s - y_s)^2}$$

The warping path has a finite length, and there is a finite number of possible warping paths. Hence, there is at least one path whose cost is minimal. We define $\text{DTW}(v, w)$ as the minimal cost of all warping paths.

In practice, the typical way to compute DTW leverages the recursive structure of the warping path:

Algorithm 1. DTW

1: **procedure** DTW(v, w) ▷ (v and w are 1-indexed; A is 0-indexed)
2:      A = new matrix $[0..n, 0..m]$
3:      $A[0, .] = A[., 0] = \infty$ and $A[0, 0] = 0$
4:      **for** $i = 1$ to n **do**
5:          **for** $j = 1$ to m **do**
6:              $A[i, j] = \delta(v_i, w_j) + \min(A[i-1, j], A[i, j-1], A[i-1, j-1])$
7:      **return** $A[n, m]$

3.2 Sparse Time Series

In contrast to dense time series, let us define a *sparse time series* as a pair of sequences with the same length, (s_i) and (v_i):

$$
\begin{aligned}
s &: \{1, \ldots, n\} \to \mathbb{R}_+ \\
v &: \{1, \ldots, n\} \to \mathbb{R}^d
\end{aligned}
\tag{1}
$$

The sequence (v_i) represents our multidimensional signal's values, like above; the novelty resides in s_i, a number describing *how long the value v_i lasts*. We call this number s_i, the *stay* of v_i. In the following, we will also denote a sparse time series as $\{(s_1, v_1), \ldots, (s_n, v_n)\}$.

For example, every dense time series (v_i) is exactly represented by the sparse time series with the same values v_i and all stays $s_i = 1$. As another example, the 2D dense time series $\{(0.5, 1.2), (0.5, 1.2), (0.3, 1.5)\}$ is equivalent to the 2D sparse time series $\{(2, (0.5, 1.2)), (1, (0.3, 1.5))\}$.

3.3 Coarse-DTW

We may now introduce the Coarse-DTW algorithm. It takes two sparse time series: (s_i, v_i) of length n, and (t_j, w_j) of length m. The main idea behind Coarse-DTW is the 'aggregation' of very similar samples in time and space. As such, it shares similar aspects with the approach developed in [2] for symbolic time series (Fig. 1).

Algorithm 2. Coarse-DTW

1: **procedure** Coarse-DTW$((s, v), (t, w))$
2:      A = new matrix $[0..n, 0..m]$
3:      $A[0, .] = A[., 0] = \infty$ and $A[0, 0] = 0$
4:      **for** $i = 1$ to n **do**
5:          **for** $j = 1$ to m **do**
6:              $A[i, j] = \min(\ s_i.\delta(v_i, w_j) + A[i-1, j],$
7:                       $t_j.\delta(v_i, w_j) + A[i, j-1],$
8:                       $\phi(s_i, t_j).\delta(v_i, w_j) + A[i-1, j-1]\ )$
9:      **return** $A[n, m]$

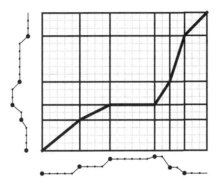

Fig. 1. A warping path in Coarse-DTW. We superimposed the sparse time series (bigger points) on top of their equivalent dense time series (smaller points). The coarse, thick grid is the Coarse-DTW matrix, whereas the underlying thin grid is the classical DTW cost matrix.

Coarse-DTW takes advantage of the sparsity in the time series to calculate costs efficiently. However, because the points last for different amount of time, we must adapt the classical DTW formulation in order to account for the stays s_i and t_j of each point into the aggregate cost calculation.

Obviously, when a point lasts for a long time, it should cost more than a point which lasts for a brief amount of time. For this reason, the pure cost $\delta(v_i, w_j)$ is multiplied by some quantity, called *weight*, linked to how long the points last, as in lines 6–8 of the algorithm. The goal of this subsection is to explain why we set those weights to s_i, t_j, and $\phi(s_i, t_j)$ respectively.

One Coarse-DTW iteration actually relates to a batch of DTW iterations in a *constant-cost sub-rectangle*. Indeed, suppose that we are operating on two pairs of subsequent points in a sparse time series, say, (s_i, v_i), (s_{i+1}, v_{i+1}) on one time series and (t_j, w_j), (t_{j+1}, w_{j+1}) on the other. If the time series were not sparse, as in classical DTW, there would be several repetitions of the first point v_i, namely s_i times, until it moves to the next value v_{i+1}. Similarly w_j would be repeated t_j times. In the DTW cost matrix, this would create an $s_i \times t_j$ sub-rectangle where all costs are identical because they match the same values; the constant cost here being $\delta(v_i, w_j)$; this is our constant-cost sub-rectangle (see Fig. 2).

The choice of weights s_i and t_j in lines 6 and 7 is motivated as follows: when we advance one time series without advancing the other, we want a lengthy point to cost more than a brief point. In the DTW constant-cost sub-rectangle, advancing the first time series is like following a horizontal subpath, whose aggregated cost would be $\delta(v_i, w_j)$ on each of its s_i cells. This sums up to $s_i.\delta(v_i, w_j)$, which is why the weight is chosen to be s_i in line 6. An analog interpretation holds for a vertical subpath of t_j cells.

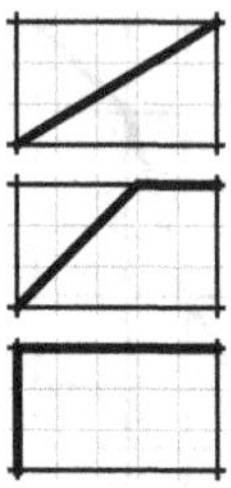

$$\phi_{\mathrm{diag}}(s_i, t_j) = \sqrt{s_i^2 + t_j^2}$$

$$\phi_{\max}(s_i, t_j) = \max(s_i, t_j)$$

$$\phi_{\mathrm{stairs}}(s_i, t_j) = s_i + t_j - 1$$

Fig. 2. Three choices for the function ϕ, in a constant-cost sub-rectangle of width s_i and height t_j.

For the third case (line 8), namely advancing *both* time series, choosing a weight for the cost is less obvious. The question is: which weight should we set for a path joining the top-right corner to the bottom-left one, in a constant-cost sub-rectangle? This question is captured by $\phi(s_i, t_j)$, the weight of the cost in this situation. We propose three choices for ϕ, all of which have a geometrical interpretation in the classical DTW cost matrix.

Our first proposition for ϕ seeks to mimic the behavior of classical DTW. In the constant-cost sub-rectangle (of size $s_i \times t_j$), we know that a path minimizing the aggregated cost is the same as one minimizing the number of cells; precisely because all cells have the same cost. Furthermore, the minimal number of cells is exactly $\max(s_i, t_j)$; take, for example, a path going diagonal until it reaches the opposite size and then completing the remaining route on a line (see Fig. 2, middle).

Instead of choosing the weight inspired from DTW, which only approximates a diagonal, we can also choose the weight to be the true diagonal of the sub-rectangle, leading to $\phi_{\mathrm{diag}}(s_i, t_j) = \sqrt{s_i^2 + t_j^2}$.

Finally, we will also consider the choice of $\phi_{\mathrm{stairs}}(s_i, t_j) = s_i + t_j - 1$, amounting to a version of classical DTW where only horizontal and vertical paths would be allowed (like stairs, hence the name). Note that it should be used only in cases where sparse time series admit stays of 1 or more (this will be the case with our downsampling algorithm introduced in the next section).

4   Downsampling

In this section, we seek to transform a dense time series (u_i) into a sparse time series (s_i, v_i); the goal is to detect when series "move a lot" and "are rather static", adjusting the number of emitted points accordingly. We propose a downsampling algorithm, called *Bubble*, which essentially collapses a block of several similar values into a single value, augmented with the duration of this block.

Bubble downsampling can be described in a simple form as follows:

Algorithm 3. Bubble Downsampling

1: **procedure** BUBBLE(v, ρ)   ▷ $\rho \geq 0$
2:     $i_{\text{center}} = 1$ ▷ initialize bubble center
3:     $v_{\text{center}} = v_1$
4:     $v_{\text{mean}} = v_1$
5:     **for** $i = 2$ to n **do**
6:         $\Delta v = \delta(v_i, v_{\text{center}})$ ▷ distance to center
7:         $\Delta i = i - i_{\text{center}}$ ▷ find the stay
8:         **if** $\Delta v \geq \rho$ **then**   ▷ does the bubble "burst"?
9:             **yield** $(\Delta i, v_{\text{mean}})$ ▷ emit stay + point
10:            $i_{\text{center}} = i$ ▷ update bubble center
11:            $v_{\text{center}} = v_i$
12:            $v_{\text{mean}} = v_i$
13:        **else**
14:            $v_{mean} = (\Delta i \times v_{mean} + v_i)/(\Delta i + 1)$ ▷ update mean
15:    $\Delta i = n - i_{\text{center}} + 1$ ▷ force bursting last bubble
16:    **yield** $(\Delta i, v_{\text{mean}})$

The idea behind Bubble downsampling lies on the following approximation: consecutive values can be considered equal if they stay within a given radius ρ for the distance δ. We can picture a curve which makes bubbles along its path (see Fig. 4), hence the name. Concretely, the algorithm emits a sparse time series, where each stay is the number of consecutive points contained in a given bubble, and each value is the mean of the points in this bubble (Fig. 3).

The parameter ρ represents the tradeoff between information loss and density. A large ρ emits few points, thus yielding a very sparse time series, but less accurate; a smaller ρ preserves more information at the expense of a lower

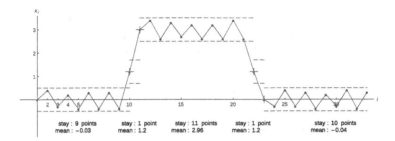

Fig. 3. Bubble downsampling applied on a 1D time series (blue, solid) with $\rho = 0.5$. The 1-bubbles are represented by their 1-centers (red crosses) and their 1-boundaries (red, dashed lines). The sparse time series emitted is $\{(9, -0.03), (1, 1.2), (11, 2.96), (1, 1.2), (10, -0.04)\}$. (Color figure online)

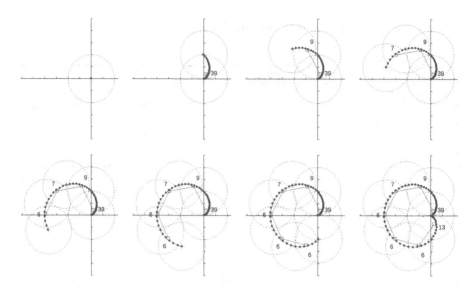

Fig. 4. Bubble downsampling progressively applied on a 2D time series (outer blue line with dots) with $\rho = 2.0$, along with the sparse time series emitted (inner green line with squares). Again, the 2-bubbles are represented by their 2-centers and their 2-boundaries (red crosses and dashed circles). Numbers indicate the stays. Notice how stays take into account the slowness at the beginning of the signal. (Color figure online)

downsampling ratio. The degenerate case $\rho = 0$ will output a clone of the original time series with no downsampling (all stays equal to 1). Because speed is a direct consequence of sparsity in Coarse-DTW, a good middle value for ρ must be found, so that time series are as sparse as possible while retaining just the right amount of information.

5   Optimizations on Coarse-DTW

DTW suffers from a slow computation time if not implemented wisely. For this reason, several optimizations have been designed [13]. The first classical optimization is to avoid a squared root computation in the distance δ. Typically, we would choose

$$\delta(x, y) = \|x - y\|_2^2 = \sum_{s=1}^{d}(x_s - y_s)^2$$

instead of its square root counterpart.

The next optimizations we considered are called *lower bounds*, designed to early-abandon computations. This kind of optimization mostly makes sense in a classification scenario along with a k-Nearest Neighbor (k-NN) classifier. In the case of 1-NN, as the classification goes on we can track the "best-so-far" distance; if a sample's lower bound exceeds the best-so-far, the computation can be stopped because it is guaranteed not to be a candidate for the nearest neighbor.

The first lower bound LB_{Kim} is based on the following remark: whatever the warping path found by DTW, both time series' first and last points will be matched together. More formally,

$$
\begin{aligned}
DTW(v, w) &= \sum_{(i,j) \in \gamma} \delta(v_{i_k}, w_{j_k}) \\
&= \delta(v_1, w_1) + \cdots + \delta(v_n, w_m) \\
&\geq \delta(v_1, w_1) + \delta(v_n, w_m)
\end{aligned}
\tag{2}
$$

where the ellipsis is a sum of positive numbers. The equation would not be satisfied if both $n \leq 1$ and $m \leq 1$, but fortunately this special case would lead to a trivial computation of DTW rendering this lower bound useless.

In the case of Coarse-DTW, the cost of matching the first points is:

$$
\phi(s_1, t_1).\delta(v_1, w_1)
$$

indeed, the first matching is done diagonally because $A[0,1] = A[1,0] = \infty$. Then, the cost of matching the last points is $\min(s_n, t_m, \phi(s_n, t_m)) . \delta(v_n, w_m)$.

Therefore, for all pairs of time series (one of which having at least two points), the following inequality stands:

$$
\text{Coarse-DTW}(v, w) \geq \phi(s_1, t_1).\delta(v_1, w_1) + \min(s_n, t_m, \phi(s_n, t_m)).\delta(v_n, w_m) \tag{3}
$$

in which the right-hand side is the LB_{Kim} lower bound adapted to Coarse-DTW.

Another lower bound, known as LB_{Keogh}, has enabled consequent speedup of DTW computation [13]. It is based upon the calculation of an envelope; however this calculation is not trivially transferable to the case of multidimensional time series simply by generalizing the uni-dimensional equations. Thus, we will unfortunately not consider it in our study.

However, a cheap bound can be evaluated several times as DTW progresses as follows: for any row i, the minimum of all cells $A[i,.]$ is a lower bound to the DTW result. Indeed, this result is the last cell of the last row, and the sequence mapping a row i to $\min_j A[i,j]$ is increasing, because the costs are positive. Hence, during each outer loop iteration (i.e., on index i), we can store the minimum of the current row and compare it to the best-so-far for possibly early abandoning. This can be transposed directly to Coarse-DTW without additional modifications.

6   Kernelization of CoarseDTW

Besides the fact that DTW and CoarseDTW are not metrics (they do not comply with the triangle inequality), it is furthermore not possible to directly derive a positive definite kernel from such elastic distances. Hence, their use in kernel approaches such as Support Vector Machines (SVM) is questionable and the experience shows that directly substituting DTW into a Gaussian kernel, for instance, does not lead to satisfactory results [18].

Recent works [7,18] propose new guidelines to regularize kernels constructed from elastic measures similar to DTW. Following the line of regularization proposed in [18], an instance of positive definite kernel deriving from the CoarseDTW (K_{cdtw}) measure can be translated into the Algorithm 4, which relies on two recursive terms, namely K_{xy} and K_{xx}.

The main idea behind this line of regularization is to replace the operators min and max (which prevent the symmetrization of the kernel) by a summation operator ($\sum$). This leads to consider, not only the best possible alignment, but also all good (or nearly best) paths by summing up their overall cost. The parameter ν is used to control what we mean by a good alignment, thus penalizing more or less alignments too far from the optimal ones. This parameter can be easily optimized through a cross-validation.

The proof for the positive definiteness of K_{cdtw} is very similar to the one given in [18] for the regularized DTW kernel, except that the local kernels $e^{-\nu \cdot \xi(s(p),t(q)) \cdot \delta_E^2(v(p),w(q))}$, where $\xi(s(p),t(q))$ stands for $s(p)$, $t(q)$ or $\phi(s(p),t(q))$ should be understood as a positive definite kernel defined on the set of constant time series of varying lengths. Note that if the two time series in argument are not sparse (this is the case when no downsampling is applied), the K_{cdtw} kernel corresponds exactly to the regularized DTW kernel described in [18].

Algorithm 4 is based on the following conventions: $\forall p \geq 0$, if $p > m = |(s,v)|$ then $s(p) = s(m)$ and $v(p) = v(m)$ and similarly $\forall q \geq 0$, if $q > n = |(t,w)|$ then $t(q) = s(n)$ and $v(q) = v(n)$.

Algorithm 4. KCoarse-DTW

1: **procedure** KCOARSE-DTW$((s,v),(t,w))$
2:     K_{xy} = new matrix $[0..n, 0..m]$
3:     K_{xx} = new matrix $[0..n, 0..m]$
4:     $K_{xy}[0,.] = K_{xy}[.,0] = 0$ and $K_{xy}[0,0] = 1.0$
5:     $K_{xx}[0,.] = K_{xx}[.,0] = 0$ and $K_{xx}[0,0] = 1.0$
6:     **for** $i = 1$ to n **do**
7:         **for** $j = 1$ to m **do**
8:             $K_{xy}[i,j] = \frac{1}{3}(\exp(-\nu.s_i.\delta(v_i,w_j)) \cdot K_{xy}[i-1,j]+$
9:                 $\exp(-\nu.t_i.\delta(v_i,w_j)) \cdot K_{xy}[i,j-1]+$
10:                 $\exp(-\nu.\phi(s_i,t_j).\delta(v_i,w_j)) \cdot K_{xy}[i-1,j-1])$
11:             **if** $i < m$ **and** $j < n$ **then**
12:                 $K_{xx}[i,j] = \frac{1}{3}(\exp(-\nu.s_i.\delta(v_i,w_i)) \cdot K_{xx}[i-1,j]+$
13:                     $\exp(-\nu.t_i.\delta(v_i,w_i)) \cdot K_{xx}[i,j-1])$
14:             **if** i == j **then**
15:                 $K_{xx}[i,j] + = \frac{1}{3}\exp(-\nu.\phi(s_i,t_i).\delta(v_i,w_i)) \cdot K_{xx}[i-1,j-1]$
16:     **return** $K_{xy}[n,m] + K_{xx}[n,m]$

6.1   Normalization of KCoarse-DTW

As KCoarse-DTW (in short K_{cdtw}) evaluates the sum on all possible alignment paths of the products of local alignment costs $e^{-\nu \cdot \xi(s(p),t(q)) \cdot \delta_E^2(v(p),w(q))} \leq 1$, its values can be very small depending on the size of the time series and the selected value for ν. Hence, K_{cdtw} values tend to 0 when ν tends towards ∞, except when the two compared time series are identical (the corresponding Gram matrix suffers from a diagonal dominance problem). As proposed in [18], a manner to avoid numerical troubles consists in using the following *normalized* kernel:

$$\tilde{K}_{\text{cdtw}}(.,.) = exp\left(\alpha \frac{\log(K_{\text{cdtw}}(.,.)) - \log(\min(K_{\text{cdtw}}))}{\log(\max(K_{\text{cdtw}})) - \log(\min(K_{\text{cdtw}}))}\right)$$

where $\max(K_{\text{cdtw}})$ and $\min(K_{\text{cdtw}})$ respectively are the max and min values taken by the kernel on the learning dataset and $\alpha > 0$ a positive constant ($\alpha = 1$ by default). If we forget the proportionality constant, this leads to take the kernel K_{cdtw} at a power $\tau = \alpha/(\log(\max(K_{\text{cdtw}})) - \log(\min(K_{\text{cdtw}})))$, which shows that the normalized kernel $\tilde{K}_{\text{cdtw}} \propto K_{\text{cdtw}}^{\tau}$ is still positive definite ([3], Proposition 2.7).

7 Results

7.1 DTW vs. Coarse-DTW in 1-NN Classification

In this first setup we considered the classification accuracy and speed of various labeled time series datasets. The classifier is 1-NN and we enabled all optimizations described earlier that apply to multidimensional time series, namely: early abandoning on LB_{Kim} and early abandoning on the minima of rows. The distance chosen is the squared version, $\delta(x, y) = \|x - y\|_2^2 = \sum_{s=1}^{d}(x_s - y_s)^2$. We report only the classification time, not the learning time.

Dataset MSRAction3D [16] consists of 10 actors executing the same gestures several times, with 60 dimensions (twenty 3D joints). To classify this dataset, we cross-validated all possible combinations of 5 actors in training and 5 in test, thus totaling 252 rounds.

The dataset uWaveGestureLibrary_[XYZ] comes from the UCR time series database [11]. It can be considered as three independent uni-dimensional datasets, but we rather used it here as a single set of 3-dimensional time series. The interest is obvious: in 1-NN DTW classification, we went from individual 1D errors of respectively 27.3 %, 36.6 % and 34.2 %, down to only 2.8 % when the three time series sets are taken together.

Finally, for the sake of comparison, we also ran our tests on the other UCR time series datasets at our disposal. It should be noted that they are all unidimensional, however we exclusively considered them as multidimensional time series which *happen* to have a dimension of $d = 1$. This means in particular that some of the traditional lower bounds such as LB_{Keogh} cannot be used, only the multidimensional-enabled ones described earlier.

For each dataset, we ran the classification once with DTW to obtain a reference value both time- and accuracy-wise. Then, we ran Coarse-DTW, with several values of ρ, as follows: the dense time series are first downsampled with Bubble into sparse time series, according to the current ρ, and then classified

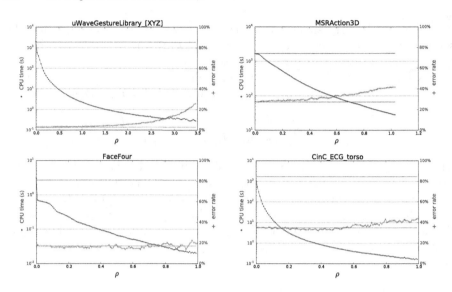

Fig. 5. 1-NN classification time and error rate of Coarse-DTW as ρ increases. For reference, DTW results are shown as horizontal bars (independent of ρ).

with Coarse-DTW. The time and error rate was measured at every run. In Fig. 5 we show the full results for a few datasets.

A general trend can be observed (Fig. 5): as ρ increases, classification time decreases. However, this comes at the expense of a higher error rate. This is expected: indeed, downsampled time series contain less information than their dense counterparts. Now, we can observe that some time series allow ρ to increase quite a bit (and therefore classification goes much faster) before the accuracy really degrades.

In order to quantify this effect, we proceed as follows. We first set a threshold on the error rate. Here, we select the threshold to be 2 % (absolute error) above our reference, the DTW error rate. (For example, if the DTW error rate were 27.1 %, we would set the threshold at 29.1 %, which might or might not be acceptable depending on the user's constraints.) Then we find the value of

$$\rho^* = \max\{\rho \mid \forall \rho' \leq \rho, \mathrm{err}_{\rho'} \leq \mathrm{err}_{\mathrm{DTW}} + 2\%\} \tag{4}$$

which represents the last acceptable value before the error rates first goes above the threshold (the "breakout"). The CPU time associated with the run of ρ^* is likely to be below the DTW CPU time, which is why we define the speedup as their ratio:

$$\mathrm{speedup} = \frac{\mathrm{CPU\ time}_{\mathrm{DTW}}}{\mathrm{CPU\ time}_{\mathrm{Coarse\text{-}DTW\ at\ }\rho^*}} \tag{5}$$

Furthermore, we tested each of the three possibilities for ϕ. Of all three, we selected only the ρ^* value giving the best time. The values of ρ^* and the speedup are summarized in Table 1, along with the winning ϕ.

Table 1. Performance of Coarse-DTW (for a threshold at $+2\%$ abs. err.) compared to DTW, in 1-NN classification (datasets from [11,16]).

Dataset	d	Time DTW	Time Coarse-DTW	Speedup	Best ϕ
uWaveGestureLibrary_[XYZ]	3	1850 s	0.769 s	2413.3x	ϕ_{stairs}
MSRAction3D	60	1710 s	428 s	4.0x	ϕ_{max}
Adiac	1	21.0 s	13.0 s	1.6x	ϕ_{stairs}
Beef	1	1.35 s	0.014 s	93.5x	ϕ_{max}
CBF	1	3.18 s	0.0393 s	80.9x	ϕ_{diag}
ChlorineConcentration	1	73.2 s	14.0 s	5.2x	ϕ_{max}
CinC_ECG_torso	1	1690 s	0.413 s	4100.7x	ϕ_{max}
Coffee	1	0.479 s	0.139 s	3.5x	ϕ_{max}
DiatomSizeReduction	1	3.81 s	0.241 s	15.8x	ϕ_{max}
ECG200	1	0.258 s	0.012 s	20.7x	ϕ_{max}
ECGFiveDays	1	2.34 s	0.283 s	8.2x	ϕ_{max}
FaceAll	1	73.3 s	21.5 s	3.4x	ϕ_{max}
FaceFour	1	2.69 s	0.031 s	85.8x	ϕ_{stairs}
FacesUCR	1	42.7 s	7.46 s	5.7x	ϕ_{max}
FISH	1	47.1 s	38.0 s	1.2x	ϕ_{max}
Gun_Point	1	0.653 s	0.108 s	6.1x	ϕ_{diag}
Haptics	1	445 s	0.860 s	516.7x	ϕ_{max}
InlineSkate	1	1790 s	0.548 s	3276.1x	ϕ_{diag}
ItalyPowerDemand	1	0.236 s	0.103 s	2.3x	ϕ_{stairs}
Lighting2	1	17.0 s	0.440 s	38.6x	ϕ_{stairs}
Lighting7	1	4.66 s	5.21 s	0.9x	ϕ_{max}
MALLAT	1	1460 s	6.408 s	228.4x	ϕ_{max}
MedicalImages	1	2.92 s	0.261 s	11.2x	ϕ_{max}
MoteStrain	1	1.14 s	0.0480 s	23.7x	ϕ_{max}
NonInvasiveFetalECG_Thorax1	1	9820 s	516 s	19.0x	ϕ_{max}
NonInvasiveFetalECG_Thorax2	1	9720 s	310 s	31.3x	ϕ_{max}
OliveOil	1	3.15 s	1.43 s	2.2x	ϕ_{diag}
OSULeaf	1	59.3 s	2.16 s	27.4x	ϕ_{stairs}
SonyAIBORobot_Surface	1	0.465 s	0.245 s	1.9x	ϕ_{max}
SonyAIBORobot_SurfaceII	1	0.902 s	0.150 s	6.0x	ϕ_{stairs}
StarLightCurves	1	44700 s	58.6 s	763.0x	ϕ_{max}
SwedishLeaf	1	19.0 s	11.5 s	1.7x	ϕ_{max}
Symbols	1	21.8 s	1.91 s	11.4x	ϕ_{max}
synthetic_control	1	1.97 s	0.624 s	3.2x	ϕ_{max}
Trace	1	2.36 s	0.00636 s	371.3x	ϕ_{max}
TwoLeadECG	1	0.827 s	0.0869 s	9.5x	ϕ_{max}
Two_Patterns	1	371 s	0.668 s	556.4x	ϕ_{max}
wafer	1	158 s	0.402 s	392.1x	ϕ_{max}
WordsSynonyms	1	87.4 s	4.61 s	18.9x	ϕ_{max}
yoga	1	581 s	4.78 s	121.7x	ϕ_{max}

Additionally, our study aimed to search for the best ϕ function for the diagonal weight. We can conclude from Table 1 that the most satisfactory is ϕ_{max}, offering the best ratio accuracy/time. Actually, it appears from our experience that ϕ_{diag} was good enough accuracy-wise but was too slow due to the square root. Thus, we recommend selecting ϕ_{max} by default.

7.2 SVM Classification with KCoarse-DTW

We also tested the accuracy of our regularized version, KCoarse-DTW, normalized as described in Sect. 6.1, with different values of ρ to see how accuracy degrades with approximation.

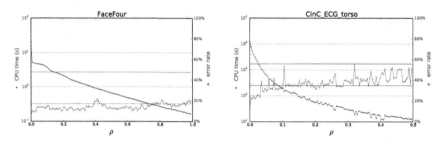

Fig. 6. SVM classification time and error rate of our regularized kernel, KCoarse-DTW. For reference, 1-NN DTW results are shown as horizontal bars (top: CPU time, bottom: error rate).

With KCoarse-DTW and with very small values of ρ, we are in general able to outperform 1-NN DTW. We must add that this was not the case for all time series when ρ increases, so this really depends on the nature of the time series in question.

In Fig. 6, we present two datasets where the regularized kernel performed better. (For FaceFour, the same (C, σ) was found for $\rho = 0$ and reused afterwards, whereas on CinC_ECG_Torso, there was a new grid search for each ρ.) The behavior is comparable to 1-NN classification with Coarse-DTW, except we start at $\rho = 0$ with a lower error rate. Then accuracy degrades as expected. SVM takes usually more time to run than 1-NN, but KCoarse-DTW helps by making it possible to decrease the classification time.

8   Conclusions

Not only have we transposed DTW into Coarse-DTW, a version accepting sparse time series, but we have also developed Bubble, an extremely efficient, streamable algorithm to generate such sparse time series from regular ones. By coupling those two mechanisms, we were able to discover that time series can be classified much faster in nearest-neighbor classification; the user can reach the desired tradeoff between speed and accuracy, by tuning the parameter ρ in the downsampling algorithm. Some time series are far more subject to downsampling than others, and therefore results can differ depending on which context time series originate. For example, smooth time series like gestures present a considerable ability to be downsampled, producing good results in classification speedup.

We also explored the regularization of Coarse-DTW, for use as an SVM kernel. For some time series, results were encouraging, giving classification results much better than 1-NN. As it was expected, the accuracy degraded as the downsampling radius ρ increased, giving once again the user the ability to choose a suitable tradeoff between speed and accuracy.

Coarse-DTW and Bubble have a great potential to be used in a variety of scenarios beyond offline classification; for example, they are totally suitable to reduce time series storage space, or also to reconize learnt patterns within a multidimensional stream. Finally, in an embedded context, where energy is scarce, the speedup offered by Coarse-DTW can also be interpreted as a saving in CPU cycles, which can be tremendously helpful.

Acknowledgements. This study was co-funded by the ANRT agency and Thales Optronique SAS, under the PhD CIFRE convention 2013/0932.

References

1. Al-Naymat, G., Chawla, S., Taheri, J.: Sparsedtw: a novel approach to speed up dynamic time warping. In: Proceedings of the Eighth Australasian Data Mining Conference, AusDM 2009, Darlinghurst, Australia, vol. 101, pp. 117–127. Australian Computer Society Inc., Australia (2009)
2. Apostolico, A., Landau, G.M., Skiena, S.: Matching for run-length encoded strings. In: 1997 Proceedings of the Compression and Complexity of Sequences, pp. 348–356, June 1997
3. Berg, C., Christensen, J.P.R., Ressel, P.: Harmonic Analysis on Semigroups: Theory of Positive Definite and Related Functions. Graduate Texts in Mathematics, vol. 100. Springer, New York (1984)
4. Chakrabarti, K., Keogh, E., Mehrotra, S., Pazzani, M.: Locally adaptive dimensionality reduction for indexing large time series databases. ACM Trans. Database Syst. **27**(2), 188–228 (2002)
5. Chen, L., Ng, R.: On the marriage of Lp-norm and edit distance. In: Proceedings of the 30th International Conference on Very Large Data Bases, pp. 792–801 (2004)
6. Chu, S., Keogh, E.J., Hart, D.M., Pazzani, M.J.: Iterative deepening dynamic time warping for time series. In: Grossman, R.L., Han, J., Kumar, V., Mannila, H., Motwani, R. (eds.) Proceedings of the Second SIAM International Conference on Data Mining, Arlington, VA, USA, 11–13 April 2002, pp. 195–212. SIAM (2002)
7. Cuturi, M., Vert, J.-P., Birkenes, O., Matsui, T.: A kernel for time series based on global alignments. In: IEEE ICASSP 2007, vol. 2, pp. II-413–II-416, April 2007
8. Fréchet, M.: Sur Quelques Points du Calcul Fonctionnel. Thèse, Faculté des Sciences de Paris (1906)
9. Gudmundsson, S., Runarsson, T.P., Sigurdsson, S.: Support vector machines and dynamic time warping for time series. In: 2008 IEEE International Joint Conference on Neural Networks, IJCNN 2008. IEEE World Congress on Computational Intelligence, pp. 2772–2776, June 2008

10. Itakura, F.: Minimum prediction residual principle applied to speech recognition. IEEE Trans. Acoust. Speech Sig. Process. **23**(1), 67–72 (1975)
11. Keogh, E.J., Xi, X., Wei, L., Ratanamahatana, C.A.: The UCR time series classification-clustering datasets (2006). http://wwwcs.ucr.edu/eamonn/time_series_data/
12. Keogh, E., Chakrabarti, K., Pazzani, M., Mehrotra, S.: Dimensionality reduction for fast similarity search in large time series databases. J. Knowl. Inf. Syst. **3**, 263–286 (2000)
13. Keogh, E., Ratanamahatana, C.A.: Exact indexing of dynamic time warping. Knowl. Inf. Syst. **7**(3), 358–386 (2005)
14. Keogh, E.J., Pazzani, M.J.: Scaling up dynamic time warping for datamining applications. In: Proceedings of the Sixth ACM SIGKDD International Conference on Knowledge Discovery and Data Mining, KDD 2000, pp. 285–289. ACM, New York, NY, USA (2000)
15. Lemire, D.: Faster retrieval with a two-pass dynamic-time-warping lower bound. Pattern Recogn. **42**(9), 2169–2180 (2009)
16. Li, W., Zhang, Z., Liu, Z.: Action recognition based on a bag of 3D points. In: Proceedings of IEEE International Workshop on CVPR for Human Communicative Behavior Analysis, pp. 9–14. IEEE CS Press (2010)
17. Marteau, P.F.: Time warp edit distance with stiffness adjustment for time series matching. IEEE Trans. Pattern Anal. Mach. Intell. **31**(2), 306–318 (2008)
18. Marteau, P.-F., Gibet, S.: On recursive edit distance kernels with application to time series classification. IEEE Trans. Neural Netw. Learn. Syst., 1–14 (2014)
19. Marteau, P.-F., Gibet, S., Reverdy, C.: Down-Sampling coupled to elastic kernel machines for efficient recognition of isolated gestures. In: International Conference on Pattern Recognition, ICPR 2014, pp. 336–368. IEEE, Stockholm, Sweden, August 2014
20. Patel, P., Keogh, E., Lin, J., Lonardi, S.: Mining motifs in massive time series databases. In: Proceedings of IEEE International Conference on Data Mining, ICDM 2002, pp. 370–377 (2002)
21. Sakoe, H., Chiba, S.: A dynamic programming approach to continuous speech recognition. In: Proceedings of the 7th International Congress of Acoustic, pp. 65–68 (1971)
22. Sakurai, Y., Yoshikawa, M., Faloutsos, C.: FTW: Fast similarity search under the time warping distance. In: Proceedings of the Twenty-Fourth ACM SIGMOD-SIGACT-SIGART Symposium on Principles of Database Systems, PODS 2005, pp. 326–337. ACM, New York, NY, USA (2005)
23. Salvador, S., Chan, P.: Toward accurate dynamic time warping in linear time and space. Intell. Data Anal. **11**(5), 561–580 (2007)
24. Shou, Y., Mamoulis, N., Cheung, D.W.: Fast and exact warping of time series using adaptive segmental approximations. Mach. Learn. **58**(2–3), 231–267 (2005)
25. Velichko, V.M., Zagoruyko, N.G.: Automatic recognition of 200 words. Int. J. Man-Mach. Stud. **2**, 223–234 (1970)
26. Kim, S.W., Park, S., Chu, W.W.: An index-based approach for similarity search supporting time warping in large sequence databases. In: ICDE, pp. 607–614 (2001)
27. Yi, B.-K., Faloutsos, C.: Fast time sequence indexing for arbitrary Lp norms. In: Proceedings of the 26th International Conference on Very Large Data Bases, VLDB 2000, pp. 385–394. Morgan Kaufmann Publishers Inc., San Francisco, CA, USA (2000)

Author Index

Printed in the United States
By Bookmasters